The
Which?
Book of House Plants

The
Which?
Book of House Plants

Published by Consumers' Association
and Hodder and Stoughton

The Which? Book of House Plants is
published in Great Britain by
Consumers' Association
14 Buckingham Street,
London WC2N 6DS

Editor:	Lizzie Boyd
House Editor:	Roger Davies
Design:	Turner Wilks Dandridge Ltd.
Photography:	Peter Higgins
Illustrations:	Craig Warwick, Linden Artists
	Anne Savage
Contributors:	Gillian Beckett
	Kenneth A. Beckett
	Peter Black
	Richard Gilbert
	Gwen Goodship
	Alyson Huxley
	Anthony Huxley
	John Negus
	Alan Toogood

**The Publishers also wish to acknowledge the help and assistance
provided by:** A-Z Botanical Collection Ltd.
Walter Blom and Sons Ltd.
Holly Gate Nurseries Ltd.
Royal Botanic Gardens, Kew
Thomas Rochford and Sons Ltd.
Paul Temple Ltd.
Geest Horticultural Group Ltd.

First Edition
© Consumers' Association 1979
First Revise 1980

ISBN 085202 167 4

Typesetting by
Lowe & Carr Ltd., Leicester
Colour Separations by
Lumarcolour Litho Reproductions Ltd., Peterborough
Printing and binding in Great Britain by
Hazell Watson & Viney Ltd., Aylesbury

Foreword

The last decade has seen a steadily growing interest in plants for indoor gardening. This has been spurred partly by the improved environment of many homes – central heating, better insulation, lighter rooms – and partly by a vigorous campaign by commercial growers.

In preparing this book the publishers have been anxious to select only those plants which can be correctly termed house plants and which can be expected to thrive in average home conditions. For this reason several types, which are offered commercially as house plants but which in fact require greenhouse cultivation for at least part of the year, have been excluded.

Availability as well as ease of cultivation has also influenced the choice of plants. The majority of those described and illustrated are readily obtainable at garden centres and florists. Department stores, supermarkets and chain stores are useful sources. A few – certain bromeliads or orchids, for example – may have to be obtained from specialist nurseries.

The cost of starting or enlarging a house plant collection is inevitably hard to estimate. Much depends on locality, the size of plants purchased, their general state of health and current popularity. A plant may seem cheap at a cost of pence compared with another of similar size but priced in pounds. The difference is usually that the former is of temporary or short-term value only or it may be a young slow-growing plant that will take many years to reach maturity. The more expensive plants are often established

plants, or they may have taken many years to raise.

The book has been divided into three parts to help beginners and experienced house plant gardeners alike. Part One discusses the cultural needs of plants in general, and the various ways in which existing conditions in the home can be improved or adapted.

Part Two describes individual plants in more detail, with an accompanying illustration of one or more of the most popular plants in each genus. This A-Z guide has been divided into separate sections according to plant groups. However, some foliage plants have additional attraction in bearing flowers, and many flowering plants are also endowed with handsome leaves.

If you are about to start a plant collection, choose those subjects recommended as being of easy cultivation. Once you have discovered which plants will thrive under your care and in your home, you can move on to more demanding species. If a particular type of plant appears to be doing exceptionally well, you might decide to specialise in, for instance, ferns or succulents.

In Part Three you will find hints and suggestions on using plants as part of your interior designs. Ultimately, of course, these become a question of personal taste and preference. A successful indoor garden depends not on the quantity of plants, but on the pleasure you derive from tending those of your choice and within your capabilities.

Contents

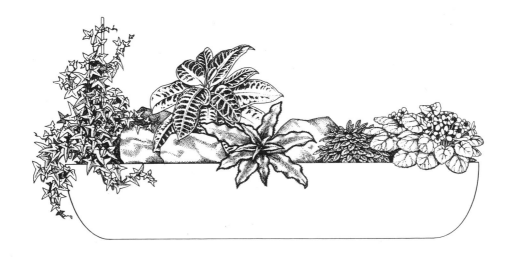

Part One

Choosing and Caring for Indoor Plants

Shopping for house plants

Healthy foliage and flower buds, sturdiness, size and age rather than exotic looks and dramatic impact are pointers to good buys

Before you purchase any plant draw up a list of those you can be reasonably sure will do well in your home and set out to buy one of them. Consult the illustrations and tables in this book so that you have an idea what the plant you intend to buy should look like.

It is always safest to buy tropical plants – most foliage and many flowering plants belong in this category – during the summer months of the year when they are in active growth. If you buy during the winter, insist that the plants are properly wrapped, or bring several sheets of newspaper with you.

Avoid open market stalls and shops with outside displays in wintry weather; the sudden transformation from icy winds to indoor dry warmth is sure to spell an early demise. At the other extreme be equally careful about the so-called impulse buys, often displayed at the check-outs of many supermarkets. Plants which look pale and jaded have probably been suffering in a dry atmosphere, and no amount of tender care can invigorate them at home if the roots have already dried out.

A healthy plant is the key to good buying, but how do you recognise a healthy plant? It should first of all be sturdy, with the leaves spaced at regular intervals and of a uniform colour. Pale, long growths at the top of a mature plant indicate an extended period spent in badly lit and overwarm conditions.

Floppy leaves are an indication of root trouble, usually extreme dryness or rotting through waterlogging. In neither case is the plant likely to survive. Look closely at the compost; if it shrinks away from the pot sides so that the plant can be lifted out to reveal a tangled mass of roots and dry soil, reject it in favour of one firmly anchored in evenly moist compost.

Apart from sturdy stems and fresh-looking leaves, another sign of a well-grown plant is its habit. In general, the top growth should be just wider than the pot diameter, except of course, on erect, single-stemmed plants, such as mother-in-law's tongue *(Sansevieria)*, and most cacti and other succulents.

On flowering plants check that there are plenty of buds coming along – a plant which sheds its opened blooms on the way home is hardly a good buy.

Finally, the size and age of a plant determine its price. Fast-growing and generally short-lived plants, such as tradescantias, are in the lower price ranges, but even so it is advantageous to buy small plants.

On the other hand, young plants, less than 10 in high, of slow growers such as palms and cordylines, though reasonably priced, are not necessarily good buys. They will take many years to reach a useful size and during that time will need extra nursing.

With few exceptions buying house plants by mail-order is a risky business. You will have no chance of seeing the plant before you buy and no guarantee that it will not suffer in transit.

Bonsai trees
More and more shops are displaying these charming miniature trees, tempting the unwary buyer with their masses of tiny apple or cherry blossoms or picturesquely gnarled pine trunks. By all means admire them, but resist buying – the price itself is a good deterrent – unless you have a garden or large terrace or balcony.

Bonsais are *not* suitable as house plants; they are miniature replicas of perfectly hardy forest and garden trees and will only flourish in the open air.

Tools and equipment

Only a few – and inexpensive – tools are needed for the routine tasks of keeping an indoor garden in good trim

Little equipment is needed for the care of house plants other than the inevitable pots. One essential, however, is a watering can, and there are a few points to consider when buying one. As it may have to be used for a plant high on a wall or for a hanging basket, buy one of the special cans with a long spout, wider at the bottom than the top and fitted with a fine detachable watering rose.

The joints on a watering can should be secure and fit snugly to avoid drips and spills on floors and carpets. Check that the handle is in a comfortable position by watering an imaginary plant at eye level.

A can should have a capacity of no more than half to three-quarters of a gallon or it will be too heavy to handle; one that holds less than two pints will involve endless trips to the kitchen.

Small compact pressurised sprayers are readily available, and one which holds a pint or less is quite adequate for all indoor purposes. It is worth-while investing in two sprayers, keeping one for water with which to mist spray plants and one for insecticides. Mark both clearly.

Narrow-bladed secateurs are useful for cutting off faded blooms and leaves, and a small fork and trowel for loosening the surface of the pot compost are handy though not essential – an old kitchen fork and spoon will do equally well.

For climbing plants you will need supports of some kind – canes, ready-made trellis or moss poles – and string or proprietary plant ties for attaching the stems. Upright young plants can be fixed with rings to slender, green-coloured sticks until they are sturdy enough to grow unaided.

At the expensive end of the scale are such sophisticated items as self-watering pots, air and soil moisture gauges and maximum-minimum thermometers.

TOOLS FOR AN INDOOR GARDEN

A basic kit for house plants includes drip saucers for the pots, string or plant ties and a long-spouted watering can. Miniature garden tools are useful.

11

Composts and soil mixtures

Choose between loam or peat mixtures, according to preference. Both are sterilised, nutritious and free of disease and weed spores

A well-balanced potting mixture is essential for all plants grown under the restricted and unnatural conditions of pot culture. Garden soil, however fertile, is totally unsuitable and should never be brought into the house.

Apart from the fact that garden soil often harbours insect grubs or eggs and disease and weed spores, the essential nutrients are never present in the correct amounts or ratios.

For all indoor garden purposes purchase proprietary composts of reputable brands. On a large scale it may be economical to mix your own composts provided that you can sterilise the soil and obtain the necessary base fertiliser and chalk or limestone.

The best known composts for pot plants were developed by the John Innes Institute in the 1930's, originally for its own research purposes. As their potential became obvious, the formula was made generally available, and as no patent was ever taken out the three various types can be made up by any manufacturer simply by following the formulas.

One of the basic ingredients of the John Innes composts is loam, that high-quality layer of soil found directly under the turf in mature meadows. Not surprisingly loam is now difficult to come by, and inferior soils are sometimes used, resulting in inferior composts. John Innes, and other loam-based composts, can be extremely good when bought from reputable suppliers, but may fall short of the high standard originally set by the inventors. The other ingredients are peat, sand and fertilisers.

John Innes potting composts are offered as No. 1, 2 or 3, the numbers referring to the amount of fertiliser that has been added. The

quantity in potting compost No. 1 is ideal for seedlings and young plants growing in small pots.

For established plants, a greater amount of fertiliser is needed and No. 2 supplies this, while No. 3, which predictably has three times as much fertiliser as No. 1, is used for plants which make a lot of growth in a short time, and for large plants in large pots.

If you can obtain good, medium-textured loam it is possible to make potting mixtures at home, to the John Innes formula. Loam must be sterilised before use.

Electric sterilisers are available from large garden suppliers, or you can improvise your own steamer by using a covered roasting tin and baking the loam in the oven at 180°F for 30 minutes.

The sterilised, cooled loam is then mixed with good moss peat and washed coarse sand in the proportions of seven parts (by volume) of loam to three parts of peat and two of sand. John Innes base fertiliser, made up of hoof and horn, superphosphate of lime and sulphate of potash, can be bought ready mixed.

To every 8 gallons of John Innes potting mixture No. 1, add 4 oz of base fertiliser, with $\frac{3}{4}$ oz of ground chalk for all but lime-hating plants. For No. 2 and 3 mixtures, double and treble respectively the amounts of fertiliser and chalk.

Peat-based composts

Because of the variability of loam-based composts, considerable research has been done into those based on peat, particularly in America where loam has never been freely available.

Loamless composts are made of moss peat, sometimes mixed with sand, and again with fertilisers added. Fertilisers are even more important than with loam-based

COMPOSTS AND SOIL MIXTURES

composts as neither peat nor sand contains more than a minimal amount of plant food.

Peat-based mixtures have the great advantage that they are light in weight. A bag of peat compost weighs far less than an equal-sized bag of sugar which can be quite a consideration if it has to be carried home from the shops. It also makes for lighter-weight pots, important when they have to be moved for cleaning or to another position.

For large plants the lack of weight in peat-based composts can cause problems as the pot and its contents must be heavier than the rest of the plant if the whole thing is not to become top-heavy and fall over. This problem can be overcome by making sure that the container is a solid one, or by putting a few weights inside a plastic or glass-fibre pot.

Probably the greatest drawback to a pure peat compost is that it creates watering problems. The compost should be placed in the pot only loosely, and as long as it is kept moist, all is well, but if it is allowed to become dry, it shrinks and leaves a space between the root ball and the edge of the pot.

Once peat compost has shrunk, any subsequent water will simply pour through the empty space and out through the bottom drainage holes while the plant's vital roots remain dry. If this happens the only remedy is to stand the pot in a bucket of water, immersed to just below the level of the pot rim, and leave it there for half-an-hour, then lift it out to drain thoroughly.

The problem has been recognised by the makers of peat composts, and it is now possible to buy packs in which the peat contains a special wetting agent. Such composts are expensive but, until you have confidence in your watering, are undoubtedly useful.

A second drawback to all-peat composts is again concerned with watering, for when thoroughly wet, they dry out only slowly. This situation is aggravated if the compost has been firmed too much so that the vital air spaces have been filled.

Only the lightest pressure should be used when filling pots with peat mixtures, and ideally they should be merely shaken down and not pressed at all.

For plants which need a continuously moist growing medium, peat is excellent, but it is certain death to most pot plants if their roots are kept waterlogged for any extended period. The solution to this problem lies in the addition of grit or sand which will open up the peat and ensure good drainage.

Most house plants thrive in a freely draining compost, and some proprietary loamless composts are available ready mixed with sand. If you are growing a wide selection of house plants, it is more convenient to buy a pure peat compost and a bag of grit and mix the two in the proportion of three parts peat, by volume, to one of grit.

Buy granite or flint grit, not limestone which is detrimental to a number of house plants; it should be of a fine grade, with a diameter of about ⅛ in. The bag should also stipulate that the grit has been washed so that it is free of dust and bacteria; it must be angular, unlike the rounded pebbles sold for aquaria.

If you choose sand to mix with peat instead of grit, make sure that it has been specifically prepared for potting. This will mean that it has been washed and all the fine silty particles removed. Even then many sands, even those termed coarse, tend to be small-grained, and this can cause the air spaces in the compost to become clogged.

Weeds should never be a problem in commercial composts; loam-based mixtures have been sterilised before marketing, and peat is usually weed-free. Any small weed seedlings with very narrow leaves appearing in peat composts will probably be heather or rush and can be pulled up with no problem. Both loam and peat composts are also disease-free.

Bulb fibre
This is a sterile weed-free medium formulated for growing bulbs for a once-only display. It serves to keep the plants erect by supporting their roots as well as holding the moisture they need.

Bulb fibre contains none of the foods that are necessary for a plant which is to continue blooming year after year, and can therefore not be used for perennial bulbs which need a freely draining compost. Bulbs grown in fibre or water jars are discarded after they have flowered, unless garden space is available where they can grow on for a few years until they have recovered enough to flower again, this time in the garden.

Bulb fibre is sold in the dry state, in plastic bags. It needs to be thoroughly wetted before use; the quickest way is to puncture the bag in several places and immerse it in a bucket of warm water for several hours until thoroughly moist. Remove excess moisture by squeezing the fibre in your hands.

Other composts
Details of the more specialised composts used for growing ferns and orchids, bromeliads and cacti are given in the relevant chapters. The necessary components, such as leaf-mould, shredded bark and osmunda fibre can be bought in small packs, usually complete with instructions.

13

Pots and containers

The right pot for the right plant creates a pleasing unity, with trailers in hanging baskets and epiphytes growing on tree branches

The days are long gone when the mention of house plants brought to the mind a picture of a cottage window sill with rows of clay pots, each in its own ill-matched saucer. Today, the range of pots, pans, boxes and baskets made specifically for the display of indoor plants is enormous, and the clever use of a pot within a pot allows almost any container which matches the general decor to be pressed into service.

Clay versus plastic

Whatever the method of ornamental display, the pot is still the basic item, and at once two alternatives present themselves: clay or plastic? Both have their fervent advocates, who will brook no objective considerations of their respective merits and drawbacks.

The chief difference between the two materials is that clay is porous and plastic is not. Both types of pots are always provided with drainage holes in the bottom, though clay pots have only one large single hole, and plastic pots have several holes or rectangular slits. However, only water evaporating through the sides can make any appreciable difference.

Soil in clay pots will dry against the sides as well as from the top, but in plastic pots this does not happen. This factor may seem relatively marginal, but that little extra moisture at the side of any overwatered plastic pot can tip the balance if the plant is already ailing, especially in an all-peat compost.

For plants which require really sharp drainage, clay pots have a slight advantage; otherwise use plastic containers with extra grit in the compost.

Plastic pots may be clay-coloured, green, brown, black or white and are also available in stronger colours. But remember that few plants are set off to advantage in a gaudy pot, though this is a matter of personal taste. Most clay pots come in the traditional terra cotta colour, but

HEAVY AND LIGHT-WEIGHT FLOWER POTS

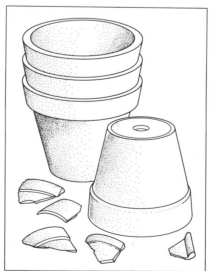

Old-fashioned clay pots need a layer of broken crocks beneath the potting compost to keep it free-draining.

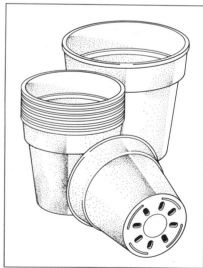

Plastic pots are pierced with several drainage holes, making crocking unnecessary; water does not evaporate.

more decorative ones can be found, usually sold as porous pots and made from different clay mixtures. They are rather more expensive than ordinary clay pots and the even cheaper plastic pots.

Self-watering pots

Single pots can be stood in specially made saucers, available to match the pots, or on any old deep saucers according to taste. Filled with gravel and water so that the base of the pot is just above the water level, such saucers help to keep the air humid.

Self-watering pots are in effect double pots with a small water reservoir in the bottom from which the compost is kept moist through capillary action. Water is added as required through a filling shaft built into one side, with indicator levels and often automatic overflow devices. Liquid feeds are added, when necessary, directly to the water reservoir.

Self-watering pots, made from rigid plastic or glass-fibre, are available in a wide range of sizes and shapes, from single-pot sizes to large group arrangements, and in several colours and simulated wood finishes. They are valuable for office displays and during the holidays, as the plants are kept watered automatically, but in permanent use they have the disadvantage that in some cases the compost is kept too wet for the plants to thrive.

Decorative containers

If you dislike the look of plain clay and plastic pots and prefer containers to fit in with the decor of the room, the answer is to use a pot within a pot. This method of growing indoor plants not only has more eye appeal, but also serves to raise the immediate air moisture.

In double-potting the plant, potted in its permanent clay or plastic pot, is set inside a decorative container and the space between the two is filled with moist peat, both around the sides and underneath if necessary to raise the potted plant to an effective level. Any container can be used that is waterproof and shaped so that it will hold a pot, from ornate vases to modern ceramics, from antique copper or pewter bowls, if you are fortunate enough to have one, to modern glass-fibre designs.

It is sensible to line china containers with polythene as peat can stain the inside. This also applies to metal containers as the continuous dampness of the peat can cause some metals to corrode, and a number of plants do not thrive if their roots are in close contact with metal, particularly copper.

Line all decorative containers with heavy-duty household foil, then polythene because growing roots are surprisingly strong and quite capable of puncturing an ordinary polythene lining. With such a carefully assembled lining, even non-waterproof containers, such as basket-ware, can be used; the basket can first be lined with coloured paper or cloth to complement the general colour scheme of the room.

Double-potting

The layer of damp peat between the two pots will serve to keep the compost moist and, if the outer container is large enough, will provide a little but valuable humidity from the surface of the damp peat.

In double pots vigorous plants will quickly send out roots into the surrounding peat, and these should not be allowed to grow too large or the plant will be weakened when the roots finally have to be broken off for re-potting. Ideally take the pot out of its container once a month and trim off any visible roots while they are small.

Large and deep decorative containers are ideal for displaying a number of plants, each in its individual pot, sunk in the peat until the top is level with the container surface. Old cooking utensils and china wash basins are now collectors' items, but containers of modern design, often in glass-fibre or simulated wood material, are readily available and comparatively inexpensive.

It is advisable to line old containers with a protective double layer of plastic foil as the china may have a slight crack where water from the permanently moist peat will leak on to furniture.

The advantage of leaving the plants in their individual pots is the ease with which they can be removed from the container, either to make a more effective arrangement or to replace a plant which is not thriving. This is far more difficult if they are planted directly in a container or plant trough where the roots become interwoven.

It is essential that all plants in a group have similar needs in respect of warmth and water. Light can be slightly modified by setting one end nearer a source of light, but this can only be marginal, and sun and shade plants should not be grouped together.

Shallow containers, such as old meat dishes or trays can be filled with a light layer of peat for moisture-loving plants, or a spread of pebbles upon which the pots are stood without taking up moisture from the water. This keeps the pebbles wet and helps to create humidity. In such a display the pots, which are visible, at least until foliage begins to cover them, should be of identical material or colour. Try to use at least one trailing plant in the group so that the stems can sprawl among the pots and eliminate the regimented look of a number of separate pots.

There are also many decorative plant holders, often in wrought iron, which hold a single pot; when buying check that the one being considered will hold the pot you have in mind. Otherwise buy one to fit it, plant pots are by no means standard in their rim sizes.

Hanging baskets
Hanging containers make attractive forms of display. Various types and sizes are available, but it is essential that they are equipped with a drip tray to prevent splashes on the carpet.

Pots suspended in macramé work are becoming increasingly popular; cane and basket containers can also be used – in fact anything that will effectively support a pot, with a drip tray and its plant. A suspended pot can be surprisingly heavy, especially after watering, and will need a strong hook to bear the weight.

The siting of hanging containers may pose problems; the centre of a window embrasure is obvious; roof beams in old houses may seem ideal, but the ceilings are usually so low that a hanging basket would often cause an obstruction. A curtain rod can be fixed across a corner and attached to the walls with two brackets; alternatively use a free-standing pole support, made especially for this purpose or fashion one yourself from an old standard lamp.

Floor displays
Tall plants make striking focal points provided they are in scale with the surroundings. For free-standing floor displays the double-pot method is recommended;

decorative half tubs are particularly useful, but make sure that the container is heavy enough to support the growing plant – glass-fibre containers, for example, are very light-weight.

When space is limited, a climber can be trained, from floor level, up sticks or strings, while many of the tropical evergreens which put out stem roots, such as *Philodendron, Monstera* and *Scindapsus,* are best grown on moss poles. These can be bought, in various sizes, from most florists' shops and garden centres, and consist of a stick wrapped around with sphagnum moss held in place with thin wire. A similar pole can be made from fine chicken wire, shaped into a tube and filled with moss. In both cases the plants should be grown in ordinary pots and the poles or wire cylinders firmly anchored in the compost. Keep the moss poles permanently moist with frequent sprayings of tepid water.

A mass of foliage can become extremely heavy and topple over pot and container. Place the support in the pot before adding compost and setting the plant in position, then wedge the moss pole with more compost. For very large poles, it may be advisable to anchor them further with large stones.

For smaller and less permanent displays of climbers, three or four canes can be inserted in a pot and held together at the top in tripod fashion. Or wires pushed into the compost can be shaped into balloon-like structures or loops. Quick-growing annuals are particularly suitable for growing on such supports.

Bark slabs and tree trunks
Some unusual containers are made from small sections of tree trunks which are split and hollowed out so that only a slab of bark remains.

The cavity is filled with a moisture-retentive material such as pulverised bark and held in place with sphagnum moss and thin wire. Many orchids and some ferns grow successfully on such slabs mounted on wall hooks.

Another effective support is the skeleton part of a columnar cactus, sometimes available from curio shops. This has a regular and attractive pattern of holes which are stuffed with sphagnum moss. A climbing plant will push its aerial roots through the holes and provide an eye-catching display.

Not all plants need containers; in the wild many bromeliads and orchids grow on tree branches, gaining their nourishment from small particles of organic debris lodged in the bark of their hosts. They are in no way parasitic, using the branches on which they grow simply for support.

In the home epiphytic plants can be grown effectively in hanging baskets, particularly orchids such as *Dendrobium, Cattleya* and *Laelia,* but they and many of the bromeliads also thrive on a decorative tree branch laid on a waterproof surface or in a shallow tray, perhaps filled with moss and stones to simulate a landscape. Try to find a piece of driftwood with rough corrugated bark, which will hold the questing roots, moss and water better.

Choose a suitable perch on the branch for each plant to be sited, then take a handful of sphagnum moss and into this sprinkle a small amount of good potting compost and wrap this mixture round the roots of each plant. Hold it in place with fine, green plastic-coated wire and bind the plant gently but firmly to the branch. Among the bromeliads, species of *Neoregelia, Nidularium* and *Vriesea* can be grown in this way.

General care

Regular attention to staking and tying, removing faded leaves and flowers and checking on pots and composts repays with a thriving plant community

Many house plants grow to gigantic sizes in the wild, an extreme example being the rubber plant, *Ficus elastica* 'Decora', which can exceed 100 ft in its forest home. The reason that it cannot, happily, attempt to do this in a living room is root restriction.

Basically a plant can only keep growing in size while its roots are spreading and finding nourishment, so by confining it to a small pot, it will remain small.

The necessity for keeping some plants in check makes it important that the reason for two very different, but much confused tasks of plant care – potting-on and re-potting – are understood. Potting-on involves moving a plant into a larger sized pot, and this is done when a larger specimen is wanted.

Re-potting implies the return of the plant to the same or same-sized pot, with fresh compost, the aim being to keep it healthy, while not increasing its size.

Potting-on and re-potting

Among the tasks connected with the general care of house plants, potting is perhaps the most

neglected. Plants are often allowed to become thin and leggy in exhausted soil when re-potting would have kept them strong.

If a plant does not grow as well as you think it should, knock it out of its pot and look at the root ball. To remove it from its pot, unless the plant is very large and unwieldy, place one hand over the compost, allowing the plant's stem to come between the fingers, then turn the whole thing upside down with the other hand. Tap the underside of the pot on a firm surface; this should free the plant so that the pot can be lifted off.

Large plants, which are too heavy or awkward to be handled in this way, need rather different treatment. Prepare an area on the floor by covering it with polythene or layers of newspaper, then carefully lay the plant in its pot on this. Tap around the edge of the pot, with the heel of a shoe, until the root and compost has loosened enough to slide out. If it resists, hold the base of the stem and give a not too vigorous pull.

It may happen that a plant refuses to budge, especially if it has

SEPARATING PLANT AND POT

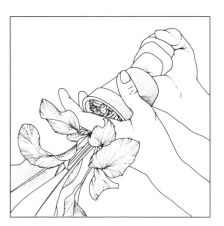

Invert pot and plant, with the fingers holding the stems and the palm steadying the compost. Tap the base

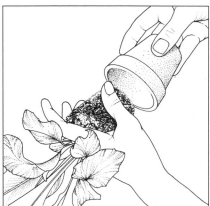

of the pot firmly and pull it away from the plant. A moist root ball slides out easier than a dry one.

Potting a cactus can be a prickly job. Use a sling of folded newspaper to hold and reposition the plant in its pot.

been in the pot for a long time. More drastic treatment is then necessary: run a long-bladed knife round the inner edge of the pot to free the roots adhering to the sides. Re-potting or potting-on of a large plant is a job for two people.

Once the plant is out of the pot, whatever its size, look at the sides of the compost. If plenty of soil and few roots are visible, look for other causes for the lack of growth, but if the pot ball is a tight mesh of roots, then the plant must be given fresh compost. Dead roots are usually the result of overwatering.

Re-potting

If the plant is already large enough, and no great increase in height or spread is desired, then it needs re-potting. Choose a clean pot of the same size and fresh compost.

To make room for fresh compost remove about a quarter of the existing soil ball and the roots within it. One of the best tools for this job is an old kitchen fork with the top of the prongs bent under; with this or a small window-box fork, scrape round the root ball, including the top, until the size is sufficiently reduced.

Put a good layer of potting compost in the new pot – and a drainage layer of broken crocks if you are using a clay pot. Set the plant on top of the compost to check the depth; add or remove compost so that, when the job is completed, there is a space equal to one seventh of the pot depth left for watering.

Hold the plant steady and trickle more compost round the sides; use a blunt stick to push it down so that all large air spaces are eliminated. Bear in mind that peat-based composts should be packed looser than the ordinary John Innes and other loam composts.

Water the re-potted plant, filling the space at the top to the pot rim so that the whole root ball is soaked through.

Potting-on

If the plant has not yet attained its full, required size, move it to a larger pot. Quick-growing plants are better moved to pots two sizes larger, but for most plants of average or slow growth, pots one size larger will be enough. The actual task of filling in with fresh compost and replacing the plant is identical

RE-POTTING TO RESTRICT TOP GROWTH

Use a fork to prise away old compost and excessively long and dead roots. Set the root ball in a clean, same-sized

pot, on fresh potting mixture and fill in round the sides and top. Firm lightly to level the compost and keep the plant

straight. Leave enough space for watering between the base of the plant and the pot rim.

Encourage bushy and compact growth by snipping off the growing points at the tips of brittle stems.

to the re-potting method, except that it is not necessary to remove any of the old compost or roots from the plant.

Once re-potting or potting-on is completed, the exhausted compost must be discarded, either spread on the garden or consigned to the dustbin. The pots should be thoroughly washed and scrubbed, ready for use again.

Pinching-out and pruning

Many house plants put a great deal of energy into developing long stems when a compact, bushy plant would be far more effective from the decorative point of view. Tradescantias and their relations, such as the bright-leaved *Zebrina*, have this natural growth habit, and in order to keep them to the desired size and shape, they need to be pinched out in the same way as greenhouse carnations and chrysanthemums.

Pinching-out implies the removal of the leading shoot where it grows away from a leaf. Simply break the stem at this point between thumb and finger nail. With growth on this stem stopped by the removal of the growing point, the plant will react by throwing out two or more stems from buds a little below the point where it was pinched. If these are subsequently treated in the same way, when long enough, a bushy plant will result.

Practically all plants can have their leading shoots pinched out and respond by branching to a lesser or greater extent.

Many climbers or tall specimen plants which are threatening to reach the ceiling can have their leading shoots removed to keep them within bounds. This pruning operation may be carried out once or twice, but eventually the lower part of the stem will become hard and woody and will lose its leaves. If this happens it is possible to cut the stem back to within 6 in of its base, and the plant will usually send up a number of shoots from this point.

Cut-back plants look unsightly until they are growing properly again, and it is a better idea to use the shoots for cuttings as soon as they are large enough. Some, such as the rubber plant, are better propagated by air layering, but in any case the old plant can be

POTTING-ON FOR LARGER PLANTS

Young plants grow steadily towards maturity given an annual shift into the next pot size. Good drainage is most important for the expanding roots, and clay pots should be well crocked. Pot in fresh compost, taking care to avoid large air spaces by shaking the pot gently to settle the soil. Firm the surface to leave room for watering.

SUPPORTS FOR CLIMBERS

Moss poles give support to climbers such as philodendrons, whose aerial roots gain an easy hold in the moss.

The weak stems of stephanotis twine gracefully round a wire loop, exposing the flowers to light and air.

Tendrils of self-clinging climbers attach themselves to trellis and quickly form a dense foliage screen.

discarded as soon as a young plant is assured. *Cissus, Dieffenbachia, Fatsia, × Fatshedera, Schefflera, Pelargonium* (geranium) and most *Ficus* species are good examples of plants that can be pruned back to provide cuttings.

Palms will not react to the above treatment, so it is important to restrict their growth once they have reached the desired height. Keep them in small pots and pot-on or re-pot only when it is absolutely necessary, and the pots are plainly full of roots.

Once palms grow too large, there is little option but to discard them or give them to friends with more room. It is possible to remove almost all palm foliage which will encourage new leaves to grow, but the second crop will be smaller than the first, and such a short-term measure is hardly worth the trouble involved.

Supporting and tying-in
Only a very few climbing house plants are self-clinging, and most will need assistance by being tied to their supports. You will soon discover that twining plants twine either clockwise or anti-clockwise, and that none is prepared to go the wrong way.

Twisted the opposite way to their natural growth habit, climbing stems will unwind and hang down until started off in the right direction. The leading tip on a climbing shoot, tied loosely to its support, will soon show the way it will climb. Tie the shoots in as unobtrusively as possible and leave a loop to allow for increasing thickness of the stem as it grows. Take the twine round the stem, then back to the string or support, in a figure of eight.

Many non-climbing plants also derive benefit from some form of support such as a cane, stick or moss pole. Insert this at the time of potting to avoid any damage to the roots. To be effective, the support should reach to the bottom of the pot, but below the top of the plant which it supports. Tie the stem with green or dark-coloured twine, in a figure of eight round support and stem as for climbing plants. Be careful not to pull the plant close to the support – the loop of twine between the two can be quite long, yet perform its job perfectly satisfactorily.

When a plant outgrows its first support, cut the ties, remove the cane from the pot and replace it with a larger one set in exactly the same hole. This is preferable to starting with a support that is too large and obvious.

For bushy and spreading plants, push small, twiggy sticks round the sides of the pot while the plant is still young; they will soon be covered by the foliage, and no tying-in is necessary.

Wire supports, chiefly used for soft-stemmed flowering plants, can be bought at most garden centres. They generally take the form of a loop with one or two 'legs' which are pushed into either side of the pot while the plant is still small. The stems will grow through the loop which keeps them upright.

Routine tasks
In addition to the daily routine of watering (see page 31), the plants and their containers should be kept tidy. This means removing any dead leaves as soon as they drop, or carefully breaking them off if they are not shed naturally. This not only improves the appearance of the plants, but also minimises any risk of infection and is particularly important in propagating and Wardian cases. Botrytis, or grey mould, can be a scourge in a damp and stagnant atmosphere.

Removing dead flowers is largely a matter of appearance, but if it is done early enough to prevent seeds from forming, it often encourages further flowers to appear.

Seeds provide an easy means of increase, and you may find it worth-while to save seed from a favourite plant in order to sow them later. In this case, leave a few flowers on the plant and check to see if the ovaries swell after the petals have fallen.

In order to obtain seeds, it will probably be necessary to hand pollinate in the absence of insects, using a tuft of cotton wool or a fine paint brush, to transfer pollen from one flower to another. If you are growing two plants of the same species, cross pollination from one to the other will make seed production more certain.

Only true species will reproduce themselves exactly from seed. Variegated forms will almost certainly produce all-green plants or ones with no green colouring at all; these will die quickly.

Home-saved seed is best sown as soon as it is gathered, but if this is not possible, store it in a cool and dry place, out of bright light.

The leaves of evergreen foliage plants show up dust as much as a piece of highly polished furniture and need regular dusting and even washing. A number of proprietary leaf cleansers and shines are on the market, but water is almost as effective and less expensive.

Never use a detergent on plant leaves, nor oil to make them glossy; both will clog the pores and damage the leaf surface. Plants with rough or hairy leaves, as well as cacti and many succulents, are best cleaned with a soft paint brush. Dust is not only a matter of appearance, it will also filter the available light and can block the pores through which the leaves take in air.

Peat composts sometimes develop a green, algal surface, particularly if kept too wet. Scrape the algae gently from the compost surface, topdress with a fresh layer of peat and avoid saturating the compost.

Hard water often causes a crusty white lime deposit on the inner pot rim and the compost surface. Scrape it off with a sharp knife and replace the top compost to improve air circulation. Soft, strained rainwater overcomes this common problem.

STAKES AND TIES FOR UPRIGHT GROWERS

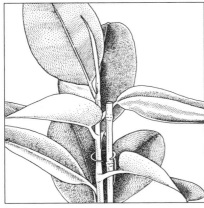

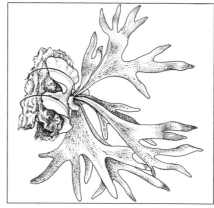

Straight stems remain erect with the aid of canes and clip-on rings that allow room for increased girth.

Branching but upright stems are better tied loosely to supports with string looped round stem and cane.

Use thin, plastic-coated wire to fix a staghorn fern and its compost to a bark slab mounted on a wall.

Natural and artificial light

Sun, the source of daylight, is essential for the growth process known as photosynthesis. Artificial light helps to maintain a steady balance

Buying a healthy plant, growing it in suitable compost and correct pot size and tending it with daily care are basic tasks of little importance unless you take into consideration the environment to which the plant is naturally inclined.

In order to cultivate plants successfully – in the home or the garden – it is important to understand and equate the native habitat of any plant. Removed from their natural surroundings, plants will have to adapt to artificial conditions; the great majority accept this if their basic needs are met.

The origin of a plant is therefore of great value in assessing its cultural requirements, for here lie the clues that will lead you to success or failure.

It is, naturally and fortunately, impossible to recreate in the home surroundings identical to the plants' homeland. The aim, though, should be to simulate to some extent conditions essential for steady and healthy growth.

The basic needs are concerned with light, heat, humidity and moisture. Of these, available light is probably the most vital as the generator of the other components. Although no green plant can live without light, the amount needed varies enormously from one species to another.

Plants in tropical and sub-tropical forests, other than trees, will rarely if ever see any continuous sunlight as the trees cast perpetual shade. Plants from these habitats have adapted in two ways, either by growing as epiphytes on the branches of trees or by accepting the gloom on the forest floor.

Epiphytes, mainly bromeliads, ferns and orchids, but also including forest cacti, get some direct sun on their high perches, though most of the light they receive is filtered through the dense foliage. In the poor light and humid air of the forest floor live numerous colourful evergreens with thin-textured leaves able to absorb what little light is available.

On the other hand, most succulents, including cacti, come from dry areas with little cloud and hours of unbroken sunlight.

These are the extremes, but to the sun lovers can be added most of the flowering and bulbous plants from temperate countries – Europe, North and South America and Australia – which flower when sunshine is uninterrupted, while those from the tropics tend to have adapted to more shady areas.

Natural light
Before placing a plant, look at all the positions available and try to divide them into the following three categories: 1) Windows that receive at least six hours' sun in June; 2) those which admit sun for two to six hours at the same time of the year, though probably none in winter; and 3) windows which get less than two hours' sun or none at all – this last category will also apply to other room areas.

The area lit from the sunny window can include up to 2 ft into the room beyond, which gives additional scope for a small plant stand or table. A tea trolley on wheels is particularly useful because of the ease with which it can be moved, and an inside window box is also effective.

The sunny window is the place for the succulents, including the majority of cacti, and for bulbs, shrubs and most of the flowering plants. Saintpaulias are notable exceptions and prone to leaf scorch in full summer sun.

If no such window is available, then it is better to ignore the light-demanding species and concentrate on foliage plants, epiphytes and tropical flowering plants. All these will do well around or close to a window which falls into the second category.

The third category is the one most people are likely to encounter. The poor amount of light, near the window and inside rooms, is, however, sufficient for the plants which grow naturally on tropical forest floors.

In addition to shade-lovers, all other plants, with the exception of the full sun lovers, can in theory grow in poorly lit positions if provided with artificial light for an average of 10–12 hours a day.

Plants that are grown solely in the natural light admitted through a window will often grow towards the light source. To prevent a lopsided appearance, the pots should be given a half turn every other day. In poor, weak light, it may be necessary to turn the pots every day. With artificial light, plants do not need to be turned to keep them straight because the light source is directly above them.

Some plants, especially azaleas and Christmas and Easter cacti, object strongly to being moved once the flower buds have formed; the accidental knock or careless turning of the plants usually result in the unopened buds dropping off.

Artificial light

In general, plants need about 12 hours of light a day while actively growing, less during the rest period. When natural light is insufficient, in duration or quality, it can be supplemented by artificial light. Ordinary electric light bulbs of sufficient power give off too much heat to be satisfactory, and the best artificial light is supplied by fluorescent tubes.

The red and violet-blue light rays in the colour spectrum are the most important for plant growth. They are supplied most efficiently by fluorescent tubes specially designed for plant growth and marketed under various brand names. The tubes are best erected in ranks of two, and on average each gives off 10 watts per square foot. The height at which the tubes should be erected varies according to the individual plant needs, but allow 9–12 in for flowering, and 18–30 in for foliage plants.

The use of reflector hoods over the tubes concentrates the light thrown on to the plants; ideally you should be able to alter the distances as growth dictates. If, for the sake of appearances, the tubes are mounted behind a pelmet, you can paint this white on the inside to reflect more light.

Artificial light is used not only to supplement daylight from a window, but can also be valuable in bringing a new focal point to a room by illuminating a normally dark area. Alcoves and niches are natural candidates for artificial lighting, as are disused fireplaces.

The average fluorescent tubes should last for a year and are best replaced when they begin to deteriorate from the ends. A faint flickering is the first sign of wear.

For positions where it is difficult or impractical to bring plants and artificial light together, a ready-made plant unit can be the ideal solution. Some units are free-standing, resembling a large tea trolley with one or more trays for the plants, lit from above by well-shaded fluorescent tubes. Others consist of a single tray beneath one hooded lighting tube and are of a size to fit a small table top.

So far beauty has lagged behind design in the construction of illuminated plant units, and many look more suitable for raising seedlings than for plant displays.

Plant illumination

While domestic, incandescent light bulbs are unsuitable as a means of supplying good artificial light, they can be used for dramatic highlighting effects at night. Small plants can be placed for a short while near a table lamp for illumination, but watch out for any signs of leaf or flower scorch.

Spotlights have their uses in large areas, such as open-plan living rooms and cavernous halls, and are particularly valuable for plants standing on a landing or the bend in a staircase. Great care has to be taken in placing the lights so that there is no risk of dazzle on the stairs themselves.

Spotlights can be fixed at floor or ceiling level to highlight an accent plant or large group display. The lights can, if necessary, be controlled with dimmer switches.

Specialised units containing banks of fluorescent lights are used in many countries, notably the United States, which experience long winters. These enable the keen amateur to grow all types of light-demanding plants, such as succulents and alpines, even in a cellar or attic with no daylight at all. At present, however, these units, at prohibitive cost, are the provenance of the dedicated amateur and outside the scope of this book.

Where any kind of artificial light is provided, check the plants carefully in the beginning to judge the intensity and heat of the light source. If the plants become pale and drawn, the light is inadequate, probably because it is placed too far away; if, on the other hand, the leaves show brown scorch marks, the light is obviously too intense.

Only by trial and error can the correct combination of plants and artificial light be achieved; the splendid effects seen in the foyers of hotels and offices are the result of many years of experimentation. No one finds perfection at first, and nothing is lost by an unsuccessful placing as long as the plants are removed as soon as they make their displeasure apparent.

Controlled flowering

Some plants, mainly those from temperate regions, are extremely sensitive to the different day and night lengths of summer and winter, the most familiar examples being chrysanthemums and poinsettias *(Euphorbia pulcherrima)*. In the wild both are late autumn-flowering and neither will begin to develop their flower buds until the nights bring more than 12 hours of darkness.

Commercial growers manipulate artificially the amount of necessary darkness so that the plants are ready for the Christmas season. Chrysanthemums, bought in bud at this season, will not flower again at the same time if kept for a second year, and they will usually develop into much taller and leggy plants. As it is virtually impossible to reproduce the controlled conditions required to produce similar plants at home, chrysanthemums are best discarded after flowering.

The more expensive poinsettias can be induced to produce their flowers and decorative bracts regularly at Christmas by the simple expedient of placing them in a dark cupboard from late afternoon until the following morning when they should be set in good, bright light. This long-night and short-day treatment should be carried out for 6-8 weeks from early autumn onwards or until the flower buds have formed. Thereafter the plants should be given normal light conditions until they begin flowering.

Place and position

Irrespective of size and outlook every room in the house can become home for at least a couple of green plants

Before you position any plant, consider two important factors: available light and warmth. These are the basic needs and essential for a plant's health and development, not merely its survival. There are, of course, other points to consider, such as humidity – which can be critical – and food and water, but these can be provided in almost any position.

Whether you are starting a collection or re-deploying existing plants to better advantage, try out the various habitats to discover which plants will feel most at home in them. In other words, choose the right plant for the right place.

Almost every room in the home offers a suitable place for a plant, and there is probably one site which is ideal for a large number. Where conditions are less than perfect, you can move plants to this environment for a spell of recuperation before returning them to their normal quarters. Even plants which prefer shady spots will benefit from a brief stay in better light as long as direct hot sun is avoided.

Never be afraid to experiment with plants, moving them around to harmonise or contrast with the decor of a room. However, pay special attention to any change this may occasion in a plant's general appearance; if it is obviously disliking its new position move it back to its former place.

Once you have decided where you want to place plants, which types appeal to you and which will thrive in the chosen positions, you can move on to more creative tasks and decide on how to use plants, singly or in groups, for the most decorative effect. See also Arranging Plants Indoors (p. 150-163).

No two homes are alike in the arrangement and use of rooms, and the following suggestions can be general guidelines only. Decorative effects and uses of indoor plants are almost as diverse as the plants themselves, but any room however dull can be brought to life with the strategic placing of even one small plant.

Halls, landings and stairways

First impressions are important, and a shapely or colourful display beyond the front door offers an immediate welcome. Unfortunately halls, passageways and staircases have a number of disadvantages for healthy plant life. They are usually dimly lighted and even in centrally heated homes tend to be subject to draughts and fluctuating temperatures. Plants for these areas must therefore be tough and undemanding.

In a small hall, a shelf or table-top can display a single plant. Trailers, such as *Chlorophytum comosum, Saxifraga stolonifera* and *Plectranthus oertendahlii*, will tolerate draughts and moderately poor light. For unheated positions near windows or glass doors which receive little or no sun, you can choose from the many attractive cultivars of the English ivy (*Hedera helix*). The outdoor and hardy maidenhair ferns (*Adiantum capillus-veneris*) are also suitable.

In draught-free and warm halls any plant suitable for ordinary room cultivation will do equally well. Otherwise *Fatsia*, × *Fatshedera*, aspidistras and *Clivia miniata* all make large sturdy specimens even in cool positions which receive no direct window light.

An unheated, brightly lit position in hall or spare bedroom, with at least an hour of sun a day in winter, is ideal for those plants which cannot tolerate too much heat at any time of year. These include most bulbs, such as hyacinths and narcissi, tulips and crocus, and temporary flowering plants, such as cyclamen, chrysanthemums and azaleas. They can, of course, be taken into a warm room by day.

Landings, and half-landings if large enough, can accommodate the same large plants as hallways and in addition such a handsome specimen as *Cissus antarctica*, provided the position is fairly warm and lit from an overhead light.

Stairways can be brightened with hanging baskets of ivies, *Ficus pumila*, ferns such as *Nephrolepis* and *Pteris* species, and the trailing tradescantias. Where light is poor, a spotlight fitted on the ceiling creates an unusual focal point as well as healthier plants.

Living rooms

Climatic conditions vary greatly, but hardly any room is without windows. These are often the first places to attract the eye and also the most obvious places for plants.

The ideal window would be double-glazed and have a radiator beneath it with a wide shelf. This combination avoids draughts and extremes of temperatures, but the plants will dry quickly and some humidity must be supplied. Such windows, with good natural light, are ideal for most succulents and cacti and for many flowering plants, such as hibiscus, poinsettias and stephanotis.

Window positions, which receive morning or afternoon sun for most of the year, suit flowering begonias, *Beloperone guttata*, calceolarias, *Impatiens* and *Sinningia* as well as azaleas and cyclamen.

North-facing and shady windows in cool or erratically heated rooms are suitable for the same plants as dull halls and passageways. If, however, the temperature remains above 65° F, a wider range of tropical foliage plants can be grown, notably *Aglaonema, Dieffenbachia, Howea* and *Maranta*, bromeliads such as *Cryptanthus* and *Neoregelia*, and, of course, African violets.

In many homes window sills are too narrow to be of any value for plant display. It is not difficult to extend them into the room with shelf conversions or even an inside window-box held on strong brackets. It this is not possible, you could adapt a movable tea trolley to a window bed. Ideally this should have a fitted top deep enough to hold pots sunk to their rims in peat.

High windows and those with a dull view can have strong glass shelves for individual pot plants fitted across them. Hanging baskets can be suspended from the window embrasure, and strong climbers can twine up the frame.

Away from windows, light is the chief limiting factor, and foliage plants will always be more successful than flowering ones. At ordinary room temperature, dull corners can be brightened with small subjects, such as *Begonia rex, Peperomia obtusifolia* and *Pilea cadierei*.

Taller plants tolerating poor light include *Ficus elastica* 'Decora', *Chamaedorea elegans*, monsteras, *Scindapsus aureus* and many philodendrons. All, however, need some light, natural or artificial.

Bathrooms

Warm bathrooms, where humidity is generally high, provide good homes for tropical plants. Artificial lighting is usually necessary as the translucent glass of bathrooms holds back a great amount of light. Talcum powder can prove a hazard, clogging plant pores and filtering light. Wipe the leaves regularly with a damp pad of cottonwool.

Where the temperature does not

The ideal home would be designed to provide comfort for people and plants alike. In this imaginary house, the living-room receives maximum light through a south-facing, unobstructed exposure. The north-facing bedroom and landing are suitable for plants thriving in cooler, dimmer positions, while the east-facing bathroom and west-facing kitchen are ideal for subjects needing indirect light and moderate heat.

fall below 65° F, *Calathea*, marantas, *Chamaedorea, Dracaena godseffiana, Fittonia* and *Peperomia* species add brilliant foliage colours and textures. For an even more exotic touch, you can try a pot or basket of cattleya orchids.

For cooler bathrooms, aspidistras and ferns are the obvious choice. Pots of sansevierias and hanging containers of ivies and *Ficus pumila* will usually succeed.

Kitchens

Kitchens are difficult to categorise as light, temperature and humidity fluctuate widely. They do have the advantage that plants will generally be observed more closely than anywhere else, and they often act as hospitals for ailing plants.

Kitchen window sills, where not occupied by pots of herbs, are traditionally crowded with smaller flowering plants, such as African violets, pelargoniums, primulas and indoor bulbs. As in living-room areas, available light governs the choice of plants, but you can hardly go wrong with the durable ivies, adaptable ferns and tough aspidistras and sansevierias.

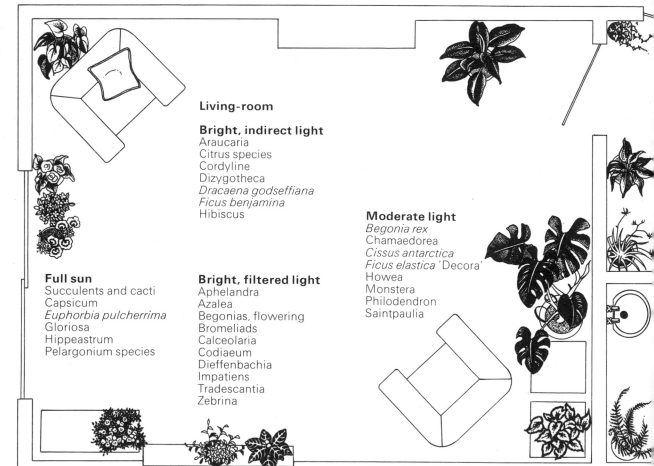

S

E

Living-room

Bright, indirect light
Araucaria
Citrus species
Cordyline
Dizygotheca
Dracaena godseffiana
Ficus benjamina
Hibiscus

Moderate light
Begonia rex
Chamaedorea
Cissus antarctica
Ficus elastica 'Decora'
Howea
Monstera
Philodendron
Saintpaulia

Full sun
Succulents and cacti
Capsicum
Euphorbia pulcherrima
Gloriosa
Hippeastrum
Pelargonium species

Bright, filtered light
Aphelandra
Azalea
Begonias, flowering
Bromeliads
Calceolaria
Codiaeum
Dieffenbachia
Impatiens
Tradescantia
Zebrina

W

Kitchen
Campanula isophylla
Ceropegia woodii
Coleus
Gynura
Impatiens
Pelargonium
Primula
Sansevieria
Tradescantia
Zebrina

Conservatory
Aphelandra
Caladium
Calathea
Codiaeum
Cordyline
Hoya carnosa
Orchids
Passiflora
Streptocarpus

Landing
Cissus antarctica
Clivia
× Fatshedera
Plectranthus

Hall
Aspidistra
Asplenium nidus
Fatsia
Ficus pumila
Hedera helix
Nephrolepis exaltata

N

Bedroom
Aspidistra   Ficus pumila
Chlorophytum   Howea
Cissus antarctica   Maranta
× Fatshedera   Sansevieria
Fatsia

Bathroom
Caladium   Peperomia
Calathea   Saintpaulia
Ferns   Saxifraga
Fittonia   stolonifera

E

Heat and humidity

The higher the temperature, the greater the need for increased air moisture or humidity – for plants and people alike

The great majority of plants that we grow indoors come from the Tropics, but this does not mean that they are all lovers of great heat. Evergreen foliage plants, together with most bromeliads and epiphytic orchids, largely originate in tropical and sub-tropical forests where the rainfall is very high.

In tropical forests many plants are protected from all but an occasional shaft of sunlight by the dense, leafy overhead canopy and from winds, hot and cold, by the dense barrier of trees. Above all, the temperature is equable, probably not fluctuating more than a few degrees on either side of 75-80°F, night or day, at any time throughout the year.

It is not difficult to recreate an even temperature in a home which has central heating. The humidity of tropical rain forests is not only impossible to copy, but would be quite intolerable for the human occupants. The air is so highly saturated with water that foliage and ground are almost constantly moist, and it is this lack of humidity that causes most problems when growing tropical foliage plants in the home.

The only plants which enjoy really high temperatures with plenty of sunshine and low humidity are the near desert species. They grow where rainfall is low or only seasonal, where cloud cover is rare, and where direct sunlight is almost continuous during daylight hours.

Most cacti and other succulents, as well as a number of annual and bulbous species not normally grown as house plants, thrive in high heat, brilliant light and dry air. These are plants for a sunny window and will benefit from a room where the temperature is much lower by night than by day as is the case in desert-like regions.

Temperature fluctuations

Rooms with intermittent heating, such as an open fire, small heaters which are only turned on when the room is occupied, or central heating which works on a time switch and is off long enough to allow the room to cool appreciably, are ideal positions for desert plants. In these conditions night temperatures can easily drop below 50°F in winter without any harm, though tropical evergreens will not tolerate such a fall in temperature.

Many flowering plants which are not hardy in this country, but which thrive indoors – species of *Begonia*, *Pelargonium* and *Impatiens* for example – come from areas which also experience cool nights after warm days. These too will be happier where the temperatures are not constantly high.

Plants which are hardy, or almost so, in parts of Britain at least, need a cool resting period once during the year. Their flowers will also last much longer if they are moved to a cool place at night. Cyclamen, azaleas, hyacinths and narcissi are among plants in this category. If there is no place where they can be kept below 50°F, but frost-free on winter nights, it is best not to attempt to grow them.

Many books on house plants, especially those published a couple of decades ago, tend to recommend excessively high temperatures for many species which are now known to grow perfectly happily in less heat. This is chiefly a legacy from the days when the plants were first introduced and grown in specially heated greenhouses, known as stove houses from their method of heating. Because of the fear of losing new, attractive and at first irreplaceable plants, they were often given intensive care.

Another source of equally high temperature recommendations

RAISING THE LEVEL OF HUMIDITY

Stand the pot on pebbles. Moisten these with water, taking care to keep the level below the pot base.

Double-potting provides the most efficient humidity. Sink the pot in peat and keep this moist.

Mist spraying should be done out of sun and at a distance that prevents the mist falling as large drops.

comes from house-plant books from the United States of America where houses are usually kept far warmer than they are in Europe.

The widely differing temperature recommendations may seem confusing until you learn to distinguish between optimum and minimum temperatures.

A plant may grow best between 59°F and 68°F, need a minimum of 50°F in winter to continue growing, but survive as long as the temperature exceeds 41°F. The 50°F temperature is the important minimum to be aimed at, but if it falls below that for short spells, the plant will not be killed as long as 41°F is maintained.

Although few rooms are rarely as cold as 41°F, it is well to remember that unless the windows are double-glazed, the temperature between a closed curtain and the glass often falls on winter nights to near freezing. Always make sure that the plants are moved into the room before pulling the curtains.

A number of foliage plants are remarkably tolerant in their temperature requirements. These are usually plants with a diversity of habitats in the wild and include *Maranta leuconeura, Aphelandra squarrosa* and several dracaenas. However, these will not be completely happy in the dry atmosphere of efficient central heating, so the problem of providing humidity is an important one and not only for the plants. Antique furniture suffers in hot, dry houses, and there is much evidence to show that moderate humidity is beneficial to human beings too.

Humidity

Humidity is the amount of water present in the air. It is usually referred to as the percentage relative humidity, i.e. 100 per cent relative humidity is when the air is completely saturated with water vapour as in a fog. The driest parts of the earth, where a few succulents are all that will survive, have a relative humidity of only 10 per cent; many deserts are between 20 per cent and 30 per cent, while the air on a pleasant English summer day will hold 40 to 50 per cent of water in the air.

In tropical forests, the relative humidity rises even more, from 60

29

Hairy-leaved plants, such as saint-paulias, object to mist sprays. They do, however, luxuriate in the humidity given off by an occasional steam bath.

per cent up to almost complete saturation at 100 per cent. For a pleasant atmosphere in the home, 40-60 per cent humidity is ideal, for people and plants.

To find out the humidity reading for any room, a hygrometer is needed. This piece of equipment resembles a thermometer and is only a little more expensive to buy. Place one in a centrally heated room with a high steady temperature, and you may be shocked to see it fall to a reading of 15 per cent. Drier than the Sahara! This is not, however, an unusual figure and will obviously not suit those tropical plants which would otherwise enjoy the warm conditions.

There are two ways of overcoming the problem of dry air. The first is to attack it on a large scale and increase the humidity of the room as a whole. The easiest, but most expensive way of doing this is to install an electric humidifier.

A humidifier works like a fan heater, with the air blowing over a permanent reservoir of water; the most efficient types have automatic controls which turn them on and off as humidity rises and falls. For the more thrifty home, a few bowls of water stood around can make a great deal of difference.

Pebble trays and double pots

At the individual plant level, there are several simple ways to increase humidity. The pot within a pot method does this very successfully, especially if the outer pot is wide enough at the top to provide a large surface of moist peat below the plant's spreading leaves. Another benefit of growing plants in this manner is that the roots are kept cool by the double layer of insulation.

Individual plants in ordinary clay or plastic pots can be stood in saucers or shallow dishes filled with pebbles and water, or with water alone if the pot is stood on an inverted pan or half pot so as to raise it above the water. It is vital that the water level remains below the top of the pebbles so that each pot can drain freely through its holes. Never allow a pot to stand in water as this will inevitably lead to rotting of the roots.

Large pebble trays – the bases of propagating trays – are ideal. Filled with pebbles kept permanently moist, a number of plants can be stood together on this humidity bed. Groups of plants conserve humidity better than solitary ones, and a group planting with the pots sunk in peat is probably the best method of all of raising and maintaining sufficient humidity.

Mist spraying

It is not easy to increase humidity for plants in hanging baskets, but a daily spraying with a fine mist of tepid water has some effect and is also beneficial as an additional measure for other plants. Spraying, which should always be done away from direct sunlight, can, however, become something of a chore with a large collection of individual plants to care for. It is much easier to arrange plants on portable trolleys which can easily be moved to the kitchen, or stand them round a trellis room-divider with a waterproof layer of tiles to catch the drips.

Mist spraying also has the advantage of washing dusty leaves; care should be taken when misting close to hairy-leaved plants.

Bottle gardens

For those plants which do best with a humidity higher than that which can be comfortably provided in a room, the enclosed case – or bottle garden – is the perfect answer. See p. 155-158.

Watering and feeding

More house plants are killed by zealous use of the watering can and by overdoses of plant food than by any other causes

Probably more advice, written and verbal, has been given on the subject of watering pot plants than on almost any other aspect of gardening. Yet it remains a constant problem for many beginners – and for quite a few experienced growers as well.

It is likely that more house plants die from overwatering than from any other cause, and underwatering would come an easy second. Luckily there are a few basic rules for watering, and if these are carefully followed at first, practice and experience should soon bring a measure of expertise.

Watering is determined partly by the state of the compost, and partly by knowing when this indicates a need for water. To establish when the compost is becoming dry, simply scratch a finger into the top inch or so of the compost to find out if there is dryness at that depth. Smaller individual plants can be picked up when they have just been watered so as to gauge the feel of the weight; experience will soon tell that a light pot signifies dry compost and the need for water.

Special moisture gauges are readily available, but such precision is rarely needed unless very demanding plants are being grown, and using them can be time-consuming. The plants themselves are sure indicators of a lack of water: if the young shoot tips and leaves show signs of wilting, and if flower buds drop off, look first at the compost to see if it is dry.

When to water

Having decided that the compost is dry, should the plant be watered at once? This is perhaps a decision which the beginner finds the greatest difficulty in making, for it is hard to resist watering a dry pot. Often, though, the correct answer is to wait for another day.

There are a number of pointers to help you decide whether to water or not. These relate to the fact that plants use a great deal of water for the development of new tissue, but relatively little if they are just 'ticking over' for the winter. At the same time, loss of moisture by transpiration, which is the plant's equivalent to perspiration, is much greater in hot, dry conditions than when temperatures are low.

As a general guide, plants in full growth, and especially in full flower, need regular watering. Foliage plants which have thin, delicate leaves need to be in a continuously moist, though never soaking wet compost.

All plants need more water when the weather is hot, or if they are in a very warm and dry atmosphere. If they are known to be pot-bound, or are large plants restricted to small pots, they will use water faster than most other plants. If a plant falls into one of these categories, then water it as soon as the compost shows signs of drying out. Fill the pot to the rim with water.

Many plants store water in their tissues, originally as an adaptation to allow them to survive long periods without rain in the wild. Succulent plants, including all the cacti except forest species, such as *Epiphyllum* and *Schlumbergera*, and evergreens with thick, fleshy leaves can all withstand periods of dryness. For these plants, the compost should be allowed to become almost dry each time before watering again.

Dormant plants

During the winter, most plants from temperate climates have a resting period when little or no new growth is made. Kept in a warm room this rhythm may be upset to a certain extent, but deciduous plants which have shed their leaves, and any others that are showing no signs of making new shoots or leaves, need very little water at this time.

Dormant tender bulbs should be kept almost dry and not watered until the new, young growth appears. The water stored in their bulbs is quite sufficient for them to start developing normally in an almost dry soil.

Most cacti and other succulents are best without any water at all during their resting periods. They should be kept in a cool place, perhaps the spare room, at this time; if they remain in a room that is warmer than is ideal, they may pucker or show signs of withering. If this happens fill the pots to the rim with water and allow to drain naturally, then keep dry as before.

All plants will need less water when kept in a cool room because loss by transpiration will be less. This also applies to enclosed cases and bottle gardens where the moisture transpired will condense on the glass sides and run back into the compost. Plants in pots sunk in moist peat should also need less regular watering in winter and at low temperatures. Take care that the surrounding peat never becomes soggy.

Methods of watering

Having decided that a plant does need watering, the final question is how to set about giving it the amount it needs. For most plants use a watering can with a narrow spout. Let the water pour gently on to the surface of the compost, with the spout resting on the pot rim to avoid making a depression in the compost round the crown.

If the plant has been potted correctly, the pot should be filled to the level of the rim once, and the compost allowed to drain naturally. If the plant stands in a saucer, tip out any water that collects there after watering.

A fine rose may be fitted to the spout of the watering can, though the resulting spray is difficult to keep under control when watering in a room. It is, however, fine for plants which can be brought to the kitchen sink.

Watering by soaking

Small pots can be watered by standing them in a bowl of water.

DIFFERENT WAYS OF WATERING

Top up the space between compost surface and pot rim at each application of water from a can.

Revive dried-out plants by soaking them in water until the compost surface is evenly moist and dark.

In addition to watering the compost, keep the central vase of bromeliads topped up with rainwater.

This is the best treatment if they are in a peat compost which has become very dry. Peat shrinks as it dries and will pull away from the edges of the pot; water will then flow between compost and pot and leave the root ball dry.

Put the pots in a bowl and fill it until the water comes about three-quarters up the sides of the pots. It will soak into the compost from below; when the compost surface is seen to be moist, remove the pots from the bowl and let them drain thoroughly.

Orchids grown on bark or on plastic chips are best treated by soaking as described above. Those grown in sphagnum moss or osmunda fibre mixture need their roots and containers immersed completely in a bowl of tepid water for 10-20 seconds, then drained as before.

It is sometimes recommended that all plants should be watered by immersion, but the result is no better than by standing the pots partially in water. Complete immersion has the distinct disadvantage that the bowl or sink fills with bits of compost which have floated from the surface.

Spray watering

Bromeliads and orchids grown on branches, and all plants on moss poles, are best watered with a fine spray from a syringe. One of the pressurised sprayers used for insecticides is ideal, but do not use the same one for killing pests and for watering, unless you are extremely careful about washing it out after use. The tiniest trace of some chemicals can be very damaging to a sensitive plant.

Pressure sprayers can also be used for misting foliage plants in a dry, warm room to increase humidity, and to freshen up a vase of cut flowers.

Bromeliads, which have a vase-like reservoir in the centre of the leaves, should have this topped up with water during the summer and at any other time if grown in a very warm room. Use rain, soft or distilled water, preferably at room temperature.

Seedlings and cuttings

Seed pans, pots and boxes should be soaked thoroughly either from a fine-rosed can or from beneath in shallow water. After being covered, they should need no more

HOLIDAY CARE OF HOUSE PLANTS

Enclosed in a polythene bag, a small plant will recycle moisture from transpiration for a few days.

Wet peat or newspaper packed round pots in a deep box will supply adequate moisture for a short period.

For longer periods, wicks leading from a tall jug conduct water to the compost by capillary action.

water until the seedlings appear. Once this happens, and the cover is removed, water in the same way to keep the compost permanently moist; the young plants will now be growing rapidly.

Cuttings should never be allowed to dry out. Look at the surface of the sand or rooting mixture used, and if it appears dry, ruffle the surface with a finger. If the grains feel separate, water well with the fine rose fitted on the can. Cuttings rooted with bottom heat should be checked every four days or so, those rooted without heat once a week.

Holiday care

Perhaps the trickiest watering problem of all is how to cope when the whole family goes away on holiday. Not everyone has a willing and knowledgeable neighbour, and the plants may have to survive by themselves for a couple of weeks.

The basic solution lies in trying to reduce loss by transpiration so as to cut down the amount of water needed, and to find a means of supplying that water without drowning the plants. The first step is to move all plants away from direct sunlight and ideally into a cool but light room. This will cut down water loss straight away.

Enclose smaller plants in polythene bags which will return the transpired water to the compost. Do this by standing each freshly watered plant, in its pot, in a large polythene bag. Tie the bag around the stem, above the compost surface, so that there is just enough space for drops of water to trickle through. This will keep the compost moist and prevent it from losing water. Tie the bag loosely over the plant, leaving a hole, about 1 inch, for air to enter. Plants enclosed in plastic bags should remain fresh for up to three weeks.

Actively growing specimens will usually make some pale, straggly shoots during this period. When routine care is resumed, cut such shoots out entirely.

Large pots and pot-bound plants do better when stood in a bowl with about 1 inch of water for each week of absence. A number of plants can be stood in the bath in this way, though it is wisest to stand them on mats or pieces of polythene so that they will not mark the enamel.

Automatic watering devices

A number of small pots can be watered automatically by a purpose-made system. Basically this consists of a central water cistern, rather like a tall jug, with a number of glass-fibre wicks which are inserted into the compost in the pots. Water is conducted through these wicks and keeps the compost moist in each pot. Similar gadgets can be improvised from large jugs and wicks of thick, soft string, plaited rug wool or purchased glass-fibre wicks.

Self-watering pots with built-in water reservoirs are useful, particularly for plants which are happy in a permanently moist compost (see page 15).

There are several fully automatic watering systems, devised for use in greenhouses, which can be conveniently adapted for the home. Whether or not it is worth going to the trouble of having a system installed depends on the individual – and the money and space available. If it will be used often through the year, then the expense, which is not excessive, will probably be worth-while.

A fully automatic watering system consists of specially designed trays which are filled with sand and kept moist through an automatic dispenser. A water

bottle designed to provide water regularly for pets can be used if the system has to function for a few days only. If the plants have to be watered automatically for a week or longer without refilling the dispenser, a special cistern, attached to the mains water supply, is needed.

The pots are screwed downwards into the sand so that this fills up the drainage holes and makes contact with the compost above. This draws up water as needed from the permanently moist sand bed. It is essential that the pots are not crocked as this would prevent the upwards flow of water. Clay pots will also need a wick in the base of the pot to make contact between the compost and the sand.

Whichever methods have been used or devised for plants during a prolonged absence, look at every plant carefully on arriving home. If necessary, soak them thoroughly before returning them to their usual positions.

Fertilisers and nutrients

When a plant is potted in fresh, properly formulated compost, it will have a supply of all the nutrients it requires ready to hand. As the months pass, so that supply will be used up. The faster a plant grows, the more nutrients it will be using, and eventually the compost is no longer able to provide all the necessary plant foods. The balance must be maintained with fertilisers.

Newly bought plants have often been fed with what is known as a slow-release fertiliser at the nursery where they were raised. This provides a supply of nutrients which will last the plant while it is on display awaiting sale, and, if the sale has been fairly prompt, for some while in the home as well.

Self-watering pots with a built-in water reservoir in the base are most suitable for plants which need a steady supply of water.

At some stage the compost becomes exhausted, and the plant will need extra nutrients to keep it healthy and thriving. A general lack of vigour is the first sign that all is not well. When this is noticed, tap the plant out of its pot, and if the root ball shows a dense mesh of roots the plant is obviously pot-bound. Once it is potted in fresh compost, this will supply the necessary nutrients.

Plants which are grown in small pots to restrict their size may show declining vigour by producing new leaves which fail to reach the size of the lower ones when mature. Variegated plants may sprout leaves lacking the usual patterns and colours. In these cases, a regular feeding programme should begin at once.

Annuals should be fed as soon as the flower buds show. Perennial flowering plants will display symptons similar to foliage plants: leaves that become duller and smaller, and flower heads with fewer flowers.

Liquid fertilisers
The easiest feed for all plants is one of the proprietary liquid fertilisers. These are applied at the time of watering. Never give a liquid feed to a dry compost; water this first and let it drain before applying fertiliser – in dry compost the chemicals may burn the roots.

Dilute all fertilisers to the maker's instructions; if different strengths are given on the label without specifying house plants, use the weakest solution recommended. Granular fertilisers and tablets are also readily available and should be sprinkled on or pushed into the compost just before watering.

Once feeding has begun, it should be continued throughout the growing season. Most plants which have not been repotted within the last six months need a regular dose of fertiliser once every fortnight. Slow-growing plants, such as *Clivia*, the Kaffir lily, should be fed less frequently, while those making very rapid growth should be fed at 7-10 day intervals. However, do not exceed the instructions on the packet as over-feeding of plants can be as detrimental as lack of nutrients.

When the plants' growth slows down, normally in autumn, feeding should be stopped and no more need be given until growth recommences the following spring. Orchids, bromeliads, cacti and other succulents can all be fed in the same way as flowering and foliage plants.

Foliar feeds
These are useful for a rapid tonic. Foliar feeds are similar to other fertilisers, but come in a soluble, easily assimilated form which is sprayed on to the plants' foliage. They are absorbed into the plant sap and become available to the plants almost at once.

As well as being invaluable where routine feeding has been neglected, foliar feeds are particularly useful for epiphytes growing on pieces of wood or climbers on moss poles which would take a long time to assimilate ordinary compost fertilisers. Such plants can be sprayed thoroughly with foliar feed or have their exposed roots sprayed with ordinary liquid feed.

If a plant, which is being fed regularly, shows signs of over-feeding, by producing larger, lush and rather floppy growth, and – in the case of a flowering plant, more foliage than flowers – cut down the frequency of fertiliser applications, but do not stop them altogether. It is a good idea to try out different brands.

New plants from old stock

Propagation from existing plants is a fascinating and inexpensive hobby, with quick results in many cases

There is an immense satisfaction to be gained from raising one's own plants from scratch, quite apart from the fact that it is cheaper than to purchase them.

Patience and care are the two main demands on the home propagator, together with a determination not to be discouraged if a batch of cuttings or a newly divided plant suddenly dies. This happens even to professional growers who then start afresh, perhaps using a different method.

Offsets and plantlets
The easiest plants to propagate and gain confidence from are those which produce offsets. These are small replicas of the parent plant which develop close to it.

Chlorophytum comosum, the spider plant, produces offsets on the long flowering stems as the flowers fade. It is a simple matter to bend the stems over and peg the small plantlets into pots of good potting compost until they have rooted and can be severed from the parent plant. Larger plantlets which have developed roots while attached to the flowering stem can be cut off and potted up at once.

Other plants, such as the commonly grown *Kalanchoe blossfeldiana* and the mother fern, *Asplenium bulbiferum,* produce plantlets on their leaves or fronds. On kalanchoes these will fall off if the plant is gently tapped. Root them in a peat and sand mixture and keep in place with a little grit sprinkled round them.

The easiest way to root fern plantlets is to peg the whole frond down on to compost and detach it from the parent plant when the plantlets have developed roots.

Many plants produce offsets as shoots, growing up from the base or crown. Some, notably the bromeliads, will begin to produce roots while they are still attached to the parent.

A bromeliad rosette normally dies after flowering, and the plant relies on offsets for its continued existence. In the wild, large clumps will eventually form, made up of dead and living rosettes.

In cultivation it is usual to remove bromeliad offsets as soon as they are about a quarter or a third the size of the mature rosette. Remove the plant from its container – or perch if being grown on

PROPAGATION FROM OFFSETS

A single chlorophytum will produce several plantlets in one season. They root easily pegged into pots.

Bromeliad offsets form roots while attached to the parent. Knock out the clump and pull the offset away.

Pot the young rooted plant at once. Nurse it into growth with extra heat and humidity, in light shade.

a tree branch — and cut the new, young plant away with a sharp knife or secateurs. Pot up at once and keep it growing in the pot until new-roots are well formed, and leaves are showing renewed and strong growth.

Once rooted, bromeliad offsets can be potted on or wired to a branch. It is possible to wire the newly severed offset directly on to a branch, but great attention is needed to keep the developing roots moist at all times.

Species of *Dracaena* and *Cordyline*, as well as bulbous plants, such as amaryllis *(Hippeastrum)*, and many cacti also produce offsets. These can all be removed from the parent and potted up as described for bromeliads.

Stem cuttings
Cuttings provide the traditional method of increasing a wide range of plants, including all those which are not so obliging as to produce offsets. Some are easy to root, others are more demanding.

The easiest cuttings to begin with are those which need little or no expertise. Many will root readily in nothing but water, such as the busy Lizzie *(Impatiens wallereana)*, the two wandering Jews *(Tradescantia* and *Zebrina)*, common ivy *(Hedera helix)* and species of *Pilea*.

Cuttings are taken from young, healthy and non-flowering stems and can be anything from 3 to 6 inches long. Use a sharp knife to cut the stem just below a leaf node, or joint, and remove all the leaves from the lower half.

Place a small piece of charcoal in a jar of water to keep it sweet, and insert the cuttings upright by pushing them through slits in a piece of foil covering the jar or wedge them with small tufts of cottonwool.

Set the jar of cuttings in a place with good light but away from direct sunlight which will heat the water too much.

When roots have formed on the cuttings and are about 2 inches long, remove them from the water, taking great care not to break the brittle roots. Pot the cuttings singly — or tradescantias and zebrinas in groups of three — in small pots of John Innes potting compost No. 1.

Keep the potted cuttings in light

ROOTING AND POTTING STEM CUTTINGS

Use a knife for cuttings of soft stems, severing cleanly beneath a node; remove the lower leaves.

Tradescantias root readily in a jar of water. Keep the weak stems erect with a support of plastic foil.

Set the rooted cuttings in small pots and firm gently round the base of the stems. Keep moist and warm.

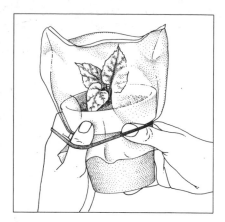

Stem cuttings root easiest in a moist atmosphere. Cover pot and cuttings with a polythene bag.

shade until they appear sturdy and begin to develop new leaves. Thereafter treat as adult plants.

Next to water, sand is the easiest rooting medium. It does, however, have the disadvantage that once the roots are growing, sand provides little nourishment for the young plants. These can quickly starve and collapse if not transferred to a potting compost. This should be done as soon as the cuttings show signs of new growth, but if this is not possible, give them a liquid feed as a temporary measure.

Another good rooting medium is a mixture made up of equal parts of peat and sand. Some cuttings will be slower to root in this mixture than in pure sand, but they can safely be left in this for an extra week or two before potting.

Most cuttings root best when given some humidity. This is easily provided by erecting a wire loop over the pot and inverting a polythene bag over it.

Plastic propagating trays complete with transparent hoods are readily and inexpensively available from garden centres, sundriesmen and large stores. They come in a wide range of sizes, and it is advis-

able to buy one a size larger than you think will be necessary; extra space is always welcome.

Hormone rooting powders
Artificial hormone rooting liquids and powders stimulate growth within cuttings and thereby help in the formation of roots. They are readily available under proprietary names and recommended for cuttings that do not normally root easily. Always follow the instructions on the label.

Propagator units
The heated propagator is another aid which is of great value, particularly when dealing with cuttings of warmth-loving species. Propagators resemble propagating trays, but are equipped with a low-powered heating element fitted in the base, or with soil-warming cables that are covered with compost. They can also be bought as a heated base for pots or trays.

Propagators usually maintain a temperature of about 68° F, but much depends on the surrounding temperature. It is wise to install a thermometer so that the temperature can be checked regularly.

HEEL CUTTINGS FROM WOODY PLANTS

Cuttings of side shoots from shrubby plants stand a better chance of rooting if taken with a heel of bark.

Trim any ragged pieces from the heel and dip it in hormone rooting powder. Insert in moist potting compost.

Heel cuttings

Stem cuttings to be rooted in a sand or peat mixture are taken and treated in the same way as those rooted in water. Cuttings of woody plants, however, are often taken with what is known as a heel: a small side shoot is pulled from the stem with a firm, downwards movement so that a small piece – the heel – of the woody stem comes away at the same time.

Stem sections

Some long-stemmed plants, such as *Aglaonema*, *Dracaena* and *Cordyline*, tend to grow leggy with age. Rather than discarding such specimens altogether, the stems can be cut crossways into 2-3 inch sections and rooted in a propagator. Make sure that they are inserted upright in the propagating case in the same direction as they grew.

It is safest to place each stem section in the compost as it is cut, burying it to half its depth, or to notch the lower edge for identification. If by chance it is impossible to tell top and base apart, lay the sections flat on the compost, covering them lightly, until one end begins to develop roots.

Rooting the cuttings

Fill a seed pan, pot or propagator tray with the chosen rooting medium and insert the prepared cuttings in small holes, 1-1½ inches deep, at a distance equal to half their length. If you set the cuttings too close, the roots may become tangled and break off when the cuttings are later separated.

Firm the compost gently round the base of each cutting with the fingers; water thoroughly and leave to drain. If you are using a seed pan or pot, it is a good idea to cover the container with a polythene bag so as to keep heat and moisture stable.

Botrytis is a quick-spreading disease which causes cuttings to rot, particularly in a moist atmosphere. Where a number of cuttings are rooted together in a propagator, it is a wise precaution to spray them with a fungicide such as Captan or Benlate. If botrytis does occur, the cuttings must be discarded. The compost should also be thrown out and the containers thoroughly scrubbed in a solution of water and household disinfectant.

Good light is essential for the encouragement of growth, but on the other hand this should not be direct sunlight. Temperatures inside a propagating case can rise alarmingly in a very short time if it is placed in full sun, and this will quickly prove fatal to the contents. The ideal position is a well-lit, north-facing window, but failing this, any window can be used as long as the propagator is covered with net curtaining or layers of muslin when exposed to the sun.

With a heated propagator unit, there is no need to provide any external warmth. For an ordinary unit, pan or pot, additional warmth can be provided by setting it on a shelf above a radiator – the ideal temperature is around 65° F. Artificial light may also be used to supplement daylight.

Leaf cuttings

Some short-stemmed, rosette-forming plants with hairy or fleshy leaves are increased from leaf cuttings. African violets (*Saintpaulia ionantha*) and small-leaved species of peperomias and begonias are propagated from young single leaves, removed with about 2 inches of leaf stalk from the parent.

Treat leaf cuttings as stem cuttings, setting them 1 inch deep in

CUTTINGS FROM HAIRY LEAVES

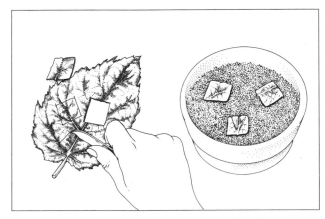

A single leaf of *Begonia rex* will yield numerous cuttings. Root the small squares in a pan set in the propagator.

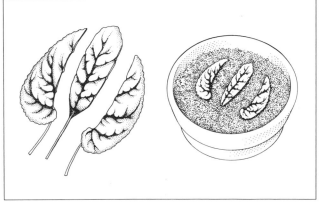

Triangular sections of peperomia leaves root better attached to a piece of leaf stalk inserted in the compost.

CUTTINGS FROM FLESHY LEAVES

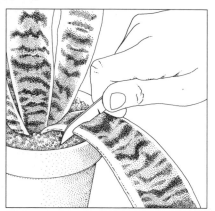

Pieces of sansevieria leaves root readily provided they are inserted in the former growing direction.

Cut a leaf into 2-3 in horizontal sections and mark the lower edge of each piece with a small notch.

Set the cuttings, lower edge down, to half their depth in moist compost. Cover with a polythene bag.

Saintpaulia leaf cuttings are inserted with a stalk to keep the leaf clear of the moist compost.

the rooting medium so that the leaves are held above the compost. Rooted in a heated propagator new plants will be produced from the base of each leaf.

Plants with larger leaves, such as *Begonia rex, Peperomia argyreia* and *P. obtusifolia,* are increased from a single leaf cut into smaller sections.

Sometimes a large leaf is left intact and a number of nicks made on the underside, at the intersections of the main leaf veins. Alternatively, cut the leaf into 1 inch squares. Lay these, underside down, on a moist rooting medium and keep them in contact with the compost with small pebbles or stones. A new plant will eventually emerge from each leaf section.

Peperomia leaf sections need a small sliver of the leaf stalk attached, and the leaves are therefore cut into triangles with one point at the stem junction.

Some succulents are most obliging in their ease of propagation from leaves. Many of the larger-leaved sedums and echeverias are easily increased by pulling off a few leaves and laying them on moist sand.

Plants with long, narrow and succulent leaves, such as *Sansevieria trifasciata,* can be propagated in a similar way to stem sections. Cut a leaf into 2-3 inch lengths and insert them vertically in the compost, after marking the base of each piece. Plants of the yellow-margined sansevieria, *S.t.* 'Laurentii' will not produce variegated offspring from this propagation method. Only by division can identical plants be obtained.

Aftercare of cuttings
Most cuttings, whether stem or leaf, kept in fairly warm conditions will root within one to five weeks, but do not despair of the few which take longer. Tend them for as long as possible and do not give up hope until they have either collapsed or become browned or blackish when they are obviously dead.

Once the cuttings are well rooted, the young plants will begin growing and must be potted-up. If they have been rooted in sand, this should be done at once. Those in peat and sand can be left for a little longer, but the larger they are, the more difficult it will be to prise the roots apart where several cuttings

SOIL LAYERING

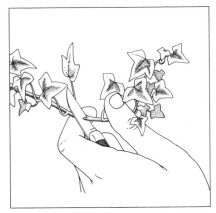

Bend a young flexible shoot close to a group of leaves; make a shallow cut half-way through the stem.

Prop the cut open and push it into a pot of compost. Keep the layer in position with a small wire loop.

When roots have formed on the buried portion, sever the layered plant from its parent in two operations.

have been rooted together. The shock of transplanting will also be greater with large cuttings.

Single cuttings in pots can be carefully knocked out, those in trays and cases are easiest lifted with a widger or small trowel. Set the rooted cuttings singly in 2½ or 3 inch pots, using an ordinary potting compost.

Small cream or yogurt pots are suitable for the first potting up provided they are given drainage holes with a sharp kitchen knife or a hot poker.

When the new plants have been potted up, return them to the same position they occupied as cuttings. Leave them for one or two weeks, until they are growing again. Thereafter, treat as adult plants, potting-on as necessary. Be particularly careful with watering until the plants are established; young roots may easily rot in saturated potting compost.

Layering

This is a convenient propagation method for plants with flexible long stems. Choose a strong-growing stem with a healthy cluster of leaves and bend it as near to the leaves as possible to avoid a leggy-stemmed plant.

Have ready a small pot of moist potting compost. Make a small slit half-way through the stem on the underside of the bend. Keep the cut open and press it into the compost, pegging it in place with a small wire loop or hair pin, then cover with a little more compost.

If the cut refuses to remain open and in contact with the compost, hold it open with a match or tiny stone. In order to facilitate rooting, dust the cut with a little hormone rooting powder.

Most climbers can be layered in this way as can some plants with trailing shoots, for example *Ficus*

pumila. Layering is a slower method of obtaining new plants than cuttings. It may take anything from one to six months to produce one new plant, but once the initial work is carried out little attention is necessary other than watering.

When the layered stem appears to be growing well, knock it out of the pot to check that good roots have developed. In this case, cut half-way through the stem about 1 inch from the new plant to begin its separation from the parent plant. After about two weeks, complete the cut and move the young plant in its pot to a position in good light, away from direct sun.

Air layering

Plants with stiff stems that cannot be bent may be air layered. This is a simpler process than it at first appears and is useful for creating a new plant from an overtall or leggy specimen of such expensive plants as *Dracaena*, *Cordyline* and the larger *Ficus* species.

Air layering is basically similar to ordinary layering, but carried out above rather than at soil level. Look first at the plant to be propagated and decide on the size of the desired new plant. Choose a point where roots should ideally form, usually about 6-8 inches from the top, though much depends on the shape of the plant being rejuvenated.

Make an upwards incision at the point chosen, terminating the cut half-way through the stem diameter. Dust or brush with hormone rooting powder or liquid, and keep the cut open with a match or toothpick.

For air layering to be successful the area around the cut must be covered with compost in which roots can develop. This is held in place with clear polythene. Use polythene tubing if it is possible to slip this over the top of the stem without damaging the leaves. Otherwise join a piece of polythene round the stem with a double fold.

Tie the tube with adhesive tape 2-3 inches below the incision and pack it with a mixture of three parts moist sphagnum moss to one of potting compost. Tie the tube at a similar distance above the cut.

After a couple of months roots should be visible through the sphagnum moss, and the stem can be cut below the polythene tube. Remove the moss carefully without damaging the roots and pot up the new plant.

The base of an air layered plant is usually unsightly and is thrown out once the new plant is growing well. But you can keep the old plant growing, cut back all stems and take the shoots it will throw out from the base as cuttings.

Division
Some plants which form a number of stems from below ground level can be divided into two or more pieces when they become too large. Aspidistras, chlorophytums, calatheas and marantas as well as many ferns can all be divided.

Knock the plant from its pot and shake it gently to dislodge the compost from the base of the stems and the root ball. This should reveal the points where stems can be divided.

Hold the top of the root ball in the hands, placing the fingers at the base of the stems, and pull the pieces apart.

Pot-bound plants with their roots a tangled mass are more difficult to divide. Try to disentangle some of the outer roots without breaking them. If this fails, a sharp knife will be necessary. Make a cut from the top of the root ball down through the outer roots and bring the cut up to the top again. Avoid cutting through the centre of the ball or the inner roots.

Trim away any roots damaged during division and pot up the pieces separately. Water sparingly at first until the divisions look healthy and appear to be growing.

For the first day or so, divided plants will probably display flagging leaves, but this is not a sign that they are dry, so resist the temptation to give more water. In this instance wilting is the plants'

AIR LAYERING A RUBBER PLANT

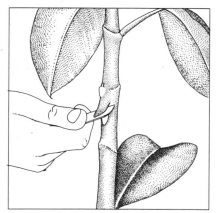

Use a sharp knife to make an upward slanting cut between two leaf nodes near the top of a leggy plant.

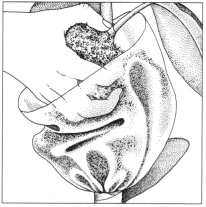

Fix a clear polythene sleeve below the cut and pack moist sphagnum moss between and round the incision.

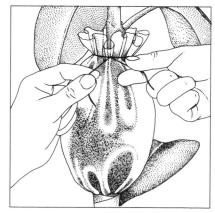

Tie the sleeve at the top; leave undisturbed until roots are visible through the moss, after some months.

way of conserving moisture and concentrating all their energies on producing new roots.

Seed propagation

Growing plants from seeds is a rewarding and inexpensive hobby, more so if the seeds are home collected. It is an easy propagation method, and even if one batch of seedlings fails to germinate – and they sometimes do, even for the professionals – little has been lost.

Seeds can be sown in pots or pans with a polythene cover or in a plastic propagator complete with lid. There are several makes of sterilised composts, with little to choose between them. Fill the container with compost and level it about $\frac{3}{4}$ inch below the rim.

Home-saved seeds should be sown as soon as they are ripe as many have a dormant period during which they will not germinate. In the wild, dormancy is often triggered off by drying and is a built-in precaution to prevent a whole season's crop of seeds germinating in unfavourable weather and dying from drought or cold.

Seeds from dry areas are usually long-lived as they may have to remain dormant for months or even years before sufficient rains arrive. Those from permanently moist climates are, however, short-lived as they have no mechanisms for surviving dry periods. Do not expect good germination rate from old seeds of tropical plants.

Sow seeds large enough to handle, with fingers or tweezers, at a distance of $\frac{1}{2}$-$1\frac{1}{2}$ inches apart. Seeds too small to handle are best scattered on the surface of the compost, while dust-like seeds are distributed most evenly if mixed with three or four times the amount of fine sand before sowing.

Dust-like seeds do not need covering with compost, though a fine sprinkling of sand may be put over them. Larger seeds should be covered with a layer of compost more or less equal to their diameter, and lightly firmed.

After sowing, water the seed containers, either with an overhead spray from a fine-rosed watering can or by standing the container in water to just below the rim. When the compost is moistened right through and dampness shows on the surface, take the container out of the water and allow it to drain.

Germination of seeds

Moisture and warmth are essential for germination. Light is not important; an airing cupboard or warm cupboard is a suitable place in which to keep the seed containers. Some form of covering is necessary so as to retain the essential moisture, and a sheet of glass or rigid polythene is fine. If the compost dries out at any time during germination, the result is almost always fatal.

Look at the containers daily to check that the compost remains moist and to remove any condensation that may have formed on the cover. After about a week watch for the first sign of germination. As soon as the seedlings appear above the compost, remove the cover and bring the container into a better lit position. Protect the seedlings from strong sun and turn the container daily to keep them growing evenly.

Artificial light will be necessary for developing seedlings if no good natural light is available. Use fluorescent strip lights as for adult plants, but suspend them about 12 inches above the seedlings. If the seedlings are known shade lovers, keep them in similar light to that enjoyed by the parent plants.

The first leaves to develop will be the cotyledons or seed leaves.

These are either single and grass-like or in pairs and rounded. On some plants they remain underground, but on the majority they come to the surface and are the first visible leaves.

The second pair of leaves on seedlings are the first true leaves, and when these appear, the time is ideal for pricking off the seedlings. If they are tricky and fragile to handle, fashion tools from small spatulas such as those which come with ice cream tubs. Cut a small notch at one end.

The thought of handling tiny plants may seem daunting, and they can be left until they grow larger. Remember that all the time the stems are extending so are the root systems, and if the seedlings are close together, roots are bound to become tangled.

Pricking off

Separating the seedlings is a matter of tapping out the whole contents of the pot or lifting out a bunch with a small trowel or widger. Shake the seedlings gently or tease them apart. It is also possible to prick off a small group of seedlings and gently pull out all the weaker ones when they have grown larger.

Large or small, the seedlings are pricked off into potting compost. Fill a container as for seed sowing, but firm it less thoroughly, and hardly at all if an all-peat compost is being used. Make holes in the compost, 1-2 inches apart, and set a single seedling in each. The holes should be deep enough for the roots to reach the bases of the holes without being cramped. Firm the compost lightly round the stems.

Once the young plants in the pot or box are touching each other and are obviously growing strongly, they are potted singly into small pots in the usual way and thereafter potted-on as necessary.

Ensuring healthy plants

Regular attention, correct watering and feeding regimen and clean surroundings are the key factors for healthy plants

Every plant which comes into the home, with the exception of those raised from seeds, will come as a purchase or gift, from shops, garden centres, nurseries or friends' collections. Any pest or disease found on plants within the house will generally have been unwittingly introduced from one of these sources.

Always buy or otherwise obtain plants with a discerning eye, and whatever their origin make sure that they are clean and healthy in every sense before mixing them with other house plants. A diseased specimen or one harbouring a pest will not only become sick itself, but may also infect healthy plants.

Examine the leaves for signs of damage or stray insects, and check especially the undersides where most pests lurk. Examine also plants brought in from the open, whether a garden or balcony. They may have attracted a stray moth or butterfly and hide a cluster of eggs waiting for the right moment to hatch.

Stems, too, should be closely scrutinised, particularly the young growing tips, favourite gathering places for aphids.

Once accepted into the plant community of the home, look carefully at each plant from time to time. There are several sources of plant pests and diseases in the home. Cut flowers are undoubtedly the worst culprits for introducing such unwelcome visitors, but winged aphids can also fly in through open windows and doors.

It is a good idea to use one room, perhaps the kitchen or bathroom, as quarantine quarters for newly obtained plants. Here they can be kept and frequently observed for a week or so, until they are given a clean bill of health. The same room can do duty as a sick bay for those showing serious symptoms.

Pests and diseases cause some problems, but most symptoms of failing plant health are the results of faulty or negligent care. Overwatering, starvation and fluctuating temperatures are common causes of collapse, all of which can be prevented by correct and regular attention.

While many plants will survive, at least for a short time, if not actually thrive in conditions less than ideal, the aim of every indoor gardener should be to encourage a flourishing plant community, not to tend a sick bay.

Recognising the signs

Wilting or falling leaves usually indicate a wrong watering routine and that a plant has either been under or overwatered, most often the latter. It may seem odd that both extremes cause the same symptoms, but both have long-term effects on the plant by preventing the roots from taking up adequate moisture.

In the case of underwatering, the necessary water has not been made available. In overwatering, the constantly wet compost has caused the roots to rot and rendered them unable to carry out their function of supplying water and nutrients.

Feel the compost, and if it is dry, immerse the pot almost to the rim in water until soaked through. Drain well and return the pot to its former place.

If the compost is soggy, knock the plant from its pot and wash the compost from the roots. Examine these carefully, and if most look white and healthy, with only a few brown roots present, the plant may be worth saving. Where most of the roots are brown, the plant is unlikely to survive.

Cut away as many of the brown roots as possible and repot the plant in moist, but not wet compost. Nurse it back to health by treating it like a cutting: enclose it in a polythene bag to improve humidity and keep it shaded.

If, after two or three weeks, the leaves still look wilted, the plant has probably died.

Vine weevils Wilting plants in correctly watered composts may suffer from root troubles of a different kind. Knock the plant out and examine the roots for signs of vine weevils, insects difficult to detect on newly acquired plants.

The visible cause is a fat, whitish grub which feeds on the roots, particularly in the centre of the ball where it is difficult to spot and dislodge. Watering with BHC will kill the pest, but usually many roots will have been lost, and it may be some time before the plant recovers, if at all.

Aphids Twisted and distorted shoots, young growing tips, leaves and even petals are likely to be the results of aphids. These tiny creatures are easily overlooked and rapidly cause severe infestations as they reproduce at an alarming rate.

Aphids, or greenfly, are tiny, soft-bodied pests, usually pale green, but also pink, pale yellow, grey or black in colour. Where only a few are spotted on a plant they can be squeezed between finger and thumb. A moderately infested plant can be wiped over with dilute liquid detergent which will usually dislodge them.

Severe infestations will need to be treated with an insecticide such as derris or diazinon. As with all insecticide sprays, the maker's instructions should be implicitly followed. Protect nearby furniture if the plant is too large to be moved, but preferably use sprays only in the garden, on the balcony or by an open window.

Mealy bugs and scale insects Next to aphids, the most common and serious pests are other sap-sucking insects such as mealy bugs. They cluster on the undersides of leaves and are recognised by the tufts of white waxy wool.

Scale insects are minute, and their presence is rarely suspected until leaves become covered with a black sticky deposit. Try to eliminate both pests by hand; spray severe infestations with an insecticide such as malathion.

Red spider mites and whiteflies Leaves mottled or spotted with yellow may be the result of visitations by red spider mites. These minute, red-spotted creatures revel in hot dry conditions.

Spray the infested plants with derris, and if this fails to destroy them, a stronger insecticide may be necessary. Malathion is probably the most reliable, but due to its obnoxious smell it should only be used outdoors or on a balcony with all doors and windows closed.

Similar symptoms can be caused by whiteflies. They are less obvious, and the first signs of their presence are often black sooty moulds which grow on the sweet secretions of honeydew. The tiny white insects may also take wing if a plant is knocked or moved.

Whiteflies are difficult to eradicate. Malathion will kill the mobile stages, but the next generations, present as eggs, larvae and pupae, will be immune. Several applications, as new flies are seen, may be necessary.

Virus diseases Yellow streaking can sometimes be seen on the leaves of narcissi, hippeastrums and several orchids. They are caused by virus diseases for which there are no remedies, and infected plants must be destroyed.

Leaf discoloration Leaves which show brown edges or patches or are variously mottled or spotted, particularly with yellow, may be reacting to a number of adverse conditions. Brown edges are often brought on by cold shocks or draughts, while brown irregular leaf patches may be due to leaf scorch, caused by too sunny a position, a close source of heat or electric light.

Azaleas which have a yellow cast to the young leaves are showing chlorosis, the result of excess lime, either in the compost or in the water. Apply iron sequestrene and water with rain or distilled water.

Loss of vigour Sometimes plants make little or no new growth or behave in a curious fashion for no obvious reason. The problems are often associated with root troubles, and may be overcome by the simple remedies of repotting or potting-on.

Foliar feeds often spur on new growth and can be seen as indicators of starvation. However, if neither repotting nor fertiliser has any visible effect, it is probable that the plant is suffering from a virus disease. No amount of care will save it, and the plant should be destroyed before it passes the disease on to other specimens in the collection.

Symptoms and treatment
Given correct growing conditions, good hygiene and regular attention, few troubles are likely to beset house plants. Where pests or diseases are suspected, move the plants into quarantine and keep them there until they have either recovered or died. The chart on pages 46-47 lists the ailments most commonly associated with indoor plants; most of these occur only as isolated incidents.

Pests, diseases and cultural disorders

Symptoms	Pest	Disease
Yellowing, mottled leaves	Red spider mites Whiteflies	Chlorosis
Leaf spots		Oedema, other fungal diseases, sooty mould, rust
Lanky growth		
Browning leaf edges		
Twisted shoot tips, curled leaves, poor growth, honeydew	Aphids Whiteflies	
White woolly clusters on foliage and leaf axils, honeydew	Mealy bugs	
White powder on leaves, stems and flowers		Mildew
Wilting leaves	Weevils	
Leaf streaks and mosaics	Bulb mites	Virus
Leaf, bud and flower drop	Red spider mites	
Lined, punctured or ragged leaves	Leaf eelworm and miners, caterpillars and earwigs	
Stunted growth	Aphids Earthworms	Virus
Sticky leaves, encrustations of waxy scales on stems and foliage	Scale insects Aphids Whiteflies	
Grey-white mould on foliage and flowers		Grey mould

Cultural Fault	Susceptible Plants	Treatment
Overwatering **Pot-bound** **Fluctuating temperatures**	**Mites:** Anthurium, Beloperone, Codiaeum, Hedera, Hydrangea, Impatiens **Whiteflies:** flowering plants **Cultural faults:** all **Chlorosis:** Rhododendron	**Mites:** insecticide sprays **Whiteflies:** insecticide sprays **Cultural treatment:** improve conditions. **Chlorosis:** apply sequestered iron; use lime-free compost and water
Sun or heat scorch	**Diseases:** Citrus, Dracaena, Pelargonium, Peperomia **Cultural faults:** all	**Diseases:** pick off damaged leaves, spray with copper, maneb or captan **Scorch:** increase air and shade
Poor light	All	**Improve conditions**
Over- and underwatering, draughts, low or high temperatures, pot-bound	All	**Improve conditions**
Pot-bound	**Aphids:** Achimenes, Anthurium, Calathea, Calceolaria, Cissus, Citrus, × Fatshedera, Fatsia, Hoya, Hydrangea, Impatiens, Jasminum, Orchids, Pelargonium, Pteris, Rhododendron, Saintpaulia, *Senecio cruentus*, Streptocarpus **Whiteflies:** see above **Cultural faults:** all	**Aphids:** destroy by hand; wipe with detergent or spray with insecticide **Whiteflies:** see above **Improve growing conditions**
	Chamaedorea, Cissus, Clivia, Codiaeum, Coleus, Dracaena, *Euphorbia pulcherrima*, Ficus, Rhoeo, Orchids, Saintpaulia, Stephanotis, etc.	Wipe with methylated spirit; wash clean. Spray with malathion
	Flowering begonias, Saintpaulia, etc.	Spray with fungicide; reduce humidity
Incorrect watering	**Weevils:** Cyclamen, Primula; **Cultural faults:** all	**Weevils:** water with BHC **Improve conditions**
	Bulbs, orchids	None. Destroy affected plants
Lack of water or humidity	**Mites:** see above **Cultural faults:** all	**Mites:** see above **Improve growing conditions**
	All	Pick off damaged leaves; spray with diazinon or BHC
Pot-bound, **lack of fertiliser**	**Aphids:** see above **Other pests, virus diseases and cultural faults:** all	**Aphids:** see above **Earthworms:** water with permanganate of potash or mowrah meal; destroy severely stunted plants **Virus:** no cure **Cultural faults:** improve conditions
	All	**Scale insects:** brush off with warm water. Spray with malathion **Aphids and whiteflies:** see above
	Foliage begonias, Campanula, Cyclamen	Remove affected parts by hand; dust with captan or thiram

Part Two

Which Plants to Grow?

Foliage plants

The majority of plants used in indoor decorating schemes, from the average homes to large open-plan offices, are chosen for the effect of their leaves. Foliage plants are valued for their enduring qualities and unchanging appearance at any time of the year.

In winter, when most plants experience a dormant period and many must be banished from living-room areas, foliage plants retain their colours and shapes, textures and patterns. In spite of having their origins in tropical and sub-tropical regions, they adapt better than any other plant group to indoor conditions and enter discreetly or dramatically into all types of interior designs.

Unlike other indoor types, foliage plants do not fall neatly into distinctive categories for they come in infinite variety, even within a single genus. *Ficus,* for example, includes such widely different plants as the upright rubber plant with oblong, leathery and glossy green leaves; the trailing *F. pumila* with tiny, heart-shaped, bright green leaves on wiry stems; and the weeping fig, *F. benjamina,* with willow-like, slender and pendent leaves along drooping branches.

Growth patterns are equally at variance: some plants are upright and sturdy, others are arching, climbing or trailing. Some grow as small shrubs, others as miniature trees, grassy clumps or as low rosettes.

Large foliage plants, such as the elegant palms, the cordylines and dracaenas, are superb as single feature plants. Shrubby, climbing, and trailing types of all-green foliage serve as evergreen backdrops and foreground covers for variegated and flowering plants. The smaller, rosette or clump-forming types assert themselves through intricate leaf patterns and textures, shapes and colour combinations. They are best viewed in isolation.

Aglaonema commutatum
'Silver Queen'

Aglaonema
(*Araceae*)

Admired for their handsome pointed leaves, aglaonemas originate in the tropical rain forests of south-east Asia. The plants form upright fleshy trunks, with long-stemmed leaves springing directly from the trunk.

Aglaonemas are shade lovers and make durable feature plants for draught-free rooms, warm sunrooms or conservatories.

A. commutatum (Chinese evergreen) bears thin leathery leaves, 6 in long, on a bushy plant up to 18 in high. In the species, the oblong midgreen leaves are flecked with silvery grey. More decorative cultivars, such as *A. commutatum* 'Pseudobracteatum', sometimes sold as 'White Rajah', and *A. commutatum* 'Silver Queen' both have larger leaves with bold white or silvery markings.

A. costatum (painted drop tongue) has long, heart-shaped leaves with striking ivory-coloured midribs. It grows slowly to 9 in high.

A. modestum is the easiest of the species to grow as a house plant. It grows quickly to a height of 3 ft. The elegant, wedge-shaped leaves, 9 in long, are a uniform midgreen colour.

Buying hints Choose plants with healthy leaves set at short intervals along the main stem. All-green species are usually more widely available from florists than the named types, and at lower prices. Variegated, 10 in tall plants are in the medium to expensive price range.

General care These are slow-growing plants and respond well to a gritty compost, such as John Innes No. 1 or 2, or a peat-based compost. No staking is necessary, and repotting is required only every two to three years or when the plants are obviously pot-bound. Avoid natural gas fumes, and draughts.

Light Naturally shade-loving, aglaonemas do best in a warm, north-facing room or similar position where bright sun cannot scorch the leaves. They are suitable for dark corners if provided with some artificial light. *A. costatum* can tolerate deeper shade than the other species.

Temperature Normal living-room temperature is ideal, and it is vital that this does not drop below 55° F at night. High day temperatures are tolerated.

Humidity Luxuriant leaf growth can be expected if the air is kept moist and warm round the plants. If daily spraying with tepid water is too much of a chore, set the pots on trays of pebbles and water so that moisture can rise among the leaves. Alternatively, use the double-pot method, packing the space with moist peat.

Watering and feeding Water freely during the growing season, from late spring to mid-summer, but keep the soil on the dry side throughout autumn and winter.

Sustain robust growth by feeding plants once a week with a dilute liquid fertiliser, from April to July or August. After repotting, do not feed for about six weeks.

Propagation Increase plants from seeds sown in spring and germinated at a temperature of 65-70° F; by division of the rootstock in March; or from rooted suckers in early summer.

Disorders Exposure to intense sunlight in summer may cause leaves to curl and show scorch marks. Red spider mites may disfigure the leaves.

Araucaria
(*Araucariacae*)

Indigenous to the Norfolk Islands in the southern Pacific Ocean, this fern-like, branched pine tree can grow to 200 ft in the wild. As a house plant, valued for its delicate foliage and horizontally tiered shoots, it is slow-growing and seldom reaches more than 6 ft in height and 3 ft in diameter. Suitable for decorating porches, halls and stairways – and outdoor patios in summer – it thrives equally well in indirect light or shade. In its homeland, it is used as the Christmas tree.

A. heterophylla (*A. excelsa*) is the only species in general cultivation. Bright green, awl-shaped needles form thickly on the tiered shoots and have a soft mossy feel on young growth. The needles grow stiffer and more prickly as they age. When the needles drop from the trunk, which supports a pyramidal arrangement of branches, they reveal a scaly bark.

Buying hints Available from garden centres and florists, plants are expensive but durable. The best buys are 12-18 in young pot plants with perfect leading shoots and symmetrically arranged tiers of bright green branches. Avoid plants with browning leaf scales and broken growing points.

General care Araucaria is a tolerant plant and grows well in a peat or loam-based potting compost. Young plants should be potted on annually until they are in 8-10 in pots. Mature plants can be kept vigorous by replacing an inch or so of the top compost.

Light Best in light shade in a well ventilated position such as a north-facing room in which the air is moist. Shield the foliage from scorching sunlight in summer.

Temperature Undemanding. Provided the temperature does not fall below 45° F in winter, the Norfolk Island pine will stay healthy and retain its bright green colour.

Humidity Moist air is essential, especially when the plants are growing strongly from spring to late summer. Set the pots on a moisture tray of pebbles and water.

Watering and feeding Water freely from March to September, whenever the soil feels dry, and encourage robust growth by feeding fortnightly with dilute liquid manure. A foliar feed will spur new growth if this is slow, especially on plants that have not been potted on.

In winter, water just enough to keep the compost from drying out, and hardly at all if the plant is kept cool.

Propagation Sow seeds in spring, or take cuttings of 3 in long side shoots in spring and summer. Both should be raised in a propagator at a temperature of about 65° F.

Disorders Few troubles affect this plant, but avoid placing it too near a radiator or bright light source which may cause the leaves to shrivel.

Araucaria heterophylla

51

Asparagus setaceus

Asparagus
(Liliaceae)

Natural climbers from Natal and other parts of South Africa, ornamental asparagus are some of the easiest and most popular house plants. Often incorrectly classed as ferns, from their fern-like appearance, the plants bear bright green leaves or phylloclades which are actually modified stems. They are ideal for training over trelliswork or netting to create a lacy backdrop to other plants.

A. densiflorus 'Sprengeri' grows up to 12 in high and spreads and arches to 2 ft. The small fern-like leaves are arranged in clusters of three. On established plants tiny star-like flowers are followed by red berries.

A. setaceus (*A. plumosus*) is probably the most widely grown asparagus. The wiry stems are set with feathery phylloclades in horizontal tiers. Vigorous, growing to 10 ft if supported on wires or netting, it is only when a plant is fully mature that it throws up climbing shoots. These can be cut out if desired to leave the plant 12 in or so high, furnished only with non-climbing stems.

Buying hints Readily available from garden centres, florists, department stores and supermarkets, the most economic buys are 6-10 in plants. These are cheap and quickly grow into fine specimens. Make sure the shoots are deep green and not turning brown and that there are several new shoots pushing up from the crown.

General care Start young plants in a peat-based compost or John Innes No. 1, in 3-5 in pots. In a year or so they will need potting on into 8 in and finally into 10-12 in pots of John Innes No. 2. Thereafter, divide old crowns to rejuvenate plants. Train over a framework of wires.

A. densiflorus 'Sprengeri' looks best in a hanging basket. Cut back fronds which turn yellow, to encourage sturdy replacements from the base.

Light Best in light shade, or away from bright hot sun. Useful plants for dull corners, where they add elegance and grace with their feathery fronds.

Temperature Plants will tolerate a wide range of temperatures and do not mind occasional drops to 40° F in winter. Try to maintain an even temperature of 55° F and avoid setting plants immediately above a radiator.

Humidity The most luxuriant growth forms in a moist atmosphere. If the air is dry, syringe the leaves with tepid water twice a day.

Watering and feeding Give plenty of water during the growing season from March to August, but ease up and only moisten the soil when it looks dry during the autumn and winter.

No feeding is necessary for two months or so after repotting, but thereafter feed the plants weekly with dilute liquid fertiliser to maintain strong growth.

Propagation Divide old congested clumps in March, potting up only outer, well-rooted healthy portions.

Disorders Red spider mites may cause the leaves to turn a dull bronze; leaves drop, and webs form.

Scale insects attach themselves to the stems, resulting in distorted growth with a sticky, sooty deposit.

Aspidistra
(Liliaceae)

Renowned for its ability to withstand extremes of temperature, bad light, neglect and other inhospitable factors, the aspidistra, beloved by the Victorians, is truly beautiful when properly cared for. It comes from China and is one of the sturdiest evergreens.

A. elatior (cast-iron plant), previously known as *A. lurida*, grows about 12 in high, and its cluster of arching and pointed leaves spreads to 2 ft across. In late summer, uninteresting dull purple flowers appear at soil level on established plants. They are of no decorative value.

Aspidistra elatior

The cultivar *A. elatior* 'Variegata' is more striking, with cream and white bands running along the deep green leaves. The stripes tend to fade if the plant is given too much fertiliser or too little light.

Buying hints Widely available from florists and garden centres, large aspidistras are by no means cheap. The best buys are young 6-8 in plants with broad, bright green leaves showing no sign of shrivelling or browning. Reject any with open centres.

The variegated aspidistra is less common and more expensive.

General care Aspidistras thrive in a peat or loam-based compost. Start young plants in John Innes No. 1 and pot on annually until they are in 10 in pots. Thereafter, replace the top layer with fresh compost as necessary. Sponge the leaves to clean them of dust.

Light While aspidistras grow best in weak light or slight shade they tolerate quite heavy shade. They are good subjects for dark halls and similar areas where draughts would cripple less sturdy house plants.

Temperature The ideal winter night temperature is 50° F, but the plants will put up with considerably lower temperatures for short spells. Conversely, full sun and high temperatures for brief periods is also acceptable.

Humidity Not essential, but growth is better where the air is moist. Use a fine mist sprayer to drench the leaves at frequent intervals during the growing season from March to August. Alternatively, set pots on trays of pebbles and water.

Watering and feeding Aspidistras are thirsty plants so water freely in spring and summer; in winter only when the soil is dry. Good drainage is essential to prevent root rot.

No feeding is necessary while plants are potted on annually, though an occasional feed added to the water spurs growth. Established plants can be fed two or three times during the growing season.

Propagation Detach rooted suckers or divide clumps in spring.

Disorders Scale insects may colonise on stems; red spider mites cause the foliage to become coppery-bronze.

Begonia
(Begoniaceae)

Begonia masoniana

Strikingly patterned and colourful leaves make the foliage begonias popular house plants. Native to moist, warm regions of south-east Asia, they make superb bathroom plants where regular doses of steam encourage them to develop luxuriant leaves.

B. masoniana (iron cross) has deeply quilted, hairy leaves on which a deep purple cross stands out vividly. The leaves are heart-shaped, 5 in across and 8 in long, on fleshy and hairy, pink-red leaf stalks.

B. rex bears slightly larger leaves, of a more angular heart shape. The corrugated surfaces have richly coloured zones of silver, cream, pink, purple and near black.

Outstanding cultivars include 'Merry Christmas', with a central heart of dark purple and pink, banded with silver; 'Silver Queen', with a network of silver veins; and 'Helen Teupel', purple pencilled with silver and pink.

Buying hints Plants around 6 in tall are generally good value for money, and readily available, in the inexpensive price range. Choose specimens with well-shaped leaves showing no signs of browning or curling. Examine leaves for fungal diseases.

General care Grow in a peat or loam-based potting compost, repotting only when roots push through the drainage holes, indicating a pot-bound state.

Light Foliage begonias prefer subdued, filtered light, so a north or east exposure suits them well. If they are set in a group arrangement in a bright sunny position, place them in the shade

Begonia rex cultivars

of taller plants. They grow well in artificial light.

Temperature Low night temperatures can prove fatal and should not drop below 50° F. Best at 60° F.

Humidity In summer particularly, a moisture-charged atmosphere is essential. Use the double-pot method. Mist sprays may cause die-back.

Watering and feeding Give water only when the soil feels dry, as begonias are liable to crown rot if the soil is soaked for any length of time. Ease up on watering in winter, apply-ing it only when the plants show obvious signs of wilting.

Maintain vigorous health with liquid feeds at fortnightly intervals.

Propagation Sow seeds in early spring at a temperature of 65° F.

Take cuttings from healthy leaves and root in a propagator.

Disorders Grey mould may cause blackish-brown blotches on the leaves. Mildew shows as downy white spots on undersides of leaves.

Root knot eelworm attacks the roots; leaves collapse and the plants die.

Caladium bicolor

Caladium
(*Araceae*)

This tuberous plant is grown for its beautifully hued, almost transparent leaves which die back to the crown in autumn. It comes from the tropical forests of South America and needs high humidity and temperatures.

C. bicolor forms a slender, airy clump, up to 15 in high, of long-stemmed leaves the shape of gigantic arrowheads or hearts. The paper-thin leaves are heavily netted and suffused with bright green, red or pink. Some are entirely white or pink, with green veins and margins.

There are several outstanding cultivars, such as the white and dark green 'Candidum'; the pinkish-red, green-edged 'Mrs. Halderman', 'Freda Hemple' and 'Rosebud'; and the pink and green 'Lord Derby'.

Buying hints Caladiums are chiefly found at garden centres from spring onwards and vary from the inexpensive to medium price range. Select 8-10 in plants with several stems arising from the crown. Avoid any with damaged, brown or shrivelled leaves.

General Care Grow caladiums singly in 6-8 in pots of moist peat or loam-based potting compost. John Innes No. 2 is ideal as it has sufficient nutrients to keep growth vigorous.

In autumn when the leaves fade, dry off plants and rest the tubers.

Light Caladiums need good light, but shade from scorching sun. Conversely, too much shade will inhibit the exotic leaf colouring.

Temperature These are tropical plants and need plenty of warmth. Spring and summer temperatures should not drop below 65° F at any time. In winter, when the tubers are resting in dry soil, the temperature can drop to 55° F.

Humidity Close and warm conditions are essential. Spray the leaves daily with water or stand the pots on trays of pebbles and water. Ideally, pack thick wads of sphagnum moss over the compost to absorb water.

Watering and feeding In summer water frequently to keep the compost evenly moist. Ease up in autumn until the soil is almost dry.

Encourage vigorous growth by spraying the leaves with a foliar feed twice weekly from late spring onwards.

Propagation Set dormant tubers in pots or boxes of peat or moss kept permanently moist. Start growth in March in a propagator case at a temperature of 65° F. When leaves appear, and roots have formed, remove the young plants from this nursery bed and pot them up.

New plants are obtained from offsets planted in March. They should make good sized tubers in two years.

Disorders Apart from aphids which may colonise on young leaves and stunt growth, few other troubles are likely.

Calathea lancifolia

Calathea
(Marantaceae)

Native to the steamy jungles of Brazil, slow-growing calatheas do best where the air is humid, ideally a bathroom or conservatory. Draughts and hot dry air cause the leaves to discolour and curl along the edges.

C. lancifolia (*C. insignis*) makes an upright plant around 10 in high and wide. The leaves, 6 in long, are patterned alternately with emerald-green and dark green. The undersides are maroon-purple.

C. makoyana (*Maranta makoyana*) is also known as the peacock plant after the striking leaf patterns. Mature height is around 2 ft. The oblong 6 in leaves, supported on thin stalks, are attractively pencilled with bright green veins and darker green "eyes" on a silver background. The undersides of the leaves are rich purple.

Buying hints Most garden centres and florists offer established plants which are generally expensive. The most economic buys are 6-8 in plants, of spreading habit and with several growing points. Pay particular attention to the leaf tips and reject any that are beginning to shrivel.

General care Grow in John Innes No. 2 compost or any peat-based brand. Start young plants in 4 in pots and pot on annually until growing in 8 in pots. Calatheas make good bottle-garden plants.

Light Bright sunlight can affect the leaf colour adversely. Position plants in light shade or away from direct sun. An ideal site is in an artificially lit glass case where the light shows up the remarkable leaf patterns.

Temperature Ordinary living-room conditions are suitable as long as the winter night temperature does not fall below 50° F.

Humidity Thriving in an atmosphere charged with moisture, this means in practice spraying the leaves daily with a fine mist. Alternatively, use the double-pot method, packing the space with moist sphagnum moss.

Watering and feeding Give plenty of water from April to August. Thereafter less is needed, but the compost must not dry out at any time.

Sustain growth by repotting in fresh compost each spring and feeding fortnightly with a dilute liquid fertiliser.

Propagation Divide crowded clumps in June and establish the divisions at a temperature of 70° F.

Disorders Aphids may weaken young leaves. Draughts cause curling foliage, and dry air is fatal.

Ceropegia woodii

Ceropegia
(Asclepiadaceae)

This plant from Natal trails slender thread-like stems set with opposite pairs of fleshy, silvery white and green leaves, purple on the underside. Easy and quick-growing, it is superb as a hanging basket plant, for edging a trough or for twining over trellis.

C. woodii is the most popular species. Commonly known as the rosary vine, the stems trail 3 ft long from a tuberous crown, with succulent heart-shaped leaves about ½ in across. Tiny, lantern-shaped, purple flowers sometimes form in summer.

Buying hints Ceropegias may need seeking out at high-class florists; 6 in plants are good, inexpensive buys. Choose those with several stems with leaves set closely and of a rich green-white appearance.

General care Loam or peat-based compost is equally suitable for this plant. A large root system takes time to develop, so the plant can be kept in a 3-4 in pot for several years.

Light Good light is essential. Whether grown in a pot or hanging basket choose a sunny position with a south or west-facing exposure.

Temperature Night temperatures in winter should never drop below 50° F. It thrives at ordinary room tempera-

55

ture, and does not mind occasional draughts though coal gas fumes should be avoided.

Humidity Ceropegia is rarely bothered by dry air as its succulent leaves are effective water storage organs. This makes it an ideal plant for hot, dry places.

Watering and feeding From April to August water freely, but let the soil become fairly dry between waterings. While the compost should not dry out in winter, give tepid water only when the surface feels dusty.

A weekly liquid feed of balanced fertiliser will encourage the curtains of slender stems to develop rapidly. Do not feed in winter when growth is slow.

Propagation Detach tiny marble-like tubers from the leaf joints and set them to half their depth in small pots of gritty compost and root at 65° F.

Alternatively, peg down stem joints in pots of composts and, when roots have formed, sever the rooted portion from the parent and pot up separately.

Disorders Few troubles affect this adaptable plant.

Chamaedorea elegans

Chamaedorea
(*Palmae*)

In its native Mexico this palm thrives in the shade of taller trees. It is one of the easier house plant palms, suitable for draught-free living-rooms. It grows fairly slowly in the early years, but as a mature plant reaches 4 ft, with feathery arching fronds 2-3 ft long.

A good tub plant, this elegant palm can be used as a centrepiece in a group arrangement.

C. elegans is often grown in dish and bottle gardens when young. The leaves, composed of 6-9 in long leaflets radiating from a stout midrib, grow straight from the central stem. The fronds are gradually shed from the lower part of trunk as the plant ages.

Buying hints Readily available from numerous sources, quality, size and price vary widely. Plants 2 ft or more tall are in the medium to very expensive price range, depending on locality. The best buys are 8-10 in plants, with several deep green fronds arising from almost the same point. Avoid any with brown-edged or discoloured leaves.

General care A peat-based compost is best. Pot on young plants annually in spring or when roots fill the pot. Ultimately, a plant may be set in a large pot or small tub.

Repotting is unnecessary for established palms, but topdress with fresh potting compost to maintain strong growth. Position mature plants strategically where they can be admired from a distance.

Light Avoid bright, direct sunlight, and choose a position with weak light or where taller plants provide shade.

Temperature Living-room temperatures are suitable for most of the year, but in late autumn and winter when the plants are resting, they prefer day and night temperatures of 50-55° F. When growth resumes in spring, bring the plants into a warmer place.

Humidity Resisting relatively inhospitable conditions of draughts and poor light, the palm objects to the dry air from the central heating. Mist the leaves twice daily with tepid water or use the double-pot method, filling the space between with peat or moss, kept permanently moist.

Watering and feeding Be careful about watering; throughout the year keep the compost just moist. If watering from the bottom, make sure to tip any surplus water from the saucer.

A dilute liquid fertiliser at fortnightly intervals, from April to August, will spur growth and encourage luxuriant leaves.

Propagation New plants are best raised from seeds sown in early spring at a temperature of 65-70° F.

Disorders Scale insects may colonise on the stem, and white cottonwool masses of mealy bugs may suck the tissues dry. Red spider mites may be troublesome in hot, dry conditions.

Chlorophytum
(Liliaceae)

Chlorophytum comosum
'Variegatum'

Probably the most widely grown foliage house plant, chlorophytum comes from South Africa. It needs a frost-free home, but is otherwise highly adaptable, tolerating heat, bright sun and shade.

C. comosum 'Variegatum', commonly known as spider plant, forms rosettes of grass-like, arching leaves, edged with green and striped white and green. They are 12-18 in long. Sometimes the stripes are reversed, the leaves being white-edged.

Mature rosettes thrust up arching flower stems which form new plants at their tips and produce more stems to create a "waterfall" of stems and small leaf rosettes. A mature plant in full cascade can reach 3 ft from tip to toe, with erect tufts of baby plants.

Buying hints Widely available throughout the year from florists, garden centres and other sources, plants up to 10 in high are generally inexpensive and good value for money. Choose specimens with well-tufted growing points, and avoid any with brown-tipped leaves.

General care This is a fast-growing plant; the fleshy rope-like roots soon outgrow a small pot and congest the surface. It is almost best to overpot, by choosing a pot size in which the plant can develop for several years before being repotted. Peat or loam-based compost is equally suitable. Stand the plant on a pedestal so that the tiers of arching leaves and shoots can be viewed from all sides.

Light One of the few house plants that does not object to bright hot sun, spider plant prefers subdued light and tolerates shade. In deep shade, though, the creamy-white stripes fade.

Temperature The minimum winter night temperature is around 45° F. High day temperatures, even 80-85° F, are not objected to.

Humidity The most luxuriant foliage is produced in a warm, moist atmosphere. Spray frequently or stand the pots on pebble and water trays.

Watering and feeding In spring and summer, while plants are making new leaves and rosettes, water freely. In winter reduce the amount of water depending on temperature; cold wet soil inhibits growth.

Feed fortnightly from spring until late summer if growth is slow, using a dilute liquid fertiliser.

Propagation Root baby plantlets in pots of gritty soil. Or divide large clumps and pot up separately.

Disorders Dry air can cause leaf tips to turn brown.

Cissus
(Vitaceae)

Cissus antarctica

A race of evergreen, long-lived climbers from tropical Australia, Java, the West Indies and South America. The handsome leaves are either entire or compounded of several leaflets. Growing rapidly to around 8 ft high, the various *Cissus* species are excellent for training on trellis, for trailing over the sides of deep troughs or cascading from hanging baskets.

C. antarctica (kangaroo vine) is the most popular species, usually grown to provide a dark green shiny curtain of toothed, oblong leaves, 4 in long and 2 in across. Easy to grow and resistant to coal gas fumes, dry air, draughts and smoke. Clinging tendrils grip readily on netting, wires or string.

C. discolor (begonia vine), quite unlike the other species, is the most decorative of the family. The velvety, spear-shaped leaves, 6 in long and 2 in across, are reminiscent of the begonia and embellished with bands of silver and green radiating from a deep green midrib; the undersides are crimson. The stems are erect and strong rather than trailing.

C. rhombifolia, formerly *Rhoicissus rhomboidea,* has softly hairy, three-lobed leaves, 4 in across. This is an

Cissus rhombifolia

accommodating climber and makes a dense screen of bright green foliage, ideal for background displays or as a room-divider.

Buying hints *C. antarctica* and *C. rhombifolia* are widely available; *C. discolor* may need seeking out from good florists. In all cases, plants around 9 in high represent inexpensive buys. Choose glossy green-leaved plants; on *C. discolor* the silvery markings should be sharply defined. Large plants of the other species are very expensive, but good value if immediate effect is required.

General care Cissus are best grown in a loam-based mixture such as John Innes No.1 for young and No.2 for established plants.

Provide a supporting structure early in the life of all plants, or they will soon become a hopeless tangle of slender stems. Pot on each year when young, and topdress plants with fresh compost when they are in 8-10 in pots.

Cut back main leaders of *C. discolor* to half or two-thirds their length in February, and reduce side shoots to short spurs a few inches long. This encourages strong new growth from the older wood.

Light Tolerant of shade, *C. antarctica* and *C. rhombifolia* are ideal for dimly-lit hallways, reception areas and similar places. *C. discolor*, however, prefers better light or the silver and white marbling may fade. All species grow in good light, but must be shaded from bright, hot sun in summer.

Temperature *C. antarctica* and *C. rhombifolia* can withstand winter night temperatures as low as 41° F, and day temperatures should ideally not rise above 65° F. *C. discolor* needs a higher winter minimum, at least 50° F at night and 70° F by day.

Humidity All species, and in particular *C. discolor*, enjoy a moist atmosphere. Where the air is dry, spray the leaves at frequent intervals.

Watering and feeding During the growing season from March to August water thoroughly but let the compost dry out between applications. Give less water in autumn and winter to avoid wet soil and the risk of root rot. Tip away any water from the saucers.

Feed with dilute liquid fertiliser at fortnightly intervals during the growing season.

Propagation Take stem cuttings in late spring and root at a temperature of 65-70° F.

Disorders Mealy bugs and aphids may cripple young leaves and growing tips. Blotchy and dropping leaves indicate dry air.

Codiaeum
(*Euphorbiaceae*)

Probably our most colourful house plant, codiaeum, commonly known as croton, presents an exciting challenge. Native to the steamy jungles of Malaysia and the Pacific Islands, it needs high humidity and a warm room to develop the exotic rainbow-tinted foliage to perfection.

C. variegatum and its variety, *pictum,* has given rise to dozens of exotic cultivars. Some have twisted and curly-edged leaves, while on others they are oblong and pointed or shaped like arrowheads. Mature plants are 2 ft high, with an erect growth habit.

Popular cultivars include 'Disraeli', whose green, lance-shaped leaves are splashed with cream and yellow and suffused with red beneath. 'Golden Ring' has marbled yellow and green leaves, spirally twisted; 'Norma' and 'Bravo' are both more robust of habit. *C. variegatum pictum* itself has leaf veins in yellow and pinkish-red.

Rich colours are a feature of all crotons, and it is common to find orange, copper, pink, green and yellow hues in one leaf.

Buying hints Readily available from most plant shops, crotons vary greatly in price, from cheap to expensive. Most economic buys are 10 in plants,

Codiaeum variegatum pictum
cultivars

but be particularly careful to check the leaves for dubious blemishes.

General care Peat and loam-based composts are equally suitable. A warm, moist, draught-free position is essential to prevent leaf drop.

Pot on each spring to avoid pot-bound roots. Pinch out growing tips to encourage branching.

Light Leaf colours are most intense in bright light though not direct summer sun. In winter, plants should be positioned where they receive as much light as possible.

Temperature It is vital that night temperatures do not drop below 60° F in winter, or the leaves will shrivel and drop. In summer, high temperatures are tolerated if the air is humid.

Humidity Atmospheric moisture is absolutely essential. Mist the leaves frequently with a fine water spray, or stand plants in pebble trays.

Watering and feeding Give plenty of water throughout spring and summer, but ease up as nights grow colder until, in winter, water is given only when the soil surface feels dry.

Feed with a dilute liquid fertiliser fortnightly from April to August.

Propagation In spring, strike 3 in long tip cuttings in sand at a temperature of 70° F.

Disorders Red spider mites cause bronzing of the leaves; mealy bugs feed on the fleshy stems and show their presence by tufts of white wool. Scale insects on the stems dry out the tissues.

Coleus
(Labiatae)

These flamboyant foliage plants from Java grow to 18 in tall and 12 in across. Popular and easy short-term house plants, they are also used for summer bedding, window boxes and tubs.

C. blumei and its many cultivars make superb plants for a cool or warm room. The nettle-like leaves, 4-6 in long and 2-3 in across, form thickly on bushy plants if the growing tips are removed. The yellow, green, pink-red or maroon leaves are usually edged with a contrasting colour.

The oak-leaved, green-edged 'Carefree' grows 9-12 in tall and has foliage richly tinted with greenish-yellow, bronze-pink, and blood-red. 'Sabre', of a similar height, has long sword-shaped leaves in jade green, scarlet, bronze and other colours.

'Old Lace' is rather different, with heart-shaped, fringed and lacy-edged leaves in apricot, red, salmon and rose.

Buying hints Coleus cultivars are on sale at most plant shops. Raised and sold as annuals, prices are generally reasonable for 6-9 in plants. Choose bushy plants, with leaves that display good colour contrasts.

General care Coleus are hungry plants and should be potted in a peat-based compost with frequent feeds or in John Innes compost No. 2 or 3. Pot on plants progressively, from 3 in to final 6 in pots.

Pinch out the tips of leaders and side shoots to encourage bushiness. Coleus are seldom kept for a second year.

Light Good light is necessary for the leaf colours to develop. Where possible set plants on a south or west-facing window sill.

Temperature Most plants are thrown out in autumn, but if over-wintered, do not let the temperature fall below 55° F for any length of time.

Humidity Dry air is fatal to these plants. Correct lack of moisture by mist-spraying plants every day.

Watering and feeding Keep plants moist throughout spring and summer, less so as autumn approaches.

If growth seems slow, apply dilute liquid fertiliser every fortnight from April to September.

Propagation Take cuttings of shoot tips in spring, late summer and autumn, or raise plants from seed sown in January. For both methods maintain a temperature of 65-70° F.

Disorders Mealy bugs and aphids suck sap from the stems.

Coleus blumei cultivars

Cordyline terminalis

Cordyline
(Agavaceae)

Used as roofing material and for hula skirts in its native Polynesia this handsome shrub makes a splendid house plant for a warm room where the air is moist, such as a draught-proof kitchen or bathroom with good light. The broad, palm-like leaves, brightly coloured, spread out like a fan from the central stem. They eventually drop to leave a trunk topped with a foliage rosette. Mature plants can reach a height and spread of 1½-3 ft.

C. terminalis, often incorrectly labelled *Dracaena terminalis,* develops oblong, pointed leaves, 2-4 in across and 1 ft long. Mature leaves are bronze-red to purple, while the young leaves are often creamy-white with pink or red margins.

Most plants are cultivars, of which the most popular is 'Tricolor', with distinct markings of creamy-white, pink and red; the leaf stalks are grooved and usually reddish-brown. 'Rededge', which is of smaller stature, has red-purple and green leaves, 9 in long.

Buying hints Widely available from all types of plant shops, it is advisable to buy from reputable sources. Small specimens, around 9 in high, are generally inexpensive; 2 ft plants are very expensive. 'Rededge' is best purchased at 5-6 in. Choose plants without traces of leaf browning and shrivelling.

General care Use a peat or loam-based compost, and 6-8 in pots for mature plants. Repot and pot on only when roots fill the pot.

Cordylines make handsome feature plants and are also used as centrepieces in group arrangements. Generally slow-growing, plants may be short-lived under less than ideal conditions.

Light Cordylines do best in bright light, but they will tolerate indirect or artificial light though with some loss of the vivid leaf tints. Shade plants from scorching sunlight in summer.

Temperature The absolute minimum night temperature is 50° F, and 55-60° F is preferable. The ideal day temperature throughout the year is 70° F.

Humidity High humidity is essential otherwise the leaves shrivel and brown. Use a fine mist sprayer at least once a day to douse the foliage. Alternatively, stand pots on trays of pebbles and water, making sure the water does not touch the base of the pots.

Watering and feeding In spring and summer when new leaves are being formed, water freely to keep the compost moist. In autumn and winter water only when the soil feels dry.

Feed at fortnightly intervals throughout the growing season, with a dilute liquid fertiliser.

Propagation Remove suckers in spring and pot up singly. Increase overgrown plants from 3 in stem sections inserted vertically in a gritty compost. Or sow seeds in spring. All three methods require the use of a propagator unit with a steady temperature of 65-70° F.

Disorders Leaf browning is common from lack of air moisture. Aphids and red spider mites may disfigure the foliage and cause leaf drop.

Cyperus
(Cyperaceae)

Easy, reliable and usually free from troubles, cyperus is a highly decorative plant from the marshes of Madagascar. It does not mind being overwatered and is an ideal subject for terrariums and hydroculture.

C. alternifolius (umbrella plant) has erect, grass-like stems 1-2½ ft high. They are topped with slender leaves, 2-3 in long, that arch like the ribs of an umbrella. Green-yellow flower clusters appear at the tops of stems in early summer.

The cultivar 'Gracilis' grows only 18 in tall. 'Variegatus', of about the

Cyperus alternifolius

same height, with leaves and stems splashed white is a striking plant.

Buying hints Small plants, 6-9 in tall, from garden centres, are inexpensive, and easy to establish. Choose plants with bright green symmetrical umbrellas and avoid any with extra large, pale green leaves, which indicate they have been forced at too high a temperature and grown in poor light.

General care Young plants are best in John Innes potting compost No. 1. Pot mature plants in a richer compost or a well-balanced peat-based compost. Repot crowded plants in spring. Cyperus can also be grown in plain water or planted in an aquarium.

Light Cyperus plants appreciate good light, even strong sunlight, and artificial light in large terrariums. They tolerate light shade and will put up with even poor light.

Temperature Aim to keep winter night temperatures above 50° F. Plants do well at ordinary room temperatures and do not object to quite severe fluctuations.

Humidity Keep the air moist by standing pots in saucers or bowls filled with water. In summer, mist spray frequently.

Watering and feeding Keep the compost soaked throughout the year; these plants are moisture lovers, and the roots should never dry out.

If growth seems slow, speed it up during spring and summer with a foliar feed applied twice weekly, or with fortnightly doses of dilute liquid manure applied to the soil.

Propagation Increase crowded plants by division in spring.

Disorders Few troubles affect these plants. Browning leaf tips usually indicate a need for repotting.

Dieffenbachia
(*Araceae*)

Dieffenbachia maculata

Easy and imposing house plants from tropical America, dieffenbachias are commonly known as dumb cane. The leaves and stems contain calcium oxalate, a poison which can cause temporary loss of speech if brought in contact with the mouth. Outstanding as single or in mixed displays, their large, broad and marbled leaves are instantly eye-catching. Rapidly forming an upright stem, 1½-4 ft high, clad with oblong leaves, allow plenty of room to grow these plants to perfection.

D. amoena has huge oblong leaves, as much as 8 in wide and up to 2 ft long. They are pale green with a regular pattern of stripes and marbling along the veins.

D. maculata (*D. picta*) bears smaller deep green, white-blotched leaves, 12 in long. Cultivars of the species are seen more frequently, notably 'Exotica' so heavily suffused with creamy-yellow that the green colour remains only in a narrow leaf edge.

Pale creamy-yellow leaves with a neat herringbone of bright ivory lateral veins is the outstanding feature of 'Rudolph Roehrs'. Several other named cultivars are available.

Buying hints Dieffenbachias are among the most popular house plants. *D. amoena* and *D. maculata* 'Exotica' can be found at almost any shop, with 10-12 in plants generally being good buys in the medium price range. Highly variegated cultivars are rarer and usually expensive.

General care Although plants begin life in 3-5 in pots, they soon make vigorous growth at normal room temperature and need repotting until they are in final pots of 10-12 in. Any proprietary peat or loam-based potting compost suits them.

Repot, in spring, when plants become pot-bound. Draughts and gas fumes are lethal.

Light Good, but filtered light suits these plants best. Shade from bright sun in summer, but place them in full light during autumn and winter or supplement with artificial light.

Dieffenbachia maculata 'Exotica'

Temperature Ordinary living-room conditions are ideal. In winter the temperature should not fall below 60° F. They can withstand, for short periods, a drop to 45° F.

Humidity A moist atmosphere is essential. Avoid placing them near radiators and other direct sources of heat. Mist the leaves daily with tepid water, or stand pots on pebbles and water or double-pot with moist peat.

Watering and feeding Keep the compost evenly moist throughout the year. In a warm living-room growth continues in winter; at cool temperatures, reduce watering.

Feed regularly, once a fortnight during spring and summer, with dilute liquid fertiliser. Do not feed in winter.

Propagation Leggy plants can be perpetuated by rooting growing tips and stem sections, 2-3 in long, in gritty compost. They require a propagator, with a temperature of 65-70° F, to root. Basal shoots from the old plant may eventually be detached and potted up, for rooting under heat.

Disorders Usually pest and disease-free. Dry air is the chief reason why leaves wither and fall. Draughts stunt growth and cause brown and yellow blemishes on the leaves.

Dizygotheca
(Araliaceae)

An elegant, delicate-leaved plant from the New Hebrides in the Pacific Ocean, dizygotheca makes a superb feature plant where its curiously thin and deeply saw-edged leaves can be admired. Slow-growing and somewhat difficult to manage in the home, dizygotheca can grow 4-5 ft tall and 3 ft across in 10 years.

D. elegantissima (Aralia elegantissima), sometimes known as false aralia, is the only common species. It grows as an upright plant, the single stems bearing slender, arching leaf stalks. Each of these is crowned with 8-10 finger-like leaflets, about 3 in long. The foliage matures through copper and dark green to near black.

Buying hints Available from high-class florists and garden centres, the best buys are 9-12 in plants, in the medium price range. Taller plants are very expensive and not necessarily in good condition. Select plants with unbroken leaders and well-spaced, healthy leaves.

General care Dizygotheca needs a draught-free place in good light. Grow in peat or loam-based compost and pot on annually, in spring, to a final 8 in size. On established plants, replace the top 3 in layer with fresh compost.

Dizygotheca elegantissima

Light Good light is necessary, especially in winter. In summer, move plants away from direct sun which can scorch the leaves. Light shade and artificial light is tolerated.

Temperature A day temperature not below 65° F is ideal throughout the year. In winter, night temperatures must not fall below 55-60° F, or the leaves will discolour and drop.

Humidity Plenty of atmospheric moisture is vital; the dry air of an average living-room is fatal to the plant. Use the double-pot method, packing the space with permanently moist peat or sphagnum moss. In addition, mist spray the leaves daily with tepid water, particularly when the temperature rises.

Watering and feeding Keep the soil just moist through the growing season from April to August; at other times water only when the compost feels dry.

Young plants, potted on annually, need no extra nutrients. Maintain growth of established plants by feeding fortnightly with a dilute liquid fertiliser during the growing season.

Propagation Raise new plants from seed sown at 70-80° F, in late winter and spring. Stem cuttings, taken in spring and summer, should be rooted in a propagator.

Disorders A dry atmosphere encourages red spider mites, aphids and scale insects.

Dracaena fragrans 'Massangeana'

Dracaena godseffiana 'Florida Beauty'

Dracaena
(*Agavaceae*)

A magnificent group of palm-like plants, dracaenas are valued for their shapes and the colours of their ornamental leaves, which vary greatly from species to species. They are widely distributed throughout tropical Africa. Some species are among the sturdiest and most long-lived of our house plants, others are superb as steamy bathroom or kitchen plants. Most grow fairly rapidly, attaining their mature height in 6-8 years. They are related to cordylines, and may sometimes be offered as such.

See *Cordyline terminalis*.

C. deremensis grows 4 ft or more high, with leaf rosettes along the erect stem. They are sword-shaped, up to 18 in long and dark green marked with pairs of silver-white stripes.

More commonly seen are such cultivars as 'Bausei', green with a solid silver-white centre, and 'Warneckii', with fine milk-white stripes along the grey-green leaves.

D. fragans grows erectly to 4 ft and spreads 2½ ft. The cultivar 'Massangeana' is the one usually seen; this has 2-3 in wide arching leaves, dark green with a broad golden centre. Other types include 'Lindenii' with green and gold leaves edged with gold.

D. godseffiana is very different. It has smaller, rounded to oblong leaves, 3 in long by 2 in across, marbled and flecked with cream and yellow. Growing 2 ft high, it is a branching plant, spreading to 1½ ft. On 'Florida Beauty', the cultivar usually grown, the white spots cover almost the entire leaf area.

D. marginata, 4 ft tall, is the easiest and toughest of the dracaenas. It bears 1½ ft long leaves in a terminal rosette on a stout palm-like stem. The attractive 'Tricolor' is variegated with thin stripes of cream and pink.

D. sanderiana, an erect species which grows to almost 2 ft, is often sold with two or three young plants in the pot. The 8 in long green leaves are edged with silver.

Buying hints Available from florists, department stores and garden centres, most dracaenas are of good quality. Depending on species and cultivar, costs of young plants come in the inexpensive to medium price range. Plants several feet high are very expensive, with named cultivars commanding the highest prices. Avoid any with leaf blemishes or white fluff which indicates mealy bugs.

General care Dracaenas can be grown in a peat or loam-based compost. Pot on in spring, when roots fill the pots, annually for the large-growing types, less frequently for *D. godseffiana* and *D. sanderiana*. Keep all plants away from draughts.

Light Good light, though not bright summer sun, is essential if dracaenas are to keep their intense colours. In shade, the leaves remain greenish and the bright hues fade. In autumn and winter give them as much light as available; a west-facing exposure or similar situation is ideal.

Temperature Aim at maintaining a winter night temperature of 50° F. *D. deremensis* and *D. fragans* need more warmth, around 55° F. Ordinary living-room day temperatures throughout the year are suitable.

Humidity A steamy atmosphere is the ideal, but hardly practicable. Mist the leaves with tepid water, preferably daily, and stand the pots on pebble and water trays.

Watering and feeding Keep the soil moist by frequent watering from spring to autumn; for the rest of the year water only when the surface looks dry.

Feed fortnightly during the growing season with dilute liquid manure.

Propagation Tip cuttings, 3 in long, can be rooted at 70° F in spring. Basal shoots, with or without roots, may be potted singly and established in a heated propagator.

Leggy stems of old plants can be cut into 3 in sections and rooted in sand.

Disorders Mealy bugs show as white, woolly skeins and result in leaf drop. Leaf spot disease may cause purple-black blotches.

× Fatshedera lizei

× Fatshedera
(*Araliaceae*)

This is a highly successful bigeneric cross that has resulted in a glossy palmate-leaved plant of great versatility. In 1912, Lizé Frères, a French nurseryman, crossed *Fatsia japonica* 'Moseri' with *Hedera helix* 'Hibernica', and the new plant was named × *Fatshedera lizei*. It is a lax, rapid climber that needs supporting; it is quite hardy and takes well to cool spots that are not particularly draught-free. × *F. lizei* grows 4-6 ft high, usually with a single stem, set with lobed leaves, up to 8 in across. Side branching from the base can be encouraged by pinching out the growing tip.

'Variegata' is an outstanding, creamy-white cultivar.

Buying hints Offered by most shops, plants are generally cheap, the best buys being 6-12 in plants. Select sturdy specimens with bright glossy leaves and short internodes. Make sure the growing tip is healthy and the foliage unblemished. Avoid pale, drawn plants which will have been grown in poor light.

General care This plant thrives in most indoor conditions: it tolerates fluctuating temperatures and extremes of light and shade. Wash the leaves occasionally to keep them glossy bright. Grow in a peat or loam-based compost and pot on every year in spring until in a final 8 in pot.

Support with a cane or moss pole. Leggy stems can be cut back to encourage new side shoots.

Light Bright light is acceptable, but the leaves develop better in light shade. An excellent plant for any room with poor light.

Temperature Thriving in a warm room, fatshedera also tolerates quite low temperatures and accepts a winter minimum of 40° F, for short periods. 'Variegata' needs a slightly higher minimum temperature and good indirect light.

Humidity A too dry atmosphere should be avoided. Spray or sponge the leaves daily or as often as possible. Or use the double-pot method.

Watering and feeding Give plenty of water during the growing season from March to September. As growth slows down for the winter, water only when the compost is dry, especially at cool temperatures.

Feed fortnightly with dilute liquid fertiliser during spring and summer.

Propagation Root 4-5 in stem cuttings from side shoots in a propagator, at a temperature of 65° F.

Disorders Aphids may occasionally be troublesome at high temperatures.

Fatsia japonica

Fatsia
(*Araliaceae*)

A parent of × *Fatshedera lizei*, this is an arresting plant prized as much for its glossy green, deeply lobed palmate leaves as for its ease of cultivation. It is hardy outdoors in mild districts. In the home it thrives in warm or cool rooms and minds neither bright light nor slight to deep shade. It grows to 4 ft high and 3 ft across as a pot plant.

F. japonica forms an upright branching plant with exceptionally long and leathery leaf stalks. The light green leaves may reach 9 in across and are composed of seven to nine lobes.

Buying hints Easily found at any type of plant shop, quality is usually good, and prices cheap. Young 6-9 in plants often have one stem only, but they are better buys than near-mature expensive specimens. Choose those with bright green leaves and sturdy stems from a central growing point.

General care Fatsia thrives in a loam-based compost such as John Innes No. 2, in which it develops fine large leaves. At maturity, it needs a 10 in pot or small tub. It also looks well as the focal plant in a deep group arrangement. Pinch out the growing tips in spring on young plants if there are no signs of natural branching.

Light Grown for its shade-tolerant qualities, fatsia suits ill-lit rooms and dull corners. At the same time it accepts good light, out of direct sun.

Temperature Extremely adaptable, fatsia will come to no harm provided the temperature remains above freezing in winter.

Humidity Not objecting to dry air, direct sources of heat should be avoided. At high day temperatures, spray the leaves for extra humidity.

Watering and feeding Water freely to keep the compost moist; in winter let it dry out slightly between applications. Give a fortnightly liquid feed in spring and summer.

Propagation Increase from rooted suckers in early spring, or from seeds sown at 65° F in March or April.

Disorders Too much heat in winter may cause curling of the leaves.

Ficus
(Moraceae)

Open the front door of any house plant gardener, and one of the first plants to greet you will be a ficus, or rubber plant. Ubiquitous maybe, but it is because of the extreme tolerance to neglect and adverse conditions, ranging from poor light to draughts and a smoky atmosphere, that this genus, which includes the edible fig tree, is so popular.

Trees and shrubs, climbers and trailers – all from south-east Asia, Australia and Africa – *Ficus* species possess a sculptural beauty and diversity that make them ideal plants for any decorating scheme.

F. benjamina, the weeping fig, is one of the most popular indoor trees. It is suitable for spacious areas, its slender woody stem reaching 6 ft. The arching branches bear glossy green, willow-like leaves, 3 in long.

F. deltoidea (F. diversifolia), also called mistletoe fig, is a slow-growing shrubby plant, to 2 ft high, with oblong, dark green leaves, dotted with brown on the upper sides, and 1-3 in across. Small yellow berries develop readily in the leaf axils.

F. elastica (rubber plant) is probably one of the most popular and durable of house plants. The species itself is rarely grown. The plant sold in shops is usually the cultivar 'Decora'. This grows with a single stem set with alternate, broad and leathery, deep green glossy leaves, up to 12 in long and 6 in wide, pointed at the tips. Pale pinkish-red sheaves enfold the young developing leaves.

Other notable cultivars are 'Doescheri', with pale green and creamy-white variegations; 'Robusta', with larger, glossy green leaves; and 'Tricolor' which has pink and creamy-white patches.

F. lyrata (F. pandurata) is known as fiddle-back fig after its magnificent leaves. Gently wavy-edged and glossy green, they are up to 18 in long and 9 in across. Fast-growing, the single stem reaches 4 ft.

F. pumila is a climbing or trailing species, with wiry stems up to 2 ft. Train it over trellis, netting or moss poles, or let it trail as a curtain over a trough, tub or hanging basket. The tiny, bright green and heart-shaped leaves are ½ in wide.

F. radicans 'Variegata' is similar in growth habit to *F. pumila*. The longer, pointed leaves have slightly wavy, cream-white edges.

Buying hints The majority of *Ficus* species and cultivars are easily found at most plant shops. Prices vary greatly, according to type and advanced growth; tree-like plants, such as *F. benjamina*, sold as 1-4 ft plants, range from inexpensive to very expensive. The popular rubber plant and its cultivars fluctuate similarly, graded by size, health, shop and locality; 9-12 in plants are usually the best and most economical buys.

F. lyrata is less common and consequently expensive, though good value as healthy 2 ft plants.

Ficus benjamina

Ficus elastica 'Robusta'

65

Ficus elastica 'Doescheri'

Ficus pumila

Tree types, such as *F. elastica* and *F. lyrata,* should have healthy growing tips and bright green, glossy leaves. Creeping, spreading kinds, such as *F. pumila* and *F. radicans* 'Variegata' should have several stems.

General care All thrive in peat or loam-based composts. Pot on young plants in small pots annually in spring, with the larger species finishing up in 12 in pots or small tubs.

Pinch out growing tips of trailing kinds from time to time to encourage bushiness and branching. *F. elastica* and *F. lyrata* may also produce side branches if the growing tip is removed.

Light All do best in good to subdued light. Direct sun, for any length of time, will cause the leaves to shrivel and fall. They are good plants for rooms with poor natural light; *F. pumila* in particular tolerates heavy shade and even some draughts.

Temperature Normal room temperatures are suitable for all species, and fluctuating temperatures are acceptable if air moisture is increased with rising heat. However, the critical winter temperatures vary: *F. elastica* 'Decora' and *F. lyrata* require an absolute minimum of 60° F, and *F. benjamina* and *F. radicans* need 55° F.

F. deltoidea and *F. pumila* can be kept as low as 50° F.

Humidity All do better when growing in a warm moist atmosphere. They will tolerate dry air, but produce better growth if mist sprayed as often as possible. Alternatively, stand the pots on trays of pebbles and water.

Watering and feeding Keep the soil of all ficus plants moist from spring to autumn – the root balls should never dry out. In winter let the soil dry out before watering; *F. elastica*, particularly, suffers if kept too moist during the dormant season.

Encourage and maintain growth with dilute liquid fertiliser fortnightly throughout spring and summer.

Propagation Increase from leaf and bud cuttings (*F. elastica* and *F. lyrata*); from air layering (*F. benjamina*, *F. elastica* and *F. lyrata*); from stem cuttings (*F. pumila*, *F. benjamina*, *F. deltoidea* and *F. radicans* 'Variegata'. All cuttings should be rooted in a propagator at 65° F.

Disorders Scale insects weaken plants by sucking the sap. Mealy bugs cause leaf drop.

Brown and yellow patches followed by leaf drop are due to dry air, persistent draughts or overwatering.

Fittonia verschaffeltii 'Argyroneura'

Fittonia
(Acanthaceae)

Not an easy plant but worth pampering for the beauty of its green or purple, silver or carmine-netted leaves. Native to Peru, it demands a warm and moist atmosphere and is best suited to a bottle garden or terrarium. Its creeping and spreading habit – 4 in high and 9 in across – makes it ideal for ground cover in conservatories and enclosed plant windows.

F. verschaffeltii bears broadly heart-shaped, 3 in long leaves prominently marked with a herringbone pattern of red to carmine veins. The popular cultivar 'Argyroneura' (snakeskin plant) has soft green leaves picked out with bright silver veins.

Buying hints Purchase plants from florists and garden centres where they can be expected to have been well cared for. Choose plants with brightly veined leaves and healthy growing tips. Avoid any with soggy, congested centres. Plants are generally inexpensive.

General care Fittonias thrive in a peat or loam-based compost. They have shallow root systems and as pot plants will do in 3-5 in pots. They are seldom repotted as they grow unkempt after three or four years. They are then started again from cuttings or divisions of the roots. To maintain the handsome leaves, cut the stems hard back in spring to encourage new growth.

A constant warm, moist and draught-free atmosphere is essential if leaves are not to shrivel and fall.

Light Fittonias do best in indirect light, and the most luxuriant leaves are produced in light shade; even deep shade is tolerated. In winter they can be moved closer to natural light.

Temperature Normal room temperatures are sufficient throughout the year. However, the winter night temperatures should not fall below 55° F.

Humidity This must be high, and unless the plants are grown in enclosed environments, set them in double pots, packed with sphagnum moss kept permanently moist. Also spray the leaves daily with tepid water, preferably rainwater.

Watering and feeding Keep the compost moist throughout the year, but watch out for waterlogging which causes root rot. At lower winter temperatures reduce watering, but do not let the soil dry out.

Feed one-year and older plants with a dilute liquid fertiliser at fortnightly intervals from March to August. Plants in closed cases should not be fed.

Propagation From tip cuttings in spring, rooted in a propagator at 70° F. Or by divisions of roots, established at the same temperature.

Disorders Few of any importance under good conditions.

Gynura
(Compositae)

Gynura aurantiaca

The two species grown as house plants differ mainly in their growing habits, one being lax and spreading, the other climbing or trailing. Rapidly growing to 3 ft high unless pinched out, gynuras are valued for their rich purple, silky-haired leaves.

G. aurantiaca, from Java, forms a spreading mound of leaves and stems up to 18 in across. The gently lobed or entire, oblong to triangular dark green leaves are 6 in long and 2 in across. They are thickly clothed with iridescent purple hairs. Groundsel-like, orange flowers appear in spring.

G. procumbens (G. sarmentosa) is native to India. The twining stems can reach 5 ft and are best supported on trellis or allowed to cascade from a hanging basket. The flowers are similar to those of *G. aurantiaca* and like those have an unpleasant smell.

Buying hints Plants around 4-6 in are usually inexpensive. Select well-branched specimens with a rich shine to their silky leaves; avoid any with woody stems and shrivelled foliage.

General care Grow in a peat or loam-based compost. Pot one-year old plants on in spring, to 6 in pots. Gynuras quickly become leggy and unkempt; they can be cut back in spring, shorten-ing side shoots to 3 in. Or new plants can be raised from cuttings.

Trail two or three plants of *G. procumbens* in a hanging basket or grow them against trellis as climbers.

Light Good light is essential to develop the purple leaf sheen. Bright light has no ill effect provided the air is moist, but give some shade in high summer to avoid sun scorch.

Temperature Ordinary room temperatures are suitable, winter night temperatures not below 50° F.

Humidity Quite dry air is tolerated, but some humidity is preferable. Do not mist spray the leaves if they are in full sun; water globules trapped by the hairs are liable to magnify the sun's rays and burn the tissues.

Watering and feeding Gynuras are thirsty plants and consume large amounts of water in summer. Less is needed in winter, sufficient to keep the compost just moist.

Encourage robust growth by feeding with dilute liquid fertiliser fortnightly throughout spring and summer.

Propagation Increase by 3 in tip cuttings, rooted in plain water or a gritty compost in a propagator at 65° F, in April. New plants can also be raised from seeds, germinated at a similar temperature.

Disorders Pests and diseases do not trouble these plants. The purple colour is lost in poor light.

Hedera helix cultivars

Hedera
(Araliaceae)

Variegated cultivars of the common and Canary Island ivy are greatly valued for bright or shady, draughty places. They are climbers that cling to their supports by tiny adventitious roots sprouting from the stems.

Ivies are useful as living screens and curtains, as carpet plants beneath shrubs and as trailers from hanging baskets, troughs and tubs. Popular and easy, ivies are, with a few exceptions, fast-growing.

H. helix (common ivy) grows wild throughout Europe. The species, from which numerous outstanding cultivars have been developed, has 3 in long and 2 in broad, three-lobed leaves, the terminal lobe being larger and more pointed than the other two.

The common or English ivy still holds its own as a tough house plant. This and all-green cultivars, such as the five-lobed 'Chicago' and the sharp-pointed 'Sagittaefolia', grow well in dark corners.

Variegated ivies include the slow-growing and small-leaved 'Adam' and 'Little Diamond', both with silver-grey leaf edges.

The widely sold grey-green 'Glacier', with silver margins, and 'Jubilee' (or 'Goldheart'), green with yellow centres, are better suited to outdoor use unless they are grown in a cool room.

'Lutzii' has almost heart-shaped leaves, heavily mottled with grey-green and yellow, while 'Buttercup' is pure golden-yellow.

Canary Island ivy is sometimes listed as a separate species (*H. canariensis*) and sometimes as a subspecies of *H. helix*. It is a rapid grower and differs in its erect habit and larger, less prominently lobed, leathery leaves. The cultivar 'Gloire de Marengo' (or 'Variegata'), green leaves variegated with silver, grey and white, is the plant usually offered.

Buying hints Ivies are readily available at all shops though varying in quality and price. Green-leaved plants, preferably with several branching stems, are cheap at up to 12 in. Variegated kinds are slower-growing and generally smaller; specimens 6-9 in wide are good value and only slightly more expensive than green ivies.

General care Grow all ivies in a peat or loam-based compost, ideally with additional lime. Repot or pot on as roots push through the drainage holes. Pinch out shoot tips to promote new stems from near the base and to encourage side shoots.

Large-leaved types are excellent for trailing on trellis, canes and strings; they need tying to their supports. Small-leaved types, green or variegated, look attractive trailing over pot edges and from hanging containers.

Light Ivies grow best in indirect or filtered light. They are tolerant of light to semi-shade, though variegated types do best where bright sun cannot shrivel the leaves. In summer, shade and ventilate plants positioned near a south-facing window where the air can heat up considerably.

Temperature Steady day temperatures of about 65° F are recommended. Low winter night temperatures, even just above freezing, will do no harm, and most ivies benefit from a rest period in winter.

Humidity A reasonable amount of air moisture results in fresh, healthy foliage. Dry air will not actually harm the plants, but often encourages pests. Spray the leaves frequently with water throughout the growing season.

Watering and feeding Keep the soil just moist in spring and summer, but water sparingly in winter when growth is slow, especially in a cool room.

During the growing season, spur growth with fortnightly feeds of dilute liquid manure.

Propagation Root tip cuttings, 3 in long, in pots of gritty compost, or in plain water at any time.

Disorders Red spider mites and aphids are encouraged by hot, dry air. Scale insects lead to sooty mould which blackens the leaves.

Heptapleurum arboricola

Heptapleurum
(*Araliaceae*)

A fairly recent introduction to house plant collections, this species from south-east Asia makes an imposing feature tree for a well-lit room. It is related to *Schefflera* and bears long-stemmed, palmate leaves on an upright stem that rapidly reaches 6 ft.

H. arboricola, sometimes offered as *Schefflera* or *Brassaia*, has a palm-like appearance. Its finger-like leaflets up to 10 in number, radiate from a 12 in long leaf stalk. Its common name is the umbrella tree.

Buying hints As yet mainly found only at florists' shops and garden centres, 12-15 in plants are in the medium price range. Choose plants with a straight leader, strong growing tip and bright green leaves.

General care Grow in a loam-based potting compost, starting young plants in 3 in pots and potting on annually in spring until in 6-9 in containers.

Left to its natural growth habit, heptapleurum grows an upright, somewhat leggy stem. By nipping out the growing tip it can be induced to branch out lower down.

Light A strong woody stem with bright glossy leaves develops in good light. Give some shade from hot sun in summer, but move into full light in autumn and winter. In poor light, heptapleurum may grow pale and drawn; site it as near as possible to a window facing south or west.

Temperature Throughout the year try to maintain a day temperature around 65° F. It is important that the winter temperature does not drop below 50° F, or the leaves will shrivel and drop.

Humidity Air moisture is beneficial; dry air is tolerated if the leathery leaves are frequently sprayed with tepid water. Alternatively, stand plants on a tray of pebbles in water.

Watering and feeding Thirsty and needing plenty of water in spring and summer, heptapleurum should be watered in winter only when the compost dries on the surface.

Fortnightly feeds of dilute liquid fertiliser invigorate growth.

Propagation Start new plants from seeds sown in a propagator in spring, at a temperature of 70° F.

Disorders Few troubles are encountered. Draughts and low winter temperatures may cause leaf drop.

Howea forsteriana

Howea
(*Palmae*)

Found only on Lord Howe Island in the south Pacific, this is a genus of only two species, formerly known as *Kentia*. Probably the easiest of indoor palms, howeas grow slowly to an eventual height of 8 ft, with a 6 ft spread. At maturity they are best suited to large rooms or conservatories.

H. belmoreana bears fans of narrow, pointed leaflets held on horizontally arching stems, 12-18 in long. The leaf fans have a spread of 12 in and can grow to 15 in long.

H. forsteriana is similar to *H. belmoreana*, but with fewer and wider leaflets which droop gracefully. It is known as the thatch palm.

Buying hints *H. forsteriana* is the more popular of the two species, and the more expensive. In both cases 2 ft plants make the best buys. Choose bright-leaved plants in 6 in pots filled with plenty of roots. Avoid impulse buys at open markets. Large and very expensive plants are also available.

General care These sculptural, enduring palms look well in glass-fibre containers and thrive in a loam-based compost such as John Innes No. 2. Pot on every two to three years when the compost becomes thick with roots, and growth starts slowing down. Established plants in 10 in pots can make do with fresh top dressing. Three or four young plants are often potted together to give a spreading effect. Set the plants in a draught-proof position.

Light Best in indirect or filtered light, howeas do not object to shade, even a poorly lit, dark situation is tolerated.

Temperature Thriving at normal room temperature and withstanding temperatures as high as 80° F, the winter night temperature should never drop below 55° F.

Humidity Dry air is acceptable at average temperatures, but the finest leaves are produced in a moist atmosphere. Spray the leaves daily with tepid water, or use the double-pot method, keeping the sphagnum moss or peat permanently moist.

Watering and feeding Howeas barely go through a resting period, and the compost should be kept moist all year round. Water freely in summer, less so in winter and let the soil dry out between waterings.

Encourage strong growth by liquid feeding every fortnight during the growing season, from April to August.

Propagation Germinate seeds in a propagator, at a temperature of 75-80° F in early spring.

Disorders Scale insects and red spider mites are the chief enemies. Remove any yellowing leaves at the base.

Maranta
(*Marantaceae*)

Maranta leuconeura 'Erythroneura'

Arrestingly decorative leaves make this spreading bushy plant from tropical America one of the most popular house plants. Related to and often confused with *Calathea* and *Ctenanthe*, marantas are generally smaller and suitable for bottle gardens or ground cover among taller plants.

M. leuconeura is commonly known as prayer plant because at night the leaves assume a vertical position and have been likened to hands held in prayer. It is almost prostrate, growing 6-8 in high, but sprawling over an area of 12 in. The rounded, oval leaves are beautifully marked with vivid brownish-purple flecks between blue-green veins, the colours darkening as the foliage matures. The undersides are purple.

There are several outstanding cultivars, including 'Erythroneura', with greenish-yellow midribs and vivid red veins bisecting the dark green leaves. 'Kerchoveana' is greyish-green and marked with red-brown spots. The leaves of 'Massangeana' fade from dark to light green at the edges, with the veins picked out in red.

Buying hints Although widely and cheaply available from stores and supermarkets, quality is variable. The best plants, around 6 in high, are found at florists' shops and garden centres, in the inexpensive to the medium price range.

General care Marantas grow equally well in a peat or loam-based compost, such as John Innes No. 2. Start plants in 3 in pots and pot on every year in spring until they are in growing in 6-8 in pots.

Light Marantas should not be subjected to bright, scorching sunlight. A north or east exposure is best, or a similar position with filtered light. In winter, give best available light.

Temperature Thriving at normal or higher room temperature, minimum winter night temperature should not fall below 50° F.

Humidity The more water that condenses on the leaves, at high temperatures, the better. Syringe the foliage with tepid water, or set several plants in a shallow container and pack moist peat round them.

Watering and feeding Keep the soil generously moist in summer, but let it dry almost out between waterings in winter when growth is slower.

Give liquid feeds every fortnight from March to August.

Propagation Root cuttings of basal shoots in spring, in a propagator at 70° F. Alternatively, divide the rhizomes and replant the portions.

Disorders Pests and diseases seldom trouble these plants. But warm dry air and dry roots cause leaf drop.

Monstera
(Araceae)

Monstera deliciosa

Superbly sculptured leaves are the outstanding feature of this Mexican climber. They are entire and heart-shaped when young, but as the plant matures intriguing perforations or splits appear.

Monstera tends to sprawl in an upward direction and where room permits is capable of reaching 18 ft. It grows rapidly, endures for many years and makes no excessive demands.

Long and arching, pencil-thick aerial roots appear from the stem joints, marring to some degree the handsome outline. They can be trained on to a moss-pole support, but are better anchored in the compost to become further channels of food to leaves and stems.

M. deliciosa is aptly named the Swiss-cheese plant after the leaf perforations. On mature plants, the bright to dark green leaves can be as much as 2 ft across, and curious, creamy-yellow flower spathes may appear.

Buying hints Widely available from all types of sources, size, price and quality vary greatly. Plants up to 18 in are most frequently offered, usually in the medium price range. For quality select plants with bright, glossy green leaves showing no signs of marginal browning.

General care Peat or loam-based composts are suitable, both with additional grit to allow the roots to breathe. Support the lax, floppy stem on a moss pole, kept damp by daily spraying with tepid water. Young plants are usually started in 5 in pots and potted on in spring.

Light The soft, light green leaves develop best in subdued or filtered light away from direct sun. In winter, give all possible light.

Temperature Monstera grows at normal room temperature and will also thrive in much higher temperatures provided the air is moist. In winter it should not be subjected to temperatures lower than 50° F.

Humidity Used to steamy jungle heat, monstera revels in high humidity. On the practical level this is supplied by spraying the leaves daily with tepid water and training the stem against a permanently moist moss pole.

Watering and feeding In spring and summer water freely, but in winter, when growth is slow, keep the compost barely moist. Excessive watering leads to root rot.

Feed young plants with dilute liquid manure fortnightly from spring to late summer and top dress large tubs with fresh potting compost.

Propagation Strike tip cuttings, with one half developed leaf attached, in gritty compost at a temperature of 75° F. Alternatively, rejuvenate overgrown plants from 3 in stem sections, inserted to half their depth in small pots of compost and rooted at 75° F.

Disorders Overwatering causes the glossy leaves to develop brownish-yellow patches.

Pandanus
(Pandanaceae)

An arching rosette of sword-shaped leaves is characteristic of this slow-growing plant from Polynesia. On young plants the rosette rises from soil level, but with age the lower leaves drop, and a short trunk develops. The resulting leaf scars resemble the threads of a screw.

Taking many years to reach a height of 4 ft, with an almost equal spread, pandanus makes an impressive feature plant for a large room.

P. veitchii is known as screw pine because the leaves are arranged spirally round the stem. Erect at first, then arching, the 3 in wide leaves grow to 2 ft long; they are dark green with creamy stripes and margined with hooked teeth.

Buying hints Pandanus needs cos-

Pandanus veitchii

setting, and it is advisable to buy plants only from reputable florists' shops and garden centres. Generally expensive, look for vigorous leaf rosettes on plants in 4-5 in pots. Reject any with blemished leaves or pale, drawn growth.

General care Best in a loam-based compost such as John Innes No. 2, screw pine needs repotting, in spring, only when roots crowd the surface soil. Ideally start with a large pot (6-8 in) and top dress with an inch or so of fresh compost each year.

Aerial roots form from the stems on four-year old plants. Known as stilt roots they serve to raise the trunk and should never be cut off. Push them into the soil to help feed the plant.

Light The plant thrives in good light all year round and needs shielding only from very hot sun in summer.

Temperature This is a critical factor.

Ideally the day temperature should be 70° F or above, with a winter night temperature not below 65° F.

Humidity Plenty of air moisture during the growing season encourages long broad leaves. Overcome dry air with the double-pot method, filling the space with peat or Forest Bark strips kept wet at all times. It is also beneficial to spray the leaves with a mixture of foliar feed and water.

Watering and feeding Never let the compost dry out during spring and summer. Water sparingly as the days grow colder and light less intense.

Propagation Increase from rooted suckers carefully cut from the base of the plant. Start growth in a propagator at 65-70° F.

Disorders Few troubles afflict this plant, but cold draughts can cause ugly blemishes on the leaves.

Peperomia
(*Piperaceae*)

Peperomia caperata

Peperomia griseo-argentea

These plants from the rain forests of tropical America display amazing diversity in the shape, colour and texture of their leaves. They are natural subjects for bottle gardens, and popular for table centrepieces and low group arrangements. Many peperomias produce slender, erect flower spikes that resemble mice tails.

P. argyreia is sometimes known as the watermelon peperomia, from the leaf colourings. It grows 9 in tall and bears 4 in shield-shaped leaves, strikingly marked with alternating silver and light green bands.

P. caperata is the most common type. The small, deeply corrugated, heart-shaped leaves form a rounded dark green tuft, 6-9 in high and wide. Creamy-white, red-stalked flower spikes are evident for much of the year.

Numerous cultivars include 'Emerald Ripple', with pink stalks to heavily quilted leaves; the similar, but dwarfer 'Little Fantasy'; and 'Tricolor', with white leaf margins.

P. griseo-argentea (*P. hederafolia*) is

similar to *P. caperata*, but the leaves, at 2-2½ in, are twice their length. They are more softly quilted, and the main veins are attractively pronounced.

P. obtusifolia (*P. magnoliifolia*) is unlike the previous species. It grows as a branched, shrubby, 6-8 in tall plant with thick and fleshy, smooth and rounded leaves. They are 3-4 in long and beautifully cream-edged in the cultivar 'Green Gold'.

The form 'Variegata' is the one most usually offered; this is cream and green with almost white young leaves.

Buying hints Peperomias are readily available from all types of plant shops and generally of good quality. Plants around 4 in high are cheap to inexpensive. Select dark green and sturdy plants and avoid any with drooping leaves, indicating some form of crown rot. Variegated kinds are usually smaller than green-leaved types.

General care Peperomias thrive in a peat-based compost. In nature they are almost epiphytic and the shallow root systems need only small pots. Repot only when pot-bound. In practice, they can stay for years in a 3-4 in pot.

Peperomia obtusifolia 'Green Gold'

Pinch out the growing tips of *P. obtusifolia* to induce a bushy habit.

Light Best in subdued light, ideally a north-facing or similar position. Light shade is suitable, and the plants must be protected from bright summer sun. In winter they will accept all available natural light.

Temperature Provided the air is moist, peperomias thrive in warm rooms. Make sure winter night temperatures do not drop below 55-60° F.

Humidity A moist atmosphere is essential for healthy growth. Plunge pots rim-deep in a large container of moist peat and moss.

Watering and feeding Care must be taken with watering. Waterlogged soil quickly leads to rot; even in spring and summer let the compost dry before watering again. In autumn and winter water enough to prevent the peat compost from shrinking.

Give a liquid fertiliser every two weeks from spring to late summer.

Propagation Root stem or leaf cuttings at a temperature of 65° F.

Disorders Overwatering can cause water-soaked spots on the leaves (oedema).

Philodendron
(Araceae)

This genus includes several hundred species of magnificent foliage shrubs and climbers from the tropical rain forests of Central and South America. A large number are grown as house plants; those described here are among the most easily grown.

Philodendrons grow as huge-leaved shrubs up to 7 ft, or develop long, sinuous trailing stems. Aerial roots form readily at the stem joints.

P. bipinnatifidum is a shrubby plant up to 4-5 ft. The deep green leaves are borne on erect leaf stalks, all arising from the crown. Mature leaves are rounded to triangular and deeply incised, up to 2 ft in length and $1\frac{1}{2}$ ft across, while young leaves are undivided and usually heart-shaped.

P. elegans is a climbing species of moderate vigour. The 2 ft long stems bear deeply cut, dark green leaves. Easy to grow, this tolerant plant deserves wider recognition.

P. erubescens climbs vigorously to more than 6 ft. It is outstanding for its copper-tinged, shield-shaped leaves, 9 in long, on purple leaf stalks.

P. 'Burgundy' is probably a form of *P. erubescens*. It is slower-growing though ultimately to the same height; the red colouring is more intense.

P. hastatum (correctly *P. domesticum*) climbs to 5 ft. Broad and succulent leaf stalks carry glossy heart or spear-shaped leaves, 7 in long.

P. laciniatum has lax climbing stems with dark green, usually three-lobed leaves. It bears some resemblance to *P. bipinnatifidum*, but needs a support.

P. scandens is probably the most widely grown philodendron. Of vigorous habit, the slender brittle stems climb or trail indefinitely unless pinched out. The dark green, heart-shaped leaves are 4 in long.

P. 'Tuxla', a fairly recent introduction, resembles *P. hastatum*, but is of stiffer, more branching habit.

Buying hints *P. bipinnatifidum* and *P. scandens* are easily found at all types of plant shops. Other species and cultivars are mainly stocked by florists and garden centres. Prices vary considerably, as does quality, and apart from the inexpensive *P. scandens*, most plants are in the medium to expensive price range and sizes of 1-3 ft.

In all cases, choose healthy-looking plants with sturdy growing points and bright green leaves. Be wary of any with damaged, blemished or yellow-blotched foliage.

General care All philodendrons grow in loam-based compost such as John Innes No. 2, or a proprietary peat compost. Start young plants in 3 in pots and pot on in spring when necessary. Non-climbing types make outstanding feature or specimen plants.

Philodendron bipinnatifidum

Philodendron 'Burgundy'

73

Philodendron scandens

Climbers need initial support in the form of moss poles, and may eventually be trained on large trellis work to create a leafy screen.

Young plants of *P. scandens* make good hanging basket subjects.

Light Philodendrons are tolerant of light shade, though in winter they should be moved as near to the light as possible. In summer, shade them from scorching sunlight. They are good plants for poorly lit areas, possibly supplemented with artificial light.

Temperature Thriving at normal room conditions, philodendrons will not tolerate low temperatures; the winter night minimum is 60° F.

Humidity A high degree of humidity is necessary for strong growth. Spray the leaves daily with tepid water or stand pots on pebble trays kept moist.

Watering and feeding Keep the compost moist at all times through spring and summer; in winter water moderately when the soil feels dry.

Encourage strong growth with fortnightly feeds of dilute liquid manure, from spring to late summer.

Propagation Root climbing species in spring from tip or stem cuttings, at a temperature of 70° F. Shrubby types are raised from seeds germinated at 75° F in spring, or from divisions of the rootstock in June. Establish these at a temperature of 70° F.

Disorders These plants are seldom troubled by pests and diseases. The brownish-yellow blotches on the leaves are due to draughts, fluctuating temperatures or overwatering.

Pilea
(*Urticaceae*)

Pilea cadierei 'Nana'

A charming group of spreading plants valued for their brightly coloured, herringbone-patterned leaves. Native to the Tropics, pileas grow no more than 8-12 in high and wide. They are easy to care for, but short-lived.

P. cadierei (aluminum plant) forms a spreading 10 in mound of lightly corrugated, silver splashed leaves. They are oval-pointed and 2 in long. 'Nana' is a more compact cultivar, and 'New Silver' ('Bronze') has silver-centred, bronzy-green leaves.

P. involucrata (*P. pubescens*) is similar to *P. cadierei*, but with copper-coloured leaves, red beneath. 'Panamiga' is an outstanding cultivar of the species with three broadly defined herringbone-like veins, grey on a bluish-silver background. It reaches a height and spread of 6-8 in.

A recent, highly decorative cultivar, variously sold as *P. mollis* or *P.* 'Moon Valley', has crimped nettle-like leaves 3 in long. They are startingly marked with bronzy-red veins on a gold-green background.

P. microphylla (artillery plant) is quite different to the previous species. It has a ferny, mossy look from the minute, scale-like leaves that clothe the branching stems. The common name is derived from the fact that the tiny flowers discharge puffs of pollen when the plant is disturbed.

Buying hints Possibly because of their low cost, pileas are not always easily found. But garden shops and department stores offer good-quality plants, 5-6 in specimens being the best buys. Choose well-branched plants with unblemished leaves.

General care Pileas grow well in 5 in pots of peat-based compost. Repot if roots fill the pots, but three- year old plants usually deteriorate and are best replaced with rooted cuttings of young shoots. Pinch out growing tips to encourage branching.

Light Best in light shade, pileas are excellent for positions away from windows or in a north or east-facing site where the air is not too dry. In summer, shade from bright hot sun, but give as much light as possible in winter. They make fine bottle-garden plants and even thrive in the light from an ordinary bulb.

Temperature Plants grow strongly at steady room temperatures of 65-70° F.

They will tolerate a winter night minimum of 55-60° F, but not draughts.

Humidity High humidity is not essential, but growth is healthier with some air moisture. Stand the pots on pebbles in trays of water, or spray the leaves frequently with tepid water.

Watering and feeding Keep the compost just moist in spring and summer.

In winter let it dry out slightly between sparse waterings.

Give fortnightly dilute liquid feeds from March to September.

Propagation Root tip cuttings in May, in a propagator at 70° F.

Disorders Bright hot sun may cause the leaves to curl; apart from that pileas rarely cause problems.

Plectranthus
(Labiatae)

Plectranthus oertendahlii

Native to South Africa, this small-leaved easy plant makes an attractive subject for a hanging basket. It is of trailing or prostrate habit, spreading to form a mat of leaves.

P. oertendahlii (Swedish ivy) is noted for its round, 1 in, boldly patterned leaves, with the main veins defined in creamy-yellow on a bronze background. The stems may trail to 2 ft, rooting where they touch the soil.

Buying hints As yet not widely available in spite of their ease of culture, young plectranthus plants around 4 in high are good value. Select well-branched plants and reject any with discoloured foliage or damaged growing tips.

General care These plants thrive in any well-balanced loam-based compost. Start them in 3 in pots and pot on annually. Ultimately plants should be in 6 in pots, or three plants growing in a 9 in pot or hanging basket. Pinch out the growing tips regularly to encourage side shoots.

Light Best in good light, but slight shade is tolerated. Place in the lightest position available in winter to prevent drawn, weak stems and leaves. Shade from hot summer sun.

Temperature Plectranthus maintains steady growth at normal room temperature and will tolerate a winter minimum of 45° F. Avoid lower temperature or leaves will curl and fall.

Humidity A dryish atmosphere is not catastrophic, but some air moisture is beneficial. Mist spray the leaves often with tepid water or use the double-pot method.

Watering and feeding Water freely and deeply throughout spring and summer, especially hanging baskets. As growth slows down give less water, but do not let the compost dry out.

Give a liquid feed once a week from April to August.

Propagation Divide large plants and pot separately in 3 in pots. Root in a warm close atmosphere.

Disorders Normally trouble-free.

Rhoeo
(Commelinaceae)

This plant, with its rosette of broad and pointed, sword-shaped leaves, is often mistaken for *Dracaena*. Native to Central America and the West Indies, it demands both heat and humidity.

R. spathacea (*R. discolor*) forms an artistic shuttlecock, 12-14 in high and wide, of strap-like leaves, dark green above and gleaming purple beneath. Tiny white flowers lie cradled within the leafy bracts, hence the common names of Moses-in-the-cradle and boat lily. In time, the lower leaves fall to reveal a squat stem. Side shoots may also form.

Buying hints Rhoeo is easily checked by fluctuating temperatures; purchase well-potted plants from warm premises. Those in 6 in pots represent good buys. Make sure the leaves are well coloured and unblemished; choose specimens with side shoots.

Rhoeo spathacea

General care A gritty peat or loam-based compost, such as John Innes No. 2, is equally suitable. Repotting is seldom necessary, and a 5 in pot will last a plant for its short life of three or four years. If plants become pot-bound, repot in spring.

Light A natural shade lover, rhoeo does best in low light and needs protection from bright hot sun. In winter set it in a better lit position.

Temperature A day temperature around 70° F ensures steady growth. Do not let winter night temperatures fall below 55-60° F.

Humidity Droplets of water on the leaves create the moist atmosphere necessary to prevent leaf curl. Particularly in summer, spray the foliage daily with tepid water and set the pot in a larger container, filling the space between with moist peat or moss.

Watering and feeding Make sure the compost is constantly moist throughout the growing season from April to September. In winter, ease up on watering, but do not let the soil dry out.

Feed fortnightly with dilute liquid manure from May to July.

Propagation Root 3-4 in side shoots in gritty compost in a propagator at 65-70° F during spring or early summer.

Disorders Mealy bugs suck the sap and cause leaves to fall.

Sansevieria
(*Agavaceae*)

Sansevieria trifasciata 'Laurentii'

Sansevieria trifasciata 'Hahnii'

Rosettes of upright, slim, fleshy and pointed sword-shaped leaves, statuesque almost, are the outstanding feature of this West African plant. There are several cultivars ranging from 6 in to 4 ft, all easy growing and enduring.

Sansevierias have become almost a legend: they will tolerate persistent neglect, dim corners and low temperatures, yet remain fresh-looking. But you can kill them – by overwatering.

S. trifasciata (mother-in-law's tongue, bowstring plant) is the type species from which most of the popular cultivars have been bred. It has stiff 3-4 ft long and narrow, leathery leaves zoned with horizontal bands of silver-grey on a dark green background.

The cultivar 'Laurentii', which is the one usually offered, has butter-yellow edges to its mackerel-banded green leaves.

'Hahnii' is much smaller, up to 6 in, and resembles the species, but the leaves form a distinct cup-shaped rosette. 'Golden Hahnii' and 'Silver Hahnii' are respectively variegated with gold-yellow and silvery-white.

Other cultivars, often unnamed, have broader, up to 4 in wide leaves, 12-15 in long, with various coloured leaf markings.

Buying hints Widely available from all types of plant shops, with 'Laurentii' the most popular, plants 1-2 ft high range from the inexpensive to expensive according to quality. Sturdy and multiple-crowned plants are impressive, up to 3 ft and very expensive. Reject plants with broken leaf points.

General care These plants thrive in a loam or peat-based compost with extra grit added. They are better under rather than overpotted and can stay in the same pot for several years without any ill effects. Repotting, when necessary, is best done in spring.

Light Sansevierias grow in light ranging from dim shade to bright sun.

Temperature Thriving at normal room temperature or higher, 65-80° F, the plants will accept a minimum winter temperature of 50° F. The smaller 'Hahnii' cultivars are slightly more tender and need a warmer spot than other types.

Humidity Dry air is no problem. The plants react by curling the leaves inwards – when they should be sprayed with tepid water.

Watering and feeding Water sparingly. Surplus water in the saucers invite rapid death. Water only when the soil is truly dry, and hardly at all in winter.

In good compost, feeding is seldom necessary. If growth is very slow, or plants have been in the pot for several years, give foliar feeds once a month during spring and summer.

Propagation Raise new plants of 'Hahnii' from leaf cuttings in May, in a propagator at 70° F, or from division.

'Laurentii' must be perpetuated from rooted offsets as leaf cuttings revert to the ordinary species.

Disorders Remarkably free from troubles, too much watering leads to root rot and death.

Saxifraga stolonifera

Saxifraga
(Saxifragaceae)

This particular saxifrage, from China and Japan, thrusts out embryo plants at the tips of arching, thread-like stems, to form a waterfall of stems and foliage. They are effective in hanging baskets, as ground-cover in tubs or troughs, and for edging.

Growing around 9 in high and 12 in across, this decorative saxifrage is a short-term plant.

S. stolonifera (*S. sarmentosa*) is popularly known as mother-of-thousands. It bears strikingly silver-veined, dark green, hairy leaves, light purple on the underside. They are borne on red, hairy leaf stalks, and are almost round, 2-3 in wide, with lobed margins. Spikes of starry, white flowers sometimes appear in summer. Baby plants are borne at the tips of the stems.

The cultivar 'Tricolor' has leaf edges demarcated in pink, red and cream.

Buying hints Young plants in 3 in pots are cheap and usually good value. Choose robust looking plants with a number of runners.

General care Grow in a peat or loam-based compost, in pots or hanging baskets. Repot in spring if pot-bound;

most plants thrive in 4-5 in pots.

Light Excellent plants for dull, poorly lit corners, provided these are draught-free. Bright light is tolerated as long as the plants are shaded from summer sun. Place in good light in winter.

Temperature Almost hardy in the open, saxifrages indoors do best in a cool room. In winter, the temperature can drop to just below freezing and should not exceed 40° F. Conversely, these plants do not mind high summer temperatures and will respond with rapid growth.

Humidity Dry air is detrimental. Spray the leaves regularly with tepid water, particularly at temperatures above 65° F. Alternatively, stand pots on pebble and water trays.

Watering and feeding Make sure the compost is kept moist at all times in spring and summer; in autumn and winter, at cool temperatures, water only when the compost dries out.

Encourage 'Tricolor' to make luxuriant foliage by feeding with liquid manure fortnightly throughout spring and summer.

Propagation In spring detach plantlets from runners and pot separately in gritty compost.

Disorders Aphids may cripple the succulent shoot tips.

Schefflera
(Araliaceae)

In its native Australia, schefflera grows as a large tree covered in spring with exquisite scarlet flowers. As a house plant it grows as a small branching tree, eventually to 6 ft tall. It is slow-growing, especially if restricted in a large pot or tub, and is suitable as a feature plant for a large room.

S. actinophylla (*Brassaia actinophylla*) is known as the umbrella tree from its elegant, broad-fingered leaves on slender stems. On mature plants, there are up to 16 leaflets on each "hand", each as much as 12 in long and 1½ in across. Young plants have only four or five fingers to each leaf. The erect main stem can sometimes be induced to branch if the growing point is nipped out at an early age.

Schefflera actinophylla

Buying hints The best buys are young plants in 5-6 in pots. They are widely available, generally of good quality and in the medium price range. Larger plants are very expensive. Avoid plants with no obvious growing point, which might mean they are blind and will not develop any further upward growth.

General care Set plants in large pots or small tubs of gritty compost such as John Innes No. 2. Pot on in spring if roots are pot-bound, choosing containers 2 in larger than before. Schefflera is suitable for hydroculture.

Light Strongest growth develops in good light, shaded from hot sun in summer. Move plants as close as possible to the light in winter. Avoid draughty and poorly lit positions.

Temperature Ordinary steady room temperatures of around 65° F are suitable. In winter try not to let the temperature drop below 55° F.

Humidity A moisture-charged atmosphere is ideal, but rarely practicable. Stand the pots inside larger ones, packing the space with moss or peat kept moist at all times. Regular spraying with tepid water is also beneficial.

Watering and feeding Keep the compost moist, but not soaked, throughout spring and summer. Give less water in winter, letting the soil dry out between waterings.

Sustain healthy growth during the growing season by fortnightly liquid feeds at the time of watering.

Propagation Raise new plants from seeds sown in a propagator at 70° F.

Disorders Rarely affected by pests and diseases. Dry air may cause brown patches on the leaves and draughts lead to leaf curl.

Scindapsus aureus

Scindapsus
(*Araceae*)

This easily-grown climber is native to tropical rain forests of the Pacific. It is closely related to *Philodendron* and like these climbs rapidly, reaching a mature height of 4-6 ft. Excellent for poorly lit positions, plants can be trained on moss poles or trail from baskets.

S. aureus (devil's ivy) is correctly classified as *Rhaphidophora aurea*, but is still commonly sold under its old name. The lax, branching stems, which climb or trail to 3-4 ft, bear leathery and glossy, ovate leaves with yellow markings. They are 4-6 in long in the juvenile stage, heart-shaped and 12 in or more on mature plants.

The cultivar 'Marble Queen' is deeply netted with creamy-white, and in 'Golden Queen' the green leaf edge is almost hidden by golden-yellow variegations.

Buying hints *S. aureus* is easily found at most plant shops, 6-9 in plants being good, inexpensive buys. The variegated cultivars are generally smaller and in the medium price range. Choose plants with several growing points and fresh-looking leaves.

General care Best grown in a peat-based compost. Support climbers on moss poles, kept moist, where they attach themselves by the aerial roots. As trailing plants, in pots or hanging baskets, growth is less vigorous.

Pot on as necessary in spring until in final 8 in pots. Thereafter renew the top 1-2 in with fresh compost or repot every two or three years.

Scindapsus are also suitable for hydroculture.

Light Excellent for poorly lit positions and tolerant of even heavy shade. Brightly variegated types need better light, but still out of direct sun in summer.

Temperature Ordinary room temperature is ideal. In winter this should not fall below 60° F and preferably not rise above 65° F while the plants experience a semi-dormant period.

Humidity Dry air inhibits growth. Spray frequently with tepid water in spring and summer and also in winter if the plants are kept at high temperatures. Alternatively, stand pots on trays of pebbles and water.

Watering and feeding Keep the compost just moist in spring and summer and let it dry out between watering. In autumn and winter water the plants sparingly.

Give dilute liquid feeds during the growing season, once a week to young plants, every two or three weeks to established specimens.

Propagation Increase from 3-4 in cuttings in summer, rooted in sand in a propagator at 70° F.

Disorders Rarely troubled by pests. Dry air causes leaf curl.

Selaginella
(Selaginellaceae)

Selaginella martensii

Branching moss-like fronds, creeping or slightly ascending, are characteristic of this humble group of plants chiefly found in tropical rain forests. They are best suited to bottle gardens or Wardian cases with high humidity. In open pots the fronds shrivel.

S. apoda (S. apus) spreads to 4 in, with pale green stems densely matted and branching. Commonly called creeping moss.

S. martensii is more vigorous, 6-12 in tall and wide, bright green and thickly matted when mature. The cultivar 'Watsoniana' has silvery-white and green variegated foliage.

Buying hints Choose only those plants which are fresh and plump, and avoid any that are dessicated and dry-looking. Plants in 3 in pots are inexpensive; they are not widely available except from nurseries.

General care Best in a close, humid environment, such as terrariums where they form a ferny floor. Selaginellas can also be tried in pans of peaty soil.

Light Place in a shady position. Bright light causes the leaves to shrivel; draughts have the same effect.

Temperature The warmer the better; at 75° F plants grow rapidly and produce the finest fronds. In winter, do not let the temperature fall below 50° F for *S. martensii* and 45° F for the hardier *S. apoda*.

Humidity A high degree of moisture is essential. Bottle gardens and closed cases are the most suitable. Stand open pans in trays with water coming just below the pans. Do not mist-spray which may blemish the foliage.

Watering and feeding Never allow the compost to dry out. Ideally use rainwater to prevent the soil from becoming sour. No feeding is necessary.

Propagation Increase from shoot tips rooted in gritty compost, in a propagator at 75° F.

Disorders Dry air and draughts cause shrivelled and discoloured leaves.

Sonerila
(Melastomataceae)

Sonerila margaritacea

Small, neat and with exquisitely patterned leaves, this Javanese gem is ideal for a bottle garden. Only one species is in general cultivation.

S. margaritacea forms a compact cluster of stems 6 in high and across. The oblong, pointed leaves are 2 in long, strikingly marbled with silvery-white spots, and the undersides are a glow of purple. 'Hendersonii' is more heavily spotted with white, and 'Argentea' even more so with silvery leaves showing hardly any green.

Buying hints Comparatively rare, sonerilas are best purchased from specialist nurseries. Those in 4 in pots are the best buys, in the medium price range. Make sure plants have several growing points and highly patterned leaves.

General care Best in a peat-based compost. Unless grown in a closed environment, choose small shallow pans, 4 in wide, to serve the plants throughout their life.

Light Thin shade or filtered sunlight suits these plants best. In summer, the shade cast by other plants is ideal, but move to better light in winter.

Temperature A very humid, warm place is essential. Aim at keeping the temperature around 70-75° F, falling no lower than 65° F in winter. Avoid draughts at all times.

Humidity Moist warmth is vital for success. Achieve this by spraying plants daily with tepid water or keeping them in a steamy kitchen or bathroom. Ideally, house them in a closed glass case.

Watering and feeding Keep the compost moist at all times, though a little less so in winter.

Give liquid feeds fortnightly from April to August.

Propagation Raise new plants from 3 in basal cuttings in spring, rooted in a propagator at 70° F. Alternatively, germinate seed at 75° F.

Disorders Dry air and draughts cause the leaves to shrivel and fall.

Syngonium podophyllum 'Albolineatum'

Syngonium
(Araceae)

The handsome three or five-lobed leaves of these plants from tropical Central and South America ensure their popularity. Commonly called goosefoot plants, they are of lax, climbing or trailing habit.

S. podophyllum has glossy green, arrow-shaped leaves, the terminal lobes larger than the relatively small side lobes. They are 8 in long and borne on long, slender leaf stalks up to 2 ft long. It does not branch freely, and the leaf stalks all develop from the central growing point.

S.p. 'Albolineatum' is more popular and differs greatly from the type species. Mature plants bear two types of leaves, the juvenile dark green, silver-marked and three-lobed leaves giving way to compound leaves of 11 leaflets. 'Green Gold' has yellow-mottled leaves, and 'Emerald Gem' is silver-white with dark green edges.

Buying hints Chiefly available from florists and garden centres, quality is generally good, with prices in the medium to expensive price range for 18 in specimens. The best buys are 10-12 in plants in 4-6 in pots. Choose plants massed with well-formed leaves and healthy growing points.

General care Syngoniums thrive in any standard peat or loam-based potting compost. Set plants in 4 in pots and pot on annually in spring until in final 6-8 in pots.

Train plants up moss poles or trellis or let them trail from baskets.

Light Best in light shade. Good light is acceptable if shading is given from strong sun in summer. Excellent plants for a room with little bright light.

Temperature Ordinary room temperature. Make sure winter night temperatures do not fall below 60° F.

Humidity Tolerant of low humidity, excessively dry air may cause shrivelled leaves. For best growth, spray the foliage with tepid water. Climbers on moist moss poles are humid enough.

Watering and feeding Keep the compost moist throughout the growing season. Even in autumn and winter, when growth slows down, the compost should never dry out.

Propagation In spring and summer, root 3-4 in stem cuttings at a temperature of 70° F.

Disorders Normally healthy, very dry air and draughts may lead to leaf drop.

Tradescantia
(Commelinaceae)

Popularly known as wandering jews – a name also given to zebrinas – these South American climbing and trailing plants are sometimes despised for their ubiquity. Several kinds are readily available, all ideal for hanging baskets or for trailing over the edges of large containers. Although past their best in a few years, they are easily propagated. All have narrow, oblong and pointed leaves often decoratively striped.

Tradescantia fluminensis

T. albiflora has green leaves, 1 in long, with cream stripes in the cultivar 'Albovittata'. 'Tricolor' has cream, pink-red and green leaves.

T. blossfeldiana is a more upright species. The narrow leaves are dark green above and rich iridescent purple beneath. 'Variegata' has cream stripes. *T. fluminensis* is similar in habit to *T. albiflora*, but with broader and longer leaves with purple undersides. Both 'Variegata' and 'Quicksilver' have leaves striped with silvery-white.

Buying hints Readily and cheaply available from all types of shops, quality is generally good. The best buys consist of three or four rooted cuttings potted together in 3 in pots. Reject any with bare, leggy bases.

General care Peat or loam-based composts are both suitable. Start several young plants in a 3 in pot and pot on progressively every year in spring. Alternatively set several plants in a hanging basket where they can cascade. Nip out growing tips to encourage side shoots.

Light The strongest coloured leaves are produced in good light. Plants will grow in light shade, but the leaves tend to become pale green. Variegated types particularly need good light.

Temperature Normal living room conditions around 65° F are ideal. Winter night temperatures should not fall below 50° F.

Humidity These plants will tolerate quite dry air, though their leaves will be smaller and less attractive. Mist spray the foliage regularly.

Watering and feeding In summer give the plants a good soaking every few days. In winter, water less often, but never let the compost dry out completely.

If growth is slow, give occasional feeds of dilute liquid fertiliser during spring and summer. Overfeeding results in loss of leaf variegations.

Propagation Tip cuttings from nipped-out shoots can be rooted in water and potted up in the growing compost at any time of year.

Disorders Excessively dry air may cause brown blemishes on leaves.

Zebrina
(Commelinaceae)

Mere botanical differences separate this trailing Mexican plant from the related *Tradescantia*. The foliage is more richly coloured, and the fleshy stems can cascade to 3 ft or more in hanging baskets.

Z. pendula (Tradescantia pendula) has 2-3 in long leaves marked with two silver bands. The undersides are rich purple and so are the stems in some instances. The cultivar 'Discolor' has bronze-green leaves edged with purple. 'Quadricolor' is even more handsome, with four colours of green, white, red and purple in vertical bands.

Zebrina pendula

Buying hints Less frequently found than tradescantias, zebrinas are available from florists at good quality and at realistic prices. The best buys are 4 in pots with several young plants.

General care These wandering jews are easy, rapid-growing plants for bright or lightly shaded positions. General cultivation is similar to that given to tradescantias.

Light Avoid too heavy shade where the leaves will lose their rich glowing colours. Good for bright sunny sites.

Temperature Best at a day temperature of 65-70° F, though less is acceptable. On winter nights, the temperature should not drop below 50° F.

Humidity High air moisture is not essential though beneficial.

Watering and feeding Water freely throughout the growing season, from April to August. Give less in autumn and winter without letting the compost dry out.

Feeding is unnecessary.

Propagation Root tip cuttings in plain water, or in gritty compost at a temperature of 60° F.

Disorders Generally trouble-free.

FERNS

Ferns have been popular house plants since early Victorian times as they will grow happily in poorly lit rooms where flowering and exotic foliage plants have only a temporary lifespan. The introduction of Wardian cases, more than a century ago, ensured constantly high humidity and steady temperatures.

In modern homes lighting has improved, rooms are warmer in winter, and humidity is easy to achieve, with the result that even tender ferns can provide year-round decoration. The varied shades of green, from pale to very dark, combined with the different frond shapes and sizes, make ferns the perfect foil in a mixed group.

Millions of years ago plant life on earth was concentrated in the fern families, and they left a legacy in the form of our present-day coal seams. Over the ages ferns have hardly changed, in contrast to the higher forms of plant life. They are dissimilar to other plant forms in that they do not flower and therefore do not reproduce by seed. Instead millions of dust-fine spores go through a complicated and prolonged propagation process to perpetuate the species.

A fern grows from a rhizome which produces roots and fronds. A frond – or leaf – comprises a stalk and a blade which may be strap-like and entire or divided into leaflets. Each division is known as a pinna and this may again be divided into pinnules.

On the underside of many leaflets are small, powdery, brown areas of varying shapes; these are the sori, or spore cases, from which new ferns will eventually develop. The position and arrangement of the sori differ according to genus and species. In *Pteris*, for example, they line the margins of the pinnules; in *Cyrtomium* they are round and irregularly scattered, while in *Asplenium nidus* they are arranged in a fish-bone pattern.

Buying hints

Before buying an indoor fern consider its decorative use. You may want it to provide a graceful background for a group planting or as a focal point in its own right. For group arrangements the smaller-growing species are most suitable, but for eye-catching displays the long-arching species are outstanding. And for sheer dramatic effect, few plants can compare with a bark-mounted staghorn fern.

Growing conditions

Ferns' natural growing conditions give valuable pointers to the indoor gardener. Fern roots may be fine or wiry, many or few, but all need good drainage and a soil high in humus. Peat or leaf-mould based composts are therefore ideal.

In the wild, ferns grow on the floor of tropical forests or on tree branches, and though filtered, light intensity is comparatively high. However, ferns have adapted well to moderate and even poor light – one of the factors which makes them such ideal and enduring house plants.

Coming from the Tropics, ferns prefer warm temperatures, but if adequate heat cannot be provided in winter they will simply stop growing for a time. This is not a true dormancy period because ferns do not drop their fronds and will quickly begin to grow again when conditions improve.

Humidity is important because ferns absorb an amazing amount of atmospheric moisture. In most cases this is adequately supplied from pebble trays, and for others with a higher humidity need by mist spraying. However, spraying should be a gentle, fine mist.

Propagation

In the wild, propagation is naturally by spore germination which takes many months. It is not easily carried out in the home and is best left to specialist nurseries. However, new plants can be raised from division of the rhizomes. Use a sharp-bladed knife to cut the rhizome into several pieces, each with at least one healthy growing point. Initially use small pots with a minimum amount of compost for the divisions. Thereafter potting on follows the usual pattern.

Adiantum
(*Polypodiaceae*)

These fairly easy ferns are native to the tropical Americas. The delicate, black frond stalks grow upright from a branching underground rhizome, with the blades divided into small leaflets. They are popularly known as maiden-hair ferns after the wiry stalks. Probably the most commonly bought indoor ferns, they succeed only if high humidity is provided. Under good conditions they will easily attain a size up to 2 ft tall and wide.

A. raddianum (A. cuneatum) has fronds up to 20 in tall, composed of finely divided blades of fan-shaped,

Adiantum tenerum

pale green leaflets. Triangular in outline, each blade may be 8 in long and 6 in wide. On mature plants the outer leaf edges are velvety-brown on the undersides where clusters of spore cases are produced.

There are several cultivars with leaflets of varying sizes and colours. 'Gracillimum', with numerous tiny leaflets, has a filigree-like appearance, while 'Fritz Luthii' has fewer, wider and curly-edged leaflets.

A. tenerum grows taller, up to 3 ft, but is otherwise similar. The leaflets are larger and often have deeply cut and wavy edges. Some cultivars are tinged with red, sometimes temporarily in young fronds which later turn green, as in 'Wrightii', and sometimes permanently as in 'Scutum Roseum'.

Buying hints Readily available from florists, garden centres and other plant shops, the best buys are 6-12 in plants which range from the cheap to the inexpensive. Young plants are preferable to large plants which are less able to accept the transition between nursery and home. Avoid plants with shrivelled fronds.

General care Adiantums prefer a well-drained peat-based compost or one made from equal parts of sterilised loam, leaf-mould and coarse sand, with the addition of broken charcoal. Repot or pot on in spring if pot-bound. Cut old fronds away at compost level.

Light Direct sunlight should be avoided, but bright light filtered through a net curtain is ideal, especially in summer. In winter, artificial light will encourage growth.

Temperature Adiantums will survive winter temperatures down to 55° F by becoming dormant. They are better kept at least 5° higher; once the temperature reaches 65° F, they need increased humidity.

Humidity Needs depend upon temperatures, but during the growing season provide extra humidity by standing pots on constantly moist pebble trays or in containers of moist peat. Unless an exceptionally fine mist can be used, avoid spraying the fronds.

Watering and feeding During active growth, water enough to keep the compost moist but not wet. At cool temperatures, reduce watering.

Give a liquid feed in spring and summer, every two weeks to peat-based composts or every four weeks to loam-based composts.

Propagation By division of the rhizomes in spring.

Disorders Low humidity causes shrivelling of fronds, and overwatering leads to rotting of the roots.

Asplenium nidus

Asplenium
(*Aspleniaceae*)

This large genus, which includes the hardy outdoor spleenwort ferns, also contains a few, widely different species that are easily grown in the home. These are native to the Far East and Australasia where they grow as epiphytes on trees. In the wild, the fronds may reach a length of more than 4 ft, but as pot plants 18 in are more likely on mature plants.

A. bulbiferum (mother fern) has fronds with black stalks and midgreen, deeply serrated and divided blades of triangular outline. A mature plant may reach a height of 2 ft, with individual blades measuring 9 in across the widest part. Characteristically the leaflets are of two types: the narrow kind bears brown spore cases at the tip, while the broader type is sterile. The common name relates to the plant's ability to produce tiny ferns from small bulbils on the leaflets; they are often so numerous that a whole frond bends in a graceful arc.

A. nidus (bird's nest fern) is completely different. The leathery fronds, which are entire and undivided and glossy apple-green in colour with a black midrib, unfurl from the centre of a rosette covered with black furry scales. Slow-growing, this fern may reach a spread of 18 in, with 2-3 in wide blades.

There are several attractive cultivars with ruffled and crested fronds.

Buying hints *A. nidus* is the most commonly found plant, while *A. bulbiferum* must be located from florists and garden centres. The latter are usually offered as 10-18 in plants, prices ranging from inexpensive to expensive. *A. nidus,* at 6-12 in high, is inexpensive to medium-priced according to quality and outlet. Check all plants for signs of pest attack, wilting or shrivelling.

General care A quick-draining fibrous compost, such as coarse peat, is ideal for aspleniums because they grow fine roots and soon become pot-bound. Pot on at any time of year as growth is continuous under good conditions.

Light Moderately bright light is necessary at all times. Hot summer sun should be avoided or the fronds become pale with brown scorch patches. The ferns will grow in shady corners if artificial light can be provided for 8-10 hours a day.

Temperature *A. bulbiferum* will tolerate winter night temperatures of 55° F; *A. nidus* will not survive below 60°. At these minimum temperatures growth will almost cease; at higher than average temperatures extra humidity must be supplied.

Humidity *A. bulbiferum* is the more tolerant of low humidity such as that released from a pebble and water tray. *A. nidus* needs additional air moisture from daily mist sprays in summer.

Watering and feeding Keep the compost permanently moist. At low temperatures let it dry out slightly between watering.

From spring until autumn give fortnightly feeds of dilute liquid fertiliser.

Propagation *A. bulbiferum* is easily increased from the tiny plantlets, rooted in moist compost at a temperature of 60-65° F. *A. nidus* can only be propagated from spores.

Disorders Scale insects may infest the stalks or undersides of the fronds. Aphids are common on *A. nidus*.

Cyrtomium
(Polypodiaceae)

This is one of the easiest and most decorative of indoor ferns, tolerant of conditions that few other plants would accept. Native to Asia, the semi-erect fronds grow slowly to 2 ft long, rising from a furry-scaled crown.

C. falcatum (holly fern) is the most popular and durable species, with glossy, dark green, leathery leaflets set alternately along a frond stalk covered with furry, brown scales. The holly-like, sharply pointed leaflets are about 3 in long. Round green spore cases form on the undersides; they ripen to brown and then shed a great number of spores.

'Rochfordianum' is a similar, but more compact cultivar.

Buying hints Young plants, 6-8 in high, are cheap or inexpensive at florists' shops and garden centres. They will look less leathery and paler green than mature plants, and are slow-growing in the early stages. They are easier to establish in new conditions. Check both sides of the fronds for any signs of pests.

General care Any proprietary peat-based compost is suitable; potting on in spring is only necessary when plants are obviously pot-bound, probably every two years. The root system is shallow, and final 6 in pots are usually adequate. In subsequent year, topdress with fresh compost.

These ferns are so tolerant of indoor conditions that they will grow throughout the year.

Light Best in bright light, but periods of poor light are tolerated. Avoid direct and hot summer sun.

Temperature Cyrtomiums will survive at a temperature down to 50° F when they will become dormant though retain their fronds. At higher temperatures growth is continuous, with corresponding needs for increased humidity and water.

Cyrtomium falcatum
'Rochfordianum'

Humidity Average to low humidity is suitable, and this is easily supplied by standing the pots on trays of pebbles and water, or by the double-pot method.

Watering and feeding While the ferns are in active growth keep the compost moist throughout the year. If the plants enter a resting phase, due to low winter temperatures, allow the compost to dry out slightly before watering again.

During spring and summer give a dilute liquid feed every two weeks.

Propagation Divide large plants in spring.

Disorders Scale insects occasionally infest fronds and stalks.

Davallia canariensis

Davallia
(Polypodiaceae)

The common names attributed to these ferns relate to the creeping furry rhizomes. These branch and quickly cover the compost surface to overhang the sides of the pots like animal paws. The fronds grow upright and one at a time from the rhizome.

Widespread from north-west Africa to Indonesia, Australia and Japan, these epiphytic ferns grow well as house plants and are ideal for hanging pots and baskets.

D. canariensis (deer's foot fern), from the Canary Islands, grows from a rhizome covered with pale golden-brown scales and looks exactly like a small furry paw. The fronds, about 1 ft tall, are made up of 6 in stalks each topped with a lacy, finely divided blade of triangular outline and 9 in wide at the base. The foliage has a soft leathery texture and midgreen colour.

D. mariesii (squirrel's foot fern), from Japan, differs only in being smaller in all respects and in having a greyish-brown rhizome. The dainty frond blades are very finely divided and mid to dark green.

Buying hints Davallias are obtainable from specialist fern nurseries and are best bought as young plants. Prices are in the expensive range, but the quality is generally excellent.

General care An open well-drained compost is essential, and a mixture of equal parts of sphagnum moss and leaf-mould makes a good anchorage for the wiry root systems. Use shallow pots or pans, or preferably hanging baskets where the rhizomes can branch and root down over the entire surface to form an attractive fern ball. Old fronds will shrivel and drop away from the rhizomes, leaving a scar like a tiny footprint.

Light These ferns will stand brighter light than many others, even to the extent of some direct sun provided shade is given at midday during the summer months.

Temperature Davallias tolerate winter temperatures down to 50° F, but will then rest and are likely to drop their fronds. A higher temperature, 60° or above, ensures continuous growth.

Humidity As epiphytes these ferns draw moisture and air from the atmosphere. If growing at 70° F or above, high humidity is essential. Provide this with daily mist sprays in addition to standing pans on constantly moist pebble trays.

Watering and feeding Except at minimum temperatures the compost should be kept constantly moist though not wet. Fern balls in hanging baskets are best watered by immersion if the surface feels dry. Drain thoroughly before returning the plants to their positions.

During the summer give a dilute liquid feed once a month.

Propagation Rhizomes root readily in a moist compost and provide the easiest method of increase. Cut off a rhizome tip, about 3 in long, and place on moist compost in a small pot. Roots may already be present, otherwise they will grow within a month if kept at about 70° F.

Disorders Low humidity causes fronds to shrivel and drop.

Nephrolepis exaltata 'Bostoniensis'

Nephrolepis
(Polypodiaceae)

Some of the most attractive ferns are found in this genus, and two in particular make spectacular focal plants. They are fairly undemanding and most handsomely displayed in hanging baskets or on free-standing pedestals. Fast-growing, they quickly encase a basket with young plants growing from numerous, thin, scurfy runners produced by the upright rhizomes. Native to the Tropics, they are sometimes known by the aptly descriptive name of ladder ferns.

N. cordifolia (erect or tuber sword fern) has nearly upright-growing fronds of light to midgreen. The leaf blades are cut to the midribs into narrow, regular segments like the rungs on a ladder. The fronds grow about 2 ft long, narrow at the base and tip, but widening at the centre to 4 in. The cultivar 'Plumosa' is less erect, and with crested or frilled frond segments.

N. exaltata (sword fern) has similarly shaped and coloured fronds which trail gracefully to as much as 6 ft. Numerous cultivars are available and more popular than the species, usually with shorter fronds often crested and feathery. Those of 'Bostoniensis', 'Rooseveltii' and 'Whitmannii' (lace fern) all grow about 3 ft long.

'Teddy Junior' is compact, growing no more than 18 in tall.

Buying hints *N. exaltata* and its cultivars are the more popular and easily available from most plant shops. The best buys are 10-12 in plants which are cheap to inexpensive. *N. cordifolia* is less common and best purchased from specialist fern nurseries; plants, 12-16 in tall, are in the medium price range but generally of good quality. In all cases, choose plants with bright green and dense fronds.

General care These ferns thrive in a coarse peat-based compost. Young plants do well in pots, but mature plants show to better advantage in hanging baskets or large pots on a pedestal. As the fronds age, some segments are liable to turn yellow, and the whole frond should be cut out from the crown. Occasionally a cultivar frond will revert to type, and this, too, should be cut out.

Light Nephrolepis do best in bright light throughout the year, with some shading from direct midday sun. Poor light can be tolerated for three or four weeks at a time if a few hours of artificial light can be given daily.

Temperature Ordinary room temperatures allow continuous growth. In winter this will cease at 50° F, and below this the ferns are likely to die.

Humidity Dry air is detrimental; at normal room temperatures sufficient humidity is supplied by daily fine mist sprays of tepid water.

Watering and feeding Keep the compost permanently moist by frequent watering. At low temperatures let it dry out slightly.

From April to September, give a dilute liquid feed every fortnight.

Propagation Tips of runners root readily in moist compost. Remove the rooted plantlets and pot them up separately.

Disorders Browning and yellowing of fronds is usually caused by dryness at the roots or low humidity, and sometimes by overwatering.

Pellaea
(Polypodiaceae)

Growing wild in many parts of the world, the most popular and frequently grown species comes from New Zealand. It is easy to grow, of moderate vigour and enduring qualities.

P. rotundifolia (button fern) is unlike other ferns. The fronds, up to 1 ft long, are prostrate and gently arching from a creeping rhizome. Almost perfectly round, leathery leaflets, $\frac{1}{2}$ in wide, are arranged on either side of the black frond stalk. They are dark green above, midgreen below and slightly serrated

Pellaea rotundifolia

except on leaflets that carry spore cases on the undersides.

Buying hints Best purchased from reputable florists and garden centres as young plants, about 6 in wide, in the inexpensive price range. Elsewhere the ferns are often included in a bowl of mixed plants.

General care Any proprietary peat-based compost can be used, on its own or mixed with leaf-mould. Pellaeas are shallow-rooting and best potted in pans or half-pots. Potting on, in spring, is only necessary when a plant is truly pot-bound. During winter, growth slows down at cool temperatures and in poor light.

Light Moderate light is adequate for these ferns although they will tolerate bright but filtered light for short periods. In summer, move the plants into the room, away from a window.

Temperature Ordinary room temperatures are suitable. In winter 50° F is acceptable, but a temperature around 60° F is essential for continuous growth.

Humidity Usually tolerant of dry air, humidity should be increased at temperatures above 60° F. Stand the pots on pebble and water trays or use the double-pot method. When 70° F is exceeded, give a daily misting with tepid water.

Watering and feeding The compost should be kept evenly moist at all times. At low winter temperatures allow it to dry out slightly.

During summer give young plants a dilute feed every fortnight.

Propagation Large plants can be divided in spring and rooted pieces of rhizome potted up separately.

Disorders Dryness at the roots and around the fronds cause shrivelling.

Platycerium
(*Polypodiaceae*)

These magnificent epiphytes come from tropical rain forests and are distinguished by their huge fronds with two distinct functions. In the home the plants need a little more care than other ferns.

P. bifurcatum (*P. alcicorne*) is aptly named the staghorn fern, from the fertile fronds, up to 2 ft wide, shaped like antlers. They emerge between fan-shaped sterile fronds which grow around the container and clasp it tightly. Both types of fronds are light to midgreen, with a covering of white velvety fur, easily spoiled by touch.

Old sterile fronds turn brown and decay, thus feeding the fern with their humus. At maturity, rich brown spore cases cover the undersides of fertile frond "tines".

Buying hints Both young and mature plants can be found at florists' shops and garden centres. Most are about 12 in and in the medium price range. Make sure that young plants have

Platycerium bifurcatum

green sterile fronds without blemishes.

General care Usually sold as pot-grown plants, staghorn ferns should ideally be grown on slabs of rough bark. Wrap a mixture of moist sphagnum moss and leaf-mould loosely round the roots. Initially, the ferns will need to be tied to the well-soaked bark with fishing line, but later the sterile fronds will hold them in place.

Mount the bark slabs on a wall or in hanging baskets. Bark-grown plants will not need to be disturbed for repotting. Fertile fronds are long-lived and only need removing from the base when brown and shrivelled.

Light Bright light, shaded from direct summer sun, is required. Winter sun will not damage the fronds.

Temperature Staghorn ferns become dormant at a winter temperature of 55° F. They will maintain growth at 60-65° F if given adequate light and humidity.

Humidity Once temperatures exceed 65° F, provide high humidity by daily misting. The large fronds can absorb a great deal of moisture.

Watering and feeding Once a week

soak the bark slabs in a bowl or sink of water for about 30 minutes; drain thoroughly and replace in position. At every fourth soaking add a liquid feed.
Propagation Remove rooted offsets in spring and set in small pots until growth is well established, or fix them to bark slabs.
Disorders Low humidity causes wilting and browning of the fronds.

Pteris ensiformis 'Evergemiensis' and *Pteris cretica* cultivars (foreground)

Pteris

(Pteridaceae or *Polypodiaceae)*

The large genus of brake ferns is widely distributed throughout tropical and sub-tropical regions, and several species make good, easy house plants. All grow from a small upright rhizome which produces numerous tufts of slender upright fronds. Most species bear fertile and sterile fronds that differ in appearance, the fertile fronds having narrow leaflets where the edges are drawn back as a protective cover for the spore cases on the frond undersides.

P. cretica (Cretan or ribbon fern) is probably the most popular species. It grows about 18 in tall, with brown frond stalks and midgreen blades divided into long, fingered leaflets. The many cultivars are more interesting, particularly 'Albo-lineata', with a narrow, creamy-white stripe along the midrib of each leaflet.

'Rivertoniana' has feathery leaflets with elongated, pointed lobes, and 'Wimsettii' and 'Wilsonii' both have leaflets with heavily crested tips.

P. ensiformis 'Evergemiensis', an outstanding cultivar of the sword brake, has two types of fronds. The fertile ones are up to 20 in long, with narrow leaflets, while the sterile fronds, 10 in long, have broader, feathery leaflets. Both types are glossy dark green, the midribs picked out in silver.

'Victoriae' is similar, but of smaller stature and more heavily variegated.

P. multifida, a slow-growing fern, is usually seen as the cultivar 'Cristata'. The arching, dark green and divided fronds have frilled crests at the tips.

P. tremula (Australian or trembling brake) is a vigorous species whose yellowish-green fronds will reach 3 ft. The triangular blades are finely cut.

Buying hints Possibly the most common ferns, easily found at most florists' shops and at garden centres. Generally of good quality, sizes vary from 6-12 in and costs from cheap to medium prices, depending on the species and cultivar. Avoid plants with limp, yellowing fronds and dry compost, and check for signs of pest attack.

General care All types grow well and fairly rapidly in a peat-based, quick-draining compost. They are best for being slightly pot-bound, but when necessary pot on, in spring, into a pot one size larger, or cut away some of the old roots and repot in the same size pot with fresh compost.

Light These ferns tolerate poor light for several weeks at a time. They do, however, thrive in good filtered light and under artificial illumination. Avoid direct, hot summer sun.

Temperature During winter, growth will slow down at 55° F, and the compost should be kept on the dry side. Ideally, provide winter temperatures around 60° F.

Humidity A high degree of air moisture is essential, especially during the main growing season from April to August, or whenever the temperature exceeds 60° F. Moist pebble trays generally supply adequate humidity.

Watering and feeding The compost should be constantly moist but not wet, or rotting will occur. In winter reduce the amount of water at cool temperatures, but never let the compost dry out completely.

Give a dilute liquid feed every fortnight from March to August.

Propagation By division of the rhizomes in spring.

Disorders Aphids and scale insects may attack young fronds. Very low humidity and dry roots result in shrivelled leaves.

BROMELIADS

The large family *Bromeliaceae*, to which the genera described here all belong, includes some of the most bizarre of all plants. A great number are native to Central and South America where they grow in the rich soil on the floor of tropical rain forests or attached by wiry roots to the trunks and limbs of trees.

Other types inhabit the edges of deserts with very dry, inhospitable conditions or grow on sea shores in almost pure sand.

Wherever bromeliads are found they have adapted their growth habits to the prevalent conditions, and they are, to some extent, able to do the same in cultivation.

Some bromeliads are naturally terrestrial, while others are epiphytic. The epiphytes are not parasitic, using the host trees or rocks solely for support. They take their nourishment from falling forest debris, such as leaves and other organic matter.

Leaf and flower characteristics

Most bromeliads have leathery, strap-like leaves arranged in a rosette shape. Each leaf may overlap its neighbour so closely that a watertight reservoir is formed, in which rain and dew collect, and on which the plant draws in times of water shortage. In some instances, such as *Cryptanthus*, the rosette is flattish and loose.

The leaves of some plants are viciously armed with hooked spines to discourage grazing animals, but epiphytic kinds have no need of such protection. More often than not they have soft and smooth leaves.

Leaf colouring and patterns are often highly attractive. A number of bromeliads have leaves overlaid with a scaly covering resembling white or silvery meal. The scales can also absorb water and help the plant through periods of drought.

With a few exceptions all bromeliads flower once only from each rosette. Having bloomed, the rosette slowly dies and is replaced by one or more offsets which develop round the base of the plants. These offshoots provide ready propagation material.

Flower shapes and sizes vary enormously, but all flowers rise from the centre of the plant, on a thickened head. In some species, this may be positioned just below the waterline in the vase, when the actual flowers peep through the water. In other cases it is borne at the end of a long flower stalk.

Low-growing, almost hidden flowers are not particularly striking, but many bromeliads with that type of inflorescence develop – in compensation as it were – rich colours in the leaves as flowering time approaches.

Plants with tall flower stems often have flamboyant bracts, or modified leaves, surrounding the flowers, and these are usually exceptionally long-lasting. Flowers may be produced or induced to occur at any time of the year.

Buying hints

Because they are slow-growing and require several years of nursery care, bromeliads are relatively expensive, but prove enduring and highly decorative. Most plants are not offered for sale until nearly mature, and many will already be in flower.

General care

Bromeliads thrive in a slightly acid, very open and free-draining compost, such as coarse peat and sharp sand, or a mixture of equal parts of leaf-mould and rough peat. The root systems are shallow, and most plants do best when grown in relatively small pots. Move on into one size larger pots every two or three years.

During the active growing season give the plants thorough waterings, but allow the compost to almost completely dry out again before the next application. Keep the reservoir-like centres filled with water, but drain stale water from the cups about every six weeks to prevent them from becoming smelly.

Feed every two weeks, from April to September, with a weak solution of a standard liquid fertiliser. It is good practice to ring the changes with different kinds of proprietary house-plant feeds.

All bromeliads should be placed in bright light, but shaded from strong summer sun, in order to develop the brilliant leaf colours fully and to encourage flowering. Although some will tolerate lower temperatures, most species need a minimum winter temperature of around 60° F.

Propagation

Increase mature plants in spring or early summer by cutting off well developed offsets. Delay this operation until they have begun to develop the characteristics of the parent plants as very young offsets are extremely difficult to root.

The best rooting medium is a mixture of equal parts peat and sand, and a 3 in pot will comfortably hold an average offset. Create a close and humid atmosphere by enclosing the potted offset in a plastic bag. Better still, keep it in a heated propagator until roots have developed, and growth is evident from the fresh looking leaves.

Once rooted, the small plants can be potted in the compost used for mature plants.

Aechmea fasciata

Aechmea

In their native Central and South America, aechmeas may be terrestrial or epiphytic and range from ground-hugging to taller than man size. The few that are freely available have attractive leaf rosettes with a capacious central reservoir, hence the popular name of urn plant. Flowers appear mainly in summer.

A. chantinii has 12-18 in long, leathery and spined leaves of a dark olive-green prominently banded with irregular stripes of silvery-grey scales. The flower stalk grows to 18 in and is topped with a spectacular arrangement of 2-3 in, pointed, orange-red and pendent bracts. The flowers themselves are red and yellow.

A. fasciata is one of the most popular bromeliads. Its grey-green, 18 in long leaves are black-spined along the edges and heavily marked with silvery-white scales. The club-shaped flower head, on a 12 in stem, is comprised of tightly packed, bright pink bracts through which peep tubular, pale blue to lilac flowers. The flower head remains attractive for about three months.

Buying hints Young plants are rarely available. Flowering-sized plants are stocked by florists and garden centres, as well as some supermarkets. They are expensive, but usually of good quality.

General care Most aechmeas are bought as flowering plants in 5 in pots. Cut down the flower spikes after they have faded and continue to water and feed the plants to encourage offshoots.

The old rosette may be cut out when past its best to allow room for two or three young plants to develop to maturity on the old root base. This makes for a multi-headed, large plant which will need a 6 or 7 in pot. Use equal parts of coarse peat and leaf-mould.

Light Grow throughout the year in bright, indirect light.

Temperature Aechmeas will tolerate a winter temperature down to 45° F, but will then enter a rest period. If possible give a minimum of 60° F.

Humidity High humidity is desirable. Spray the leaves regularly and stand the pots on moist pebble trays. Place outside in gentle rain for up to an hour during the summer months.

Watering and feeding Normal moderate watering should be reduced during winter; give only enough to moisten the compost.

Feed with a weak liquid fertiliser, monthly from March to September.

Propagation *A. chantinii* produces offsets at the end of runners. Sever these when 3-4 in high, pot in peat and sand and establish at 70° F. Offsets, 3-4 in long, of *A. fasciata* root easily in early summer, in a similar mixture and temperature.

Disorders Few troubles occur. Low winter temperature is the chief danger.

Ananas

The origin of the cultivated pineapple, *Ananas comosus,* is uncertain, but it has been cultivated in tropical America since the 16th century. The commercial plant bears 3-4 ft long, spiny-edged and sword-shaped leaves arranged in a grey-green rosette. The ornamental forms of the pineapple, bred for indoor cultivation, are compact and of slow growth. *A.c.* 'Variegatus' bears narrow leaves margined with a broad cream band and edged with red spines; in strong light the cream bands turn pink. The leaves eventually reach a length of 3 ft. Greenhouse conditions are needed for fruit production.

Some forms – one is known as the smooth cayenne – have few spines and make small decorative plants.

Buying hints Large plants are expensive to very expensive as they are likely to be several years old. Chiefly available from florists and garden centres, the average size is around 12 in. Young plants are occasionally available and are by far the best buys.

General care When repotting, which

Ananas comosus 'Variegatus'

may be necessary every other year, use a mixture of equal parts of John Innes No. 2 and coarse peat or leaf-mould. Clay pots, with their added weight, help to keep these spreading plants from being knocked over.

Light Strong light, with direct sun even in summer, brings out the full colours of the foliage.

Temperature Maintain a constant 60° F, and preferably higher, throughout the year.

Humidity Plenty of air moisture is vital. Stand large plants on wide trays with moist pebbles. Small plants can go in double pots packed with moist moss peat.

Watering and feeding Water moderately during the growing period whenever the compost begins to dry out. In winter give only enough water to prevent a bone-dry condition unless temperatures are above average.

Feed with a dilute solution of a standard liquid fertiliser, once a month, from April to September.

Propagation Suckers may appear round the base of plants at any time. Detach these in summer when they are 4-5 in high, ideally already rooted. Pot in sand and keep at 70° F in a propagator until growing well.

Considerable bottom heat is needed to induce unrooted suckers to produce strong roots.

Disorders None of any consequence.

Billbergia

Billbergia species

The genus *Billbergia* includes some of the easiest of indoor bromeliads. Native to Central and South America, they are of moderate vigour and vary considerably in size and shape. They have fewer leaves than most other bromeliads; in some species they are held closely together to form a watertight, upright cup, in others the leaves are narrow and arching.

The flowers are tubular, in pendent clusters at the tip of a 12-15 in long stem and offset by showy red or bright pink bracts. The flowers, which appear mainly in late spring and early summer, are short-lived.

B. 'Fantasia' is an American hybrid, about 12 in tall and of tubular habit. Each olive-green leaf, 2-3 in wide, is heavily marked with cream, which in bright light may assume a pinkish tinge. Bright cherry-red bracts surround the purple and red flowers.

B. horrida, up to 18 in tall, grows in an open urn shape, with narrow, black-spined and dark green leaves banded with grey scales. The erect flower head is composed of rose-pink bracts and blue-tipped, green flowers with recurving petals.

B. nutans (queen's tears) has dark green, narrow and arching leaves, 10-12 in long, arranged in a loose clump. The nodding flower clusters are yellowish-green, pink and dark blue, with bright pink bracts.

B. 'Windii' resembles *B. nutans*, one of its parents, but the green leaves, 15 in long, are covered with grey scales. The flower bracts are wider and even more striking.

Buying hints Most billbergias are relatively inexpensive from florists and garden centres. The slow-growing *B.* 'Fantasia' is more expensive. Ensure that young plants are well-rooted and not just tufts of leaves with barely any roots. Avoid those with open blooms.

General care Use 3 or 4 in pots and equal parts of coarse peat and John Innes No. 2. Pot on in spring if crowded with new growths, cutting out completely the old rosettes that have flowered.

B. nutans and *B.* 'Windii' are best stood outdoors in a sheltered place in summer; the exposure to fresh air, sun and rain encourages strong growth.

Light Grow in bright light throughout the year.

Temperature *B. nutans* and *B.* 'Windii' will accept a winter minimum temperature of 45° F without ill effect. Ideally all billbergias should be kept at around 60° F.

Humidity Stand on trays of moist pebbles.

Watering and feeding Water freely in the growing season, ideally with rainwater; in winter enough to keep the compost just moist.

Give monthly feeds of dilute liquid fertiliser, applied to the centre cups, the foliage and the compost, from March to September.

Propagation In spring and early summer remove offsets when they are 5-7 in high. Set in 3 in pots of peat and sand and root at 65° F.

Disorders Few troubles are encountered.

Cryptanthus bivittatus

Cryptanthus

Earth star is the common name for this group of ground-hugging, star-shaped bromeliads. Widely distributed throughout eastern Brazil, they thrive under all kinds of conditions, clasping almost bare rocks with sparse wiry roots in dry regions or carpeting the humid forest floor.

Most are prostrate and flat, with thin but tough, pointed leaves, 2-15 in long. Many have grey or white scales scattered over the undulating, crinkly-edged leaves which may be striped, mottled, barred or plain.

The flowers are white and insignificant, produced on short stalks in the centre of the star and usually hidden by the leaves. Offsets are borne on the tips of long stolons or tucked between the lower rosette leaves.

Several species are in cultivation and augmented by the recent introduction of brightly coloured hybrids from America. Cryptanthus are generally slow-growing, ideal for mixed plantings, shallow containers, bottle gardens and simulated tree branches.

C. bivittatus spans about 6 in, each wavy, olive-green leaf having two light green longitudinal stripes. In bright light the whole plant is suffused with deep rose-pink.

C. bromelioides 'Tricolor', up to 12 in high and 10 in across, is more upright than most and produces offsets on long stolons from the leaf axils. The leaves are striped lengthways with green, cream, white and pink.

C. fosterianus can spread to 15 in, with 2 in wide leaves of a dark copper shade irregularly crossbanded with stripes of grey scales.

C. zonatus is similar to *C. fosterianus*, but smaller, with thinner, silver-banded leaves.

Buying hints Because they are extremely slow-growing, most cryptanthus are expensive. *C. bivittatus* is the most readily available, from florists and garden centres, in the medium price range. The plants do, however, last for many years and are economical in the long run.

General care These plants have sparse and wiry roots and can be grown in quite small containers. Pot on only when obviously pot-bound. Use a mixture of equal parts of leaf-mould and coarse peat, or a standard peat-based compost.

Light Give bright, but filtered light throughout the year.

Temperature Do not allow the temperature to fall below 60° F at any time.

Humidity A high level of humidity is essential. Stand pots on moist pebble trays or grow the plants in an enclosed environment.

Watering and feeding Keep the compost moist at all times, without saturating it.

Feed with a dilute liquid fertiliser once a month from April to September, splashing it over the leaves and on to the compost.

Propagation Remove offsets during spring or early summer. Cut the stolons if necessary or push the offsets from the leaf axils with the fingers. Set them, $\frac{1}{4}$-$\frac{1}{2}$ in deep, in a mixture of sharp sand and peat and enclose in plastic bags. Keep in a closed propagator, at a temperature of 70° F until roots have formed and growth is under way.

Disorders Trouble-free.

Guzmania

Guzmania lingulata cardinalis

Guzmanias are smooth, shiny-leaved bromeliads from tropical rain forests of Central and South America. They are mainly epiphytic, with rows of pencil-like, red, brown or purple lines running the length of the leaves.

Some produce tall, branching flower spikes, others short stalks topped with star-shaped tufts of colourful floral bracts. In yet others the flower heads lie below the waterline in the central vases. The white or cream flowers are quickly finished, but the bracts are normally long-lasting.

G. lingulata, up to 12 in high, bears 15 in long, 1 in wide, grass-green leaves finely striped with purple. The 3 in star-shaped flower head is surrounded by orange or red bracts.

There are several forms, sometimes listed as separate species, such as *G.l. cardinalis,* with scarlet bracts. *G.l. splendens,* which may reach 2 ft in diameter, has leaves red above and deep purple-red below; the bracts are purplish-red.

G.l. minor is up to 12 in across, with ½ in wide, yellow-green leaves and a tuft of yellow to orange bracts. *G.l.* 'Orange Star' is similar.

G. monostachya (G. tricolor), up to 16 in tall, has lettuce-green leaves, 1 in wide and as much as 18 in long. It produces a 12 in long flower stalk tightly wrapped with pale green bracts striped with dark brown. The stripes become more pronounced round the base of the 3-4 in cylindrical, vivid scarlet flower head.

Buying hints These plants are available from many types of plant shops and range from the inexpensive to the medium-priced. Ensure that they are at the beginning of their flowering seasons and not already past their best. Choose those that are just beginning to send up tufts of colourful bracts.

General care Grow in equal parts leaf-mould, coarse peat and sharp sand, or small grit. Guzmanias are shallow-rooted, and 4 in pot sizes are usually the maximum needed. They rarely need repotting or potting on.

Light Place in bright, but filtered light throughout the year.

Temperature The minimum acceptable temperature at any time is around 65° F.

Humidity Provide a high degree of air moisture by standing pots on trays of moist pebbles as well as misting the leaves regularly.

Watering and feeding Whenever possible, use clean rainwater, topping up the central cups and watering the compost thoroughly during the growing season. In winter, keep the cups filled, but give only enough water to keep the mixture just moist.

Apply a weak solution of a general liquid fertiliser once a month from April to September. Splash this on the leaves, and add it to the cups as well as to the compost.

Propagation Detach rooted offsets in mid-spring and establish as separate young plants at a minimum temperature of 65° F.

Disorders Lack of humidity causes browning and shrivelled leaves.

Neoregelia

These rosette-shaped bromeliads, with strap-like, leathery leaves often armed with spiny edges, originate in Brazil and neighbouring countries. The flower heads of the slow-growing neoregelias appear at the water level in the central leaf cups. The flowers themselves are small, usually white or in shades of blue and purple.

The outstanding feature of these plants is the dramatic colour changes that occur in the leaves as flowering approaches. Some develop brightly coloured leaf tips, others assume brilliant pink, red or purple hues in the centre of the rosette, and these may spread over most of the leaf area.

N. carolinae is usually offered as the compact form *N.c.* 'Marechalii'. This has midgreen, 9-12 in long and 2 in

Neoregelia carolinae 'Tricolor'

wide leaves with a rose-coloured centre. The striking *N.c.* 'Tricolor' bears 12-15 in long, 1½ in wide leaves, boldly striped green, creamy-white and pink. The whole leaf area takes on a rose-pink hue at flowering time, and this lasts for nine months or more.

N. concentrica has 12-15 in long, 2 in wide pale green leaves lightly spotted with brown and purple lines; they are tipped with red and edged with tough black spines. At flowering time the centre of the leaf rosette is suffused with rich purple.

Buying hints Generally only 8-10 in high plants are available, from florists and garden centres, in the expensive price range. Mature plants are at their most attractive when they begin to flower. Plants that have just begun to colour in the centre of the rosettes are the best buys.

General care Grow in equal parts of coarse peat and leaf-mould. Repot or pot on, in April or May, only when

essential. Mature plants will flower in 6 in pots.

Light Give plants the brightest light possible at all times, even two or three hours of direct sun daily in order to develop the striking leaf colours.

Temperature Ordinary room temperatures are suitable, but in winter provide a minimum of 60° F.

Humidity Neoregelias enjoy a high level of humidity. Stand them on moist pebbles and mist spray the foliage daily during the growing phase.

Watering and feeding During the active growing season give enough water to keep the compost moist. Reduce watering from October to March, applying just enough to prevent it from drying out completely.

Feed the compost and water cups once a month with a dilute liquid fertiliser, from April to September.

Propagation In spring remove well-developed offshoots and root in a propagator at 70° F.

Disorders Normally free of problems.

Nidularium

Nidularium innocentii

Nidulariums are tropical rain forest bromeliads from eastern Brazil. Their usually glossy and pliant, strap-shaped leaves, sometimes serrated and sometimes spined, are arranged in a flat rosette about 18 in wide. The centre forms a water-holding cup, from which appears a short collaret of brightly coloured, pink, red or purple bracts. The small flowers are short-lived, but the tuft of bracts persists over a long period. Flowering can occur at any time of year.

N. fulgens has shiny, apple-green leaves mottled with darker green spots. The central bract tuft, enclosing violet blue flowers, is about 3 in across and bright cerise.

N. innocentii is similar, but with leaves that are mahogany-red above, shiny wine-red beneath. The 4 in wide, rose-red bracts are just clear of the waterline and surround small white flowers.

Several cultivars exist, the most

attractive being 'Liniatum' with a rose-red centre and bright green leaves striped with white. 'Striatum' is similar, but with broader, white or creamy-yellow stripes.

Buying hints These plants are generally expensive, but because their leaves are decorative over an extended period, they are good long-term buys. Choose 8-10 in high plants from florists' shops, selecting those which have just begun to colour.

General care Grow in a compost of equal parts of leaf-mould, coarse peat and coarse sand or grit. Repot or pot on in late spring to a final pot size of 5 in.

Light Best in bright light, filtered from hot summer sun.

Temperature While nidulariums thrive at normal room temperature, this should remain at 65° F in winter

Humidity Provide high humidity by standing pots on trays of moist pebbles. Mist the plants regularly, particularly at high temperatures.

Watering and feeding Use rainwater preferably, to fill the central cups and watering the compost to keep it evenly moist through spring and summer. During autumn and winter keep the cups filled, but water the compost only to prevent it from drying out.

Give a weak liquid feed every month from April to September.

Propagation Detach rooted offsets in mid-spring and keep in a propagator at 70° F until established.

Disorders Browning leaf tips are usually due to low humidity.

Vriesea

This large genus from tropical South America includes both epiphytic and terrestrial bromeliads, all bearing their soft and pliant, strap-like leaves in an arching rosette. Most species have leaves about 12 in long and 2 in wide. They grow to a height and spread of around 18 in.

The highly coloured flower spike appears at the top of an erect stalk, up to 18 in long; it is usually a flattened head, up to 9 in long, with notched edges from which the short-lived tubular flowers emerge.

Some vrieseas are predominantly foliage plants, valued for their ornamental leaves. The less striking flowers are often slow to appear, but the bracts persist for a long time.

V. fenestralis is a foliage type with light green leaves netted with dark green veins. The flower spike is yellow with bright green bracts.

V. hieroglyphica is also grown mainly for its leaves. These are pale green with irregular transverse bands of darker green and purple. The branched flower spike carries pale green bracts and yellow flowers.

V. splendens is the most popular vriesea, commonly called flaming sword. The leaves are dark green with wide crossbands of deep purple, particularly on the undersides. The flower head is a flattish, lance-shaped, bright red spike, up to 2 ft tall, from which the yellow flowers appear.

Several selected forms, or clones, and crosses between forms have introduced flower spikes of varying sizes and colours, and differing leaf colours and patterns. They are rarely offered by name.

Buying hints Foliage vrieseas are comparatively rare, except at high-class florists and garden centres.

V. splendens is widely available from many kinds of sources, in the medium to expensive price range. Usually only mature, 15 in and above, plants are offered. Make sure plants are just beginning to send up flowering spikes; they will remain attractive for at least three months.

General care Vrieseas are normally sold as flowering-sized plants, in 4 or 5 in pots and do not need potting on. A suitable growing medium is equal parts of leaf-mould and coarse peat.

Light Place in bright, filtered light during the summer, but move as close as possible to direct light from September to March.

Temperature Provide a minimum temperature of at least 64° F at all times of the year.

Humidity A high degree of humidity is essential. Stand pots on trays of moist pebbles, and mist spray the foliage frequently.

Watering and feeding Water generously from late spring and through summer, but give only enough water to keep the compost just moist for the rest of the year. Keep the central water cups topped up at all times.

Give a weak liquid fertiliser once a month from April to August.

Propagation Offsets on *V. splendens* – often only a single one – appear near to the flower stem in the leaf axils. In other species the offsets form round the base of the rosette. Remove all offsets when 5-7 in high and root at 70-75° F.

Commercially vrieseas are raised from seed but take several years to reach flowering size.

Disorders Normally trouble-free.

Vriesea hieroglyphica

Vriesea splendens

FLOWERING HOUSE PLANTS

Flowering house plants fall into one of three distinct groups. The best kinds are those which flower whenever growing conditions are right for them, and these plants may be in bloom for the greater part of the year. *Begonia semperflorens, Impatiens,* some pelargoniums, the saintpaulias and some streptocarpus are examples of this group.

The second group comprises plants which have only a brief and seasonal flowering period, but which are long-lived, decorative plants even when not in flower. *Aphelandra squarrosa* and *Clivia miniata* are typical examples.

The third and final group includes short-term plants, often called florists' or gift plants. They make one glorious, but relatively short-lived display and are then best thrown away. The majority are specialists' plants, needing considerable expertise and particular facilities to bring them into bloom again.

Some of these short-lived plants are annuals and will die anyway after having bloomed, and others are usually treated as annuals. Calceolarias and chrysanthemums fall into this category.

In the following plant descriptions advice is given on how to make temporary plants last as long as possible, and how to grow those which can feasibly be kept.

Buying hints

Many of the popular temporary flowering house plants are offered for sale in winter. In cold weather much damage, often undetectable at the time of purchase, can be caused to plants both in transit and while on display.

Some wholesalers dispatch their plants boxed up or wrapped in paper or polythene sleeves which protect them from cold blasts and draughty situations. However, many florists are primarily concerned with the sale of cut flowers, which must be kept cool in the shops. Potted plants, newly arrived from heated greenhouses, are rarely specially catered for.

A street market on a cold, wintry day, and the slightly more elegant counterpart, a stand outside a florist shop, are the worst places from which to buy a tender plant such as a cyclamen or poinsettia.

Always choose plants with plenty of buds rather than those in full bloom. If you are in doubt about the treatment to which plants have been subjected during bitterly cold weather, refrain from buying altogether.

Achimenes 'Little Beauty'

Achimenes
(Gesneriaceae)

These summer and autumn-flowering plants, native to Mexico and Central America, grow from scaly underground rhizomes. The growing season extends from spring to autumn and is followed by a period of dormancy.

The thin stems are weak and usually need supporting, though some naturally trailing plants are good for edging troughs and for growing in hanging baskets.

The dark green leaves are variable in shape and size, but are most often pointed ovals with toothed edges, and $1\frac{1}{2}$-$2\frac{1}{2}$ in long. The tubular or trumpet-shaped flowers, which flare out to a flat face of five-lobed petals, are 1-$2\frac{1}{2}$in across. The colours cover a wide spectrum, and some blooms have contrasting veins or markings.

A few species and many hybrids are available from specialist growers. The most successful for indoor use include 'Blue Beauty', violet-blue; 'Ambroise Verschaffelt', white with purple veining; 'Little Beauty', deep crimson-pink, yellow eye; 'Paul Arnold', violet-purple; and 'Pink Beauty'.

Buying hints Plants are best acquired as dry rhizomes, bought from bulb merchants and specialist growers in early spring. Potted, flowering-sized plants are available from florists' shops in summer, in the medium to expensive price range. Choose plants with short, bushy growth.

General care Achimenes are not the easiest house plants. If their particular needs can be met, they will flower continuously over several months.

Start rhizomes into growth in March or April, setting four to six in a 4 in pot of peat-based compost. Keep them at around 60° F. They will grow into a bushy group, 9-10 in high and wide, and need the support of twiggy sticks.

Light Place in a brightly lit position where the plants will get 3-4 hours of sun a day, but avoid hot midday sun. Bright light is essential for flower production. If necessary, augment this with fluorescent light.

Temperature While actively growing, achimenes will thrive at any normal room temperature. Store dried off plants during the winter at not less than 45° F.

Humidity Stand on trays of moist pebbles to provide high humidity.

Watering and feeding Always use tepid water. After potting water sparingly, just enough to barely moisten the compost. As growth progresses, gradually give more water and when in full growth keep the compost permanently moist.

Feed every two weeks with a high-potash liquid fertiliser from June onwards. As flowering decreases in September, cease feeding and gradually reduce watering until top growth begins to die down.

When the dormant period occurs, cut down the stems and store the pots, on their sides, after drying off, until the following spring.

Propagation Achimenes produce many new rhizomes each year. Separate these from the parent plant and pot up. A temperature of 65-70° F is needed to start them into growth.

Disorders Aphids are the chief pests.

Anthurium
(*Araceae*)

Anthurium scherzerianum

This genus from tropical America contains two species which are popular house plants. They are prized for their waxy, often brilliantly coloured spathes backing a straight or curled spadix in which the insignificant flowers are embedded.

A. andreanum (painter's palette) has short, erect stems and heart-shaped, dark green leaves, 6-8 in long. They are borne on long leaf stalks and give a plant height of up to 18 in and a spread of 12 in. The scarlet, shiny and puckered spathe is heart-shaped, 4-5 in long and 3 in wide. The slightly curved, 3 in long spadix is white.

A. scherzerianum (flamingo flower) is virtually stemless with leaves clustered together at the base. These are lance-shaped, up to 9 in long and $2\frac{1}{2}$ in wide and held on wiry, 10 in long leaf stalks. The oval spathes are brilliant scarlet, glossy and 3-4 in long. The red or orange spadix twists in a spiral. Hybrids with white, cream and pink spathes are occasionally available.

Buying hints Purchase only from reputable sources as chilling can cause irreparable damage. Mainly available from garden centres, plants vary in size from 6-18 in, and prices from medium to expensive. Check that plants are firm with plenty of roots in the pots. Choose those with young spathes.

General care Use a mixture of equal parts of leaf-mould, peat and, if available, sphagnum moss. Maximum pot size of 4-5 in is usually sufficient, with a drainage layer, to one-third the depth, of crocks or large pebbles.

Repot in March, carefully teasing the compost away from the roots. Position the plants so that the growing point is 1-2 in above the surface. As aerial roots appear round the base of the plant, pack damp moss round them to increase humidity and encourage them to penetrate the potting mixture.

Anthuriums are particularly suitable for hydroculture.

Light Place in bright but filtered light throughout the year.

Temperature Maintain a minimum temperature of 60° F at all times.

Humidity A high level of humidity is essential if these plants are to flower. Stand them on trays of moist pebbles and spray the foliage regularly.

Watering and feeding In the summer water freely to keep the compost moist. As temperatures fall, give only moderate amounts of water, but never allow the plants to become completely dry at the roots.

Feed once a month with a liquid fertiliser, from March to September.
Propagation Increase by division of crowded clumps in early spring. A temperature of at least 70° F, coupled with high humidity, is necessary to start the divisions into fresh growth.
Disorders Aphids may disfigure new leaves and young flowers. Provided the air is humid, red spider mites prove no problem, though attacks are more liable at high temperatures.

Aphelandra
(Acanthaceae)

Aphelandra squarrosa 'Dania'

One species, *A. squarrosa*, from Brazil is variously known as zebra plant, from the white-striped leaves, and as saffron spike, from the tuft of yellow bracts. It is decorative both in leaf and flower. Blooms are normally produced in autumn or at any time until February.

In the popular form *A.s.* 'Louisae' growth is robust, the main stem being fleshy, almost succulent. A well grown plant may grow 18 in high and 12 in across. The lance-shaped leaves are pointed, 8-10 in long and shiny dark green. Some curl slightly and all are marked with prominent white veins in a herringbone pattern.

The flower head is a many-sided pyramid shape of stepped and overlapping yellow bracts, often with red streaks, from which the 1-2 in long tubular and yellow flowers emerge in succession. The flower head remains decorative for around two months and smaller flower heads may appear in the leaf axils just below the main spike.

A.s. 'Dania' has paler green leaves marked with numerous white veins. It is more compact, rarely growing taller than 12 in with a spread of 9 in.

Buying hints Readily available from all types of shops, 5-10 in plants are generally of good quality and inexpensive. Examine flower spikes carefully to see that only flowers in the lower bracts have opened.

General care Aphelandras are normally sold as established plants, about 10 in high, when their flowers are about to open. If they are in pots smaller than 5 in, move them into that size, using John Innes No. 3.

Cut off the main flower spike as it fades, to encourage new, smaller flower heads below. Aphelandras are not easy to flower in the home for a second year. It is more practical to cut the plants back by half, when flowering is finished, to encourage side shoots for use in propagation.
Light Place in the brightest possible light during autumn and winter. For the remainder of the year, good but filtered light is important.
Temperature Provide a minimum temperature of 60° F throughout the year. Avoid draughts at all costs.
Humidity These plants need a high degree of air moisture. Stand them on trays of moist pebbles, and mist the foliage daily with tepid water.
Watering and feeding Never allow the potting mixture to dry out, or flagging will occur and the lower leaves fall off.

In addition to copious watering, aphelandras should be fed once a week, during spring and summer, with dilute liquid fertiliser.
Propagation Take 2-3 in long side growths and root in a propagator at a temperature of 65° F.
Disorders Aphids may attack the growing tips of plants and also collect around the developing flower heads.

Begonia
(Begoniaceae)

As a family begonias are widely distributed over Africa, Asia and South America. Some are grown principally for their leaves, some for their flowers, but most of the flowering types also have attractive foliage. It is often difficult to separate the two types.

Begonia 'Elatior' hybrid

Begonia semperflorens

The original species, from which most of today's plants are derived, differ considerably in shape, scale and ease of culture. As a general rule the more exotic a plant looks, the more difficult it is to grow in the home.

Begonias can be tuberous, rhizomatous or fibrous-rooted, and they may be perennial or evergreen.

Begonias bear male and female flowers, sometimes in one cluster and sometimes separately. Male flowers are often the more striking, with a single or several layers of petals. They last for only a few days while the female flowers remain for weeks or months. These have four petals and are distinguished by a triangular seed pod.

B. 'Gloire de Lorraine' hybrids are tuberous-rooted, up to 12 in tall and wide. They produce numerous erect stems with single $\frac{3}{4}$-1 in wide flowers in winter. Pink is the predominant colour, but yellow and orange shades are known. The green leaves are almost circular, with a concave centre.

B. 'Elatior' hybrids are also tuberous. Well-grown specimens may reach a height of 18 in and a spread of 12 in. They were raised in Germany at the beginning of this century and have been popular ever since. They bloom in winter, with semi-double or double flowers $2\frac{1}{2}$ in across. Mainly red, but pink, peach and white-flowered hybrids are also available. The dark green, shiny leaves are almost circular, with undulating edges.

B. corallina, its hybrids and some closely related and similar species belong to the fibrous-rooted, cane-stemmed group of begonias. Most produce several branched stems of considerable length, but they seldom extend beyond 4 ft as pot plants.

The lop-sided 'angel-wing' leaves are midgreen and variously spotted with silvery dots above, shaded deep wine-red beneath. Large trusses of bright coral-pink flowers, $\frac{3}{4}$ in across, appear from May to November.

B. metallica is shrubby and fibrous-rooted, up to $2\frac{1}{2}$ ft tall and $1\frac{1}{2}$ ft wide. The asymmetric leaves, 4-6 in long, are a shiny metallic green, with prominent wine-purple veins on the undersides. Small clusters of white, pink-flushed flowers appear in summer.

B. semperflorens hybrids are popular for summer bedding and as house plants, prized for their small flowers, produced throughout the year.

The newer hybrids rarely grow taller or wider than 9 in, with single or double flowers ranging from white through pink to deep red. The waxy leaves may be green or bronze.

Buying hints Small seedlings of B. semperflorens hybrids are often marketed in trays, at plant shops, garden centres and market stalls. Inexpensive, they can be selected for leaf and flower colour when only 2 or 3 in tall.

The winter-flowering, tuberous-rooted kinds are best bought in bud, inexpensive to medium-priced from florists and garden centres. Unless very good growing conditions are available, they are best disposed of when flowers fade. Beware of plants with torn or otherwise damaged leaves, any with signs of powdery mildew or any that may have been exposed, even briefly, to cold or draughty positions.

B. corallina and B. metallica can often be bought as young, 6 in plants. They are cheap and soon grow into impressive plants. Larger plants are obviously more expensive.

General care Grow in a compost made up from equal parts of John Innes No. 3 and leaf-mould or peat. Pot on the corallina types and B. metallica annually in spring until in final 8-10 in pots. Provide them with cane supports and tie the stems in place at frequent intervals. Pinch out the tips occasionally to induce side-branching.

The tuberous-rooted begonias and B. semperflorens hybrids can be flowered in 4-5 in pots. They are often treated as annuals and may be discarded after flowering or used for propagation.

Light All flowering begonias need considerably more light than their foliage relatives. In summer place them in bright, but filtered light; put them nearer to direct light in winter.

Temperature Begonias do best at moderate room temperatures, not rising above 68° F. The ideal temperature for winter-flowering begonias is around 60° F, with an acceptable night minimum of 55° F.

B. corallina and *B. metallica* will tolerate a winter minimum of 50° F.

Humidity A high degree of air moisture may encourage fungal diseases such as mildew. At rising temperatures it is sufficient to stand the pots on moist pebble trays.

Watering and feeding All begonias thrive in moist, but never sodden compost. Let it dry out slightly between applications.

Feed actively growing plants every two weeks with a high-potash liquid fertiliser.

Propagation Double-flowered and prized forms of *B. semperflorens* can be perpetuated from 2-2½ in stem cuttings, best taken from low down on the plants, in late autumn. All other kinds root relatively easily from 2-3 in tip cuttings at any time of year. Pot in peat and sand and root at 65° F.

Disorders Some species and hybrids suffer badly from mildew while other forms appear immune. Precautionary measures against this fungus disease include moderate humidity and good ventilation, though not draughts, on hot days. Avoid crowding and over-watering the plants.

Beloperone guttata

Beloperone
(Acanthaceae)

The easily grown and popular shrimp plant, *Beloperone guttata*, originates in Mexico. It forms a vigorous, twiggy, green-stemmed shrub with a height and spread of about 18 in. The soft green and faintly hairy leaves are undistinguished, but the pink or bronze overlapping floral bracts, arranged like the body of a shrimp, are borne in a striking terminal spike.

Narrow white flowers, spotted with red, appear from between the bracts, at any time between late spring and winter. The flowers are short-lived, but the bracts remain attractive for several weeks.

Buying hints Choose young, short and bushy plants no more than 6-8 in high. Garden centres and florists usually offer pots with three or four plants; they are generally inexpensive. Avoid any with long straggly stems and poor bract colour.

General care Grow in John Innes No. 3 and repot or pot on annually. Pinch out the growing tips of young plants to encourage bushy growth. Large straggly plants are better for being cut hard back in February.

Stems can be shortened by up to half and will respond with side branching.

Light Shrimp plants are best grown in bright, but filtered light during the summer. From autumn to spring move them close to direct light to initiate brightly coloured bracts.

Temperature During the growing season ordinary room temperatures are suitable. Encourage plants to take a short winter rest by keeping them at a temperature of 50° F.

Humidity These plants do not demand a high level of humidity. Growth is, however, better if the pots stand on trays of moist pebbles.

Watering and feeding Water freely while in active growth, but during the rest period give only enough to prevent the compost from drying out.

Feed established plants every week from March to September with a general liquid fertiliser.

Propagation Root 2-3 in tip cuttings in spring, in pots covered with plastic bags or in a propagator at 65° F. Remove the first few bracts and the growing tips from the rooted cuttings to build up bushy plants.

Disorders Brown or black patches on the leaves are usually a sign of over-watering. Red spider mites may attack plants in hot rooms.

Calceolaria
(Scrophulariaceae)

The hybrid calceolarias, widely sold in spring and early summer, are commonly called slipper flowers and botanically C. × herbeo-hybrida. They are grown for their broad heads of inflated, pouch-like flowers, each up to 2 in across. They come in shades of yellow, orange, pink or red and may be spotted or marked with red. The thin oval leaves, up to 6 in long, are light green and covered with soft hairs.

Most modern strains grow 9-12 in tall. They are temporary plants, discarded when past their best.

Buying hints Garden centres and florists are the main sources, with prices varying from cheap to expensive. Choose plants with plenty of unopened buds. Avoid any with damaged or marked leaves.

General care Plants purchased in small pots should ideally be moved to 5-7 in pots, filled with John Innes No. 2 and moved again to 8-9 in pots.

Nip out faded blooms with the thumb and forefinger.

Light Grow in bright but filtered light, away from direct sun.

Temperature Keep the plants as cool as possible for their short life. Avoid positions near to heating appliances.

Humidity Good humidity extends the flowering period. Stand the pots on trays of moist pebbles, but do not spray foliage and flowers; water droplets leave marks and may even encourage fungus diseases.

Watering and feeding These plants need considerable amounts of water, and the compost should be kept permanently moist though not wet.

Feed every two weeks with a general liquid fertiliser.

Propagation Home propagation is not normally practical.

Disorders Keep a careful watch for aphids which tend to congregate round the growing tips and flower buds.

Calceolaria × herbeo-hybrida

Campanula
(Campanulaceae)

One species only in this large genus is grown indoors. This is an extremely easy campanula from northern Italy, excellent for trailing over the edges of pots and baskets. It comes into bloom in July and often continues until early November.

C. isophylla trails its slender stems about 1 ft long. The fresh green leaves are almost circular, ½ in across, with slightly scalloped edges. They are held on brittle leaf stalks. Pale blue, open bell-shaped flowers, 1 in across, appear in clusters at the tips of the trailing stems and open in succession.

'Alba' is white-flowered, and the blue 'Mayi' has grey-green, cream-marked leaves covered with the softest of fine hairs.

Buying hints Campanulas are normally bought as flowering plants from florists' shops and garden centres. They are usually in the medium price range, but once purchased they yield numerous cuttings.

General care Grow in John Innes No. 3, potting young plants progressively until in 5 in pots. Alternatively, trail several plants together over the edges of a hanging basket.

Pinch off the flowers as they fade to tidy the plants and ensure continuous blooming. Cut the stems back, right to the base, after flowering and rest the plants over winter. Start plants into new growth in March or April with higher temperatures and more water.

Light Place in bright light, close to a window, but avoid direct summer sun.

Temperature High temperatures encourage soft growth and short-lived flowers. The ideal temperature during the growing and flowering season is around 60° F. For the winter rest period, 45° F is sufficient.

Humidity Stand pots on trays of moist pebbles as increased humidity counteracts high temperatures.

Campanula isophylla 'Alba'

Watering and feeding Water copiously from April to October without flooding the plants. During the rest period apply just enough water to keep the compost moist.

Give two-weekly feeds during the growing season with a standard liquid fertiliser; change this to one high in potash from mid-June.

Propagation Overwintered plants are better used for propagation purposes. In early spring, take 2 in tip cuttings and root at 65° F. Set at least three cuttings in one pot or hanging basket for a bushy effect. Division is also possible, though less satisfactory.

Disorders Waterlogging encourages grey mould and other fungus diseases.

Capsicum
(Solanaceae)

Capsicum hybrid

This genus includes the large-fruited culinary pepper from the Tropics; house plant species are grown for the decorative value of their fruits.

Most types have cone-shaped fruits, 1-2 in long, held upright in clusters at the tips of the shoots. They mature from green to red or yellow, sometimes through creamy-white and purple, and remain on the plants for many weeks.

Dwarf, bushy kinds, mainly hybrids of *C. annuum* and *C. frutescens*, are the most popular. They are of compact and dense habit, with an ultimate height and spread of 12-15 in. The leaves are 1-1½ in long, oval-pointed and dull green; the flowers are small and white. They are short-lived plants, discarded when the leaves fall and fruits shrivel.

Buying hints Young plants in 3 in pots are the best buys. They are readily and inexpensively available at all types of plant shops from early autumn.

Check that there are many small fruits.

General care Plants are normally bought in 3 or 4 in pots. If they have plenty of top growth, move them into 5 in pots, with John Innes No. 3.

Light Place in good, bright light.

Temperature Any normal room temperature suits these plants. It should not fall below 50° F at night.

Humidity Stand pots on trays of moist pebbles. Spray the foliage and flowers regularly to help the flowers set fruit and to discourage spider mites.

Watering and feeding Water generously, allowing the compost to almost dry out before applying more.

Feed plants every two weeks with a general liquid fertiliser while fruits are still developing, but stop once they are fully grown.

Propagation Capsicums are raised from seed. Seedlings and young plants need greenhouse cultivation.

Disorders Dry air encourages red spider mites. Spray the foliage regularly. When present, wash the mites off the plants.

Chrysanthemum
(Compositae)

Florists' chrysanthemums are plants of complicated hybrid origin and classified as *C. morifolium*. Until fairly recently they were treated as plants for flowering in autumn and early winter which are their natural seasons of blooming. However, commercial growers have developed special growing methods, and chrysanthemums can now be bought in flower throughout the year.

Chrysanthemums are short-day plants – blooming only when the days are short. Commercial growers control the amount of light in order to initiate flower buds. They also spray the plants with a hormone dwarfing compound which stops their naturally robust growth and keeps it down to no more than 9-12 in.

Single and double-flowered forms are available, in white, yellow, orange, bronze, red or purple. As house plants chrysanthemums are strictly temporary, though relatively long-lived

Chrysanthemum (mixed)

flowering plants, They are discarded when their flowers have faded.

Buying hints Widely available from all types of shops, including market stalls, most plants are in 5 in half-pots and generally inexpensive. Buy plants with buds just beginning to open rather than those in full flower. If buds are tightly closed they may not open.

General care These plants will not need repotting, but can stay in the pots in which they were purchased for the period that they are grown indoors. Cut off individual flowers as they fade.

Light Grow in bright filtered light. In poor light the buds may fail to open.

Temperature Keep as cool as poss-ible at all times. Plants will survive for only a short time during the warm summer months. Conversely, they are not harmed by winter temperatures down to 40° F.

Humidity During the warm months it is advantageous to stand pots on trays of moist pebbles.

Watering and feeding Keep the potting mixture permanently moist.

A dilute liquid fertiliser may be given fortnightly to plants still in bud. When the flowers open, cease all feeds.

Propagation Home propagation is pointless as the necessary, controlled conditions cannot be achieved.

Disorders Few troubles are en-countered with these plants.

Citrus microcarpa

Citrus
(Rutaceae)

The genus *Citrus*, distributed throughout eastern Asia, includes all the popular citrus fruits – lemon, orange, lime, grapefruit and tangerine – few of which are suitable for use indoors. Most prefer open-ground cultivation and often fail to flower or to set fruit under less than ideal con-ditions.

A few, however, are more amenable to indoor pot culture, and the best are listed below. All are slow-growing, with leathery, elliptic leaves and heav-ily scented, five-petalled white flowers.

C. limon (lemon) produces flowers in late spring and early summer, and 2-3 in long dark green fruits follow. These may take as long as a year to ripen and develop fully. It makes a narrow, leggy shrub, eventually up to 4 ft tall.

C. microcarpa (*C. mitis*) (calamondin) is a dwarf orange, unlikely to grow more than 18 in high with a similar spread. It may flower and fruit when quite young. Odd flowers may appear through most of the year, but the majority are borne in summer.

The 1-1½ in wide fruits appear in groups of two or three at the ends of the shoots, tending to bend down the branches. They ripen slowly from deep green to orange. Flowers, green and ripe fruits may occur on the plants at the same time.

C. taitensis, probably a hybrid orange, grows 3 ft high and 18 in wide. The flowering season is variable, but the fruits normally ripen in late autumn and early winter.

Buying hints Citrus plants are very expensive and best purchased from reputable florists and garden centres. Buy in April or May, if possible, so that plants have a chance to get used to indoor conditions before winter.

Choose plants with deep green leaves, plenty of flower buds and ideally some small fruits.

General care Grow in John Innes No. 3 and pot on into the next size pot each spring until the maximum pot size of 8-10 in is reached. Maintain a manageable size by gentle pruning, cutting out completely thin growths and shortening by up to half long shoots that spoil the symmetry.

If possible, move plants outdoors in summer. Indoors, admit fresh air dur-ing the warm months.

Light Place in really bright, lightly filtered light during the summer. For the rest of the year move them to the brightest position available.

Temperature Ordinary room temperatures are suitable. In winter the minimum should be 55° F or growth will cease.

Humidity Stand pots on large trays of moist pebbles or use the double-pot method. Spray the foliage frequently on warm days.

Watering and feeding During the growing period give enough water to make the compost moist, but never let it become saturated. Water very sparingly during the winter rest period, letting the compost dry out almost completely between applications.

Feed once a month from April to September with a liquid fertiliser.

Propagation Home propagation is not practical as most plants are grafted.

Disorders Scale insects may occur, clustering on the undersides of leaves. Aphids attack the growing tips. Both pests exude a sticky substance which may lead to the disease known as sooty mould. Leaf drop is caused by over-watering and draughts.

Clivia miniata

Clivia
(Amaryllidaceae)

Clivias are South African plants valued for their spectacular heads of orange or orange-red flowers, normally produced in spring, and for their elegant leaves. Only one species is in general cultivation and is easy, undemanding and long-lived.

C. miniata bears dark green, leathery and strap-shaped leaves arching out from the base in two opposite ranks. The tightly clasped, overlapping leaf bases eventually form a thickened 3-8 in long leek-like stem. New leaves appear from the centre of the two ranks of leaves.

Some forms have 3 in wide leaves, on others they are only 1½ in wide, but all grow to a length of 18 in, giving a spread of up to 2 ft.

The 2-3 in long, trumpet-shaped flowers number between 10 and 20 to a head and are borne on top of a stout 18 in flower stalk. Individual blooms last for only a few days but are most impressive and open in succession.

Buying hints Young unpotted, but flowering-sized plants are offered by mail order, and these are the most economical. Florists and garden centres sell clivias potted and in bud in February and March. They are generally very expensive.

General care Grow in John Innes No. 3. Clivias flower best when their fleshy roots are restricted and left alone. Pot on only into the next size pot when the thick roots congest the surface of the compost. This should be done very early in the year, just as the flower buds begin to appear. Cut off the flower head after blooms fade, but leave the stalk until it withers when it may be gently pulled out.

Light Grow in good, but filtered light, shaded from direct summer sun.

Temperature Ordinary room temperatures are suitable during the growing season. In the rest period, during autumn and early winter, a cooler position is desirable. The temperature should not fall below 50° F.

Humidity High humidity is not essential. The pots can stand on trays of moist pebbles during the growing season. Wipe the leaves free of dust.

Watering and feeding Keep the compost moist, but not wet, from March to September; give very little water in winter.

Feed once or twice a month during the growing season with a dilute liquid fertiliser.

Propagation Increase from well developed offsets rooted at 65° F. Knock the whole plant from its pot and carefully cut the offset from the parent, with as much root as possible. Set in a 5 in pot and water sparingly until new roots are active.

Disorders Watch out for mealy bugs which may congregate in the leaf axils. Failure to flower is usually caused by an insufficient or too warm resting period in winter.

Cuphea
(Lythraceae)

Cuphea ignea

One species, the cigar plant from Mexico, is an easy and popular flowering house plant. Given good cultivation it will bloom for the greater part of the year. It is short-lived, getting past its best in a couple of years, but it increases readily from cuttings.

C. ignea (cigar plant) is a bushy shrub up to 12 in high and wide. Its common name refers to the 1 in long, thin, tubular flowers that are bright red except for the very tip which is deep purple and white. They are borne from mid spring until late autumn, on short stalks arising from the leaf axils.

The 1 in leaves are glossy dark green. A rare cultivar, 'Variegata', has leaves streaked with yellow.

Buying hints Commercially cupheas are grown from seed, and it is sometimes possible to buy small seedling plants in May and June. Flowering-sized plants, available from florists and garden centres, are however inexpensive and give immediate results. Choose well-branched specimens and avoid any with drooping leaves.

General care Grow in John Innes No. 2 or 3, in 3-5 in pots. Repot or pot on in spring and pinch out growing tips on young plants regularly to encourage bushy side growth.

Around Christmas cut back one year and older plants by as much as half their growth, taking out completely any thin, straggly shoots.

Light The best position is a brightly lit window, preferably one receiving 3 or 4 hours of sun daily.

Temperature Cupheas dislike excessive heat but will grow well in normal room conditions. They will tolerate winter temperatures of 45° F.

Humidity A high level of humidity is essential. All plants should be stood on moist pebble trays, and the foliage misted daily during the growing period. Let the pebbles dry out in winter and cease misting.

Watering and feeding From April to mid-October water generously, giving enough water to thoroughly moisten the compost. During the winter rest period, and especially at low temperatures, water only enough to prevent the compost from becoming dry.

Feed growing plants once a week with a dilute liquid fertiliser, from April until September.

Propagation Increase from 2-3 in tip cuttings rooted in a propagator at 65° F during spring and early summer. Pinch out the growing tips periodically to build up bushy plants. Seedlings branch naturally, but seed sowing is rarely worth the trouble as bought plants are cheap.

Disorders Generally free of trouble.

Cyclamen
(Primulaceae)

The popular florists' cyclamens, hybrids of *C. persicum* from the Eastern Mediterranean, can be bought in flower from August through to March. They are best treated as temporary plants which, if given good growing conditions, will stay in bloom for up to 2 months but are then discarded. If a garden or balcony is available they may be rested there for the summer and started into growth again in late August.

Cyclamens grow to a height and spread of 12 in, from flattened brown tubers, and bear fleshy, heart-shaped leaves, about 6 in across, on long leaf stalks. The basic leaf colour is dark green, marbled to a greater or lesser degree with grey-green.

The 2 in long, red, pink, lilac, white or bicoloured blooms with backswept petals are held well above the foliage. Many are sweetly scented.

Large-flowered forms, sometimes with ruffled and frilled petals, are frequently offered though they are the least successful as the blooms are easily damaged. The toughest and most suitable indoor cyclamens are the minia-

Cyclamen persicum (mixed)

ture types, with small leaves and small, but still impressive flowers.

Buying hints Undoubtedly the most widely sold flowering pot plants in winter, cyclamens are cheap to medium priced. Small plants with six to eight flowers or buds are sold in 3-$3\frac{1}{2}$ in pots, larger plants in the 5 in pot size. Both are good buys for the amount of bloom they produce. If necessary, remove plants from their paper sleeves and choose those with few open flowers and plenty of buds.

Avoid any of loose habit, those with broken leaves and leaf stalks and those stood outside shops.

General care Purchased plants will grow well in the pots in which they are bought. It is vitally important to remove fading flowers and odd yellowing leaves by pulling them gently away from the base. Any stump left behind is liable to rot and set up fungal diseases.

Light Set in the best possible light during the dark winter months.

Temperature The ideal temperature for the short indoor lives of these plants is around 55-60° F. Avoid very warm rooms and do not position plants near heating appliances.

Humidity A reasonable level of humidity is required. Stand pots in decorative bowls with a 1 in layer of moist peat or pebbles. Do not spray the foliage which is easily marked.

Watering and feeding Contrary to popular belief, it is of little importance whether plants are watered from below or above. It is, however, important that the tubers are never made wet.

For watering from below, stand the pots in a bowl with 2 in of water for 20 minutes while the compost takes up the necessary water. For watering from above, guide the spout of the watering can to the side of the tuber. Whichever method is used, give water only when the compost has almost dried out, *not before*. Overwatering kills the roots.

Feed weekly with liquid fertiliser.

Propagation Commercially, plants are raised from seed, a process usually outside the amateur's scope.

Disorders Grey mould and other fungal diseases may occur. Rapid loss of flowers and leaves is usually caused by too much heat.

Euphorbia pulcherrima

Euphorbia
(*Euphorbiaceae*)

Poinsettias (*E. pulcherrima*) are particularly popular around Christmas when large numbers are sold as gift plants. They are relatively easy to keep in good condition for several weeks or months and are not even difficult to keep for another year.

What is difficult, however, is to give poinsettias the growing conditions they need to flower again. Home gardeners with limited space are advised to enjoy the plants while in flower and then to discard them.

Poinsettias are naturally tall-growing shrubs, native to Mexico. Present-day cultivars are considerably shorter, but this is because they have been subjected to treatment with a hormone dwarfing compound which restricts their growth.

The leaves are dark green with lighter veining, elliptic in shape and often deeply lobed.

The true poinsettia flowers are small, greenish-yellow and clustered together in the centre of a rosette of brightly coloured bracts. Red has for long been the most popular colour, but other forms are seen with pink or creamy-green bracts.

Buying hints Widely available from florists and garden centres, quality and price vary enormously, from cheap to very expensive. Single shoots are marketed in 3-$3\frac{1}{2}$ in pots and are the cheapest. Three cuttings are often planted together in one 5 in pot. They provide three large heads of bracts and are most effective, but also expensive.

Try to find plants with fresh bracts, recognised by the small flowers intact in the centre.

Avoid cold street markets and shops where the plants have stood in cold draughty positions.

General care Purchased plants will not need to be repotted or moved into larger pots. Staking is not necessary.

At the end of flowering, poinsettias are usually discarded. If you wish to attempt keeping them, cut the stems back to 4-6 in of the base and give the plants an almost dry rest period until May. Repot in fresh compost and start into growth with resumed watering. When shoots appear, apply weekly doses of liquid feeds.

Poinsettias are short-day plants and only initiate flowers and buds under specific conditions of darkness and light. About 2 months before you wish the plants to flower, begin a regimen of 14 hours in total, uninterrupted darkness, followed by 10 hours of daylight.

Light Give the brightest possible light in winter. In summer shade from direct sun.

Temperature These plants are amenable to a wide range of temperatures but do best and flower longest when grown at a steady 55° or 60° F.

Humidity Additional humidity is not essential, but trays of moist pebbles under the pots help to extend the plants' lives, particularly at higher than recommended temperatures.

Watering and feeding Water thoroughly, but allow the compost to dry out almost completely before the next application. In summer water more plentifully.

Fertilisers are not necessary for poinsettias grown as temporary plants.

Propagation Easily increased from 3 in tip cuttings taken in June or July and rooted at 65° F.

Disorders Excessively dry air may encourage mealy bugs and scale insects. A combination of dry air and high temperatures causes premature flower drop. Overwatering and draughts result in leaf drop.

Hibiscus rosa-sinensis

Hibiscus
(*Malvaceae*)

This rapid, fairly easy growing shrubby plant, prized for its exotic flowers, originates in China. The numerous hybrids, however, have the blood of Pacific Islands species in their make-up. The flowering season is mainly in summer and autumn, each bloom lasting only a few days, but under good growing conditions flowers may appear at any time of the year.

H. rosa-sinensis is the most widely grown species. It forms a small, branched shrub, usually with a height and spread of 3 ft in a 7-8 in pot. The coarsely toothed, oval, dark green leaves, 2-3 in long, are densely set along the stems.

The showy flowers, up to 5 in across, are trumpet-shaped and made up of five rounded petals with a prominent central column of stamens. They range in colour from deep crimson to palest pink, orange, yellow and, more rarely, pure white.

There are also several double-flowered forms and one variegated-leaved form, 'Cooperi'. This has narrower leaves marked with olive green, creamy-white and deep pink. The crimson flowers are smaller.

Buying hints Garden centres and florists are the main sources. Offered in 5 in pots, they are in the medium price range, but smaller plants with three or four branches, each with buds, are usually the best and most economical buys. They may, initially, lose their flower buds, but new ones are quickly produced.

General care Grow in John Innes No. 3. Pot on young plants annually in spring until in 5-6 in pots. Thereafter pot on only if growth is extremely vigorous; otherwise replace the top 2 in of compost.

In February prune older and established plants drastically, cutting out completely all thin spindly shoots and shortening the main stems by at least half their length.

Light Best in a position which receives 3 or 4 hours of direct sunlight daily. Shade from hot summer sun.

Temperature Ordinary room temperatures are suitable during the growing season. The plants will tolerate a minimum winter temperature of 50° F, but may then take a rest and lose some of their leaves. Ideally provide 55° F.

Humidity Although not demanding a high degree of air moisture, growing plants benefit from the humidity released from trays of moist pebbles.

Watering and feeding Water copiously during the active growing season from April to September and feed once a week with a high-potash liquid fertiliser. Stop feeding in October and gradually reduce the amount of water to encourage a winter rest.

Propagation Take 3-4 in non-flowering side shoots in early summer and root, preferably in a propagator at 64° F. Rooting is also possible in a warm room if the potted cuttings are placed in plastic bags.

Disorders Bud drop may be caused by the plants being moved around too much, by erratic watering and by too dry air. Lack of flower buds is usually due to inadequate sun and/or insufficient or improper fertilisers.

Hoya
(*Asclepiadaceae*)

Hoya carnosa

Two quite different kinds of hoya are popular as house plants: *H. bella,* a small spreading shrub from India, and *H. carnosa,* a vigorous climber native to Australia. Both are called wax flower and grown principally for their trusses of heavily scented, waxy, white or pale pink, starry flowers. *H. carnosa* also has attractive fleshy leaves.

The flowers are borne during summer on short woody stalks growing from the leaf axils. These stumps should be retained as subsequent blooms appear from the same point. New stalks also develop each year.

H. bella grows about 9 in tall, spreading to 15 in with its twiggy, pendulous branches. The leaves are 1-1½ in long, arrow-shaped and pale green, often silver spotted. The 2 in flower clusters droop near the tips of the stems.

H. carnosa begins by producing leafless stems which are later clothed with midgreen shiny, ovate leaves, 2 or 3 in long. Growth is vigorous and may reach 20 ft. The stems are usually trained round hoops of wire or over long canes pushed into the compost for support. The ideal situation for this species is a large conservatory or greenhouse. The fragrant flower trusses are up to 3 in across.

There are many cultivars with varie-gated leaves, including 'Exotica', with yellow and pink markings on a green-edged leaf; and 'Variegata', with white leaf margins.

Buying hints Young plants of *H. carnosa* with a dozen or so leaves are occasionally available, at economical prices. Hoyas are unlikely to flower before they are three years old. Flowering-sized plants, trained on wires and hoops in the case of *H. carnosa,* are marketed by florists and garden centres. Both species are expensive, *H. bella* commanding the highest prices.

Choose plants with several clusters of flowers, healthy foliage and undamaged growing tips.

General care Grow in John Innes No. 2 or 3. In spring pot on *H. bella* every other year and *H. carnosa* annually. When final pot size is reached, 5 and 10 in respectively, replace the top 2 in layer with fresh compost annually in spring. *H. bella* is best grown in a hanging container.

Light Place in bright light, ideally near a window with 3 or 4 hours of morning or late afternoon sun daily. Poor light results in lanky growth and few flowers. Avoid draughts at all costs, particularly while buds are forming.

Temperature Ordinary room temperatures are suitable. Excessive heat has the same effect as poor light.

Encourage plants to rest in winter at a temperature of 50° F.

Humidity A good degree of air moisture is essential. Syringe the leaves daily with tepid water during warm weather and stand the pots on trays of moist pebbles or embedded in peat.

Watering and feeding Give generous amounts of water during the growing season, but always allow the compost to partly dry out before the next application. During the rest period, give no more water than is necessary to stop the mixture from becoming dust dry.

Feed every month, from March to September, with a general fertiliser; from May to August change to one high in potash to encourage flowers.

Propagation Increase *H. bella* from 2-3 in tip cuttings rooted at 60-65° F. Propagate *H. carnosa* from cuttings lower down on the plant, where pairs of leaves will have already opened; or by layering. Late spring and early summer are the best seasons.

Disorders Hoyas rarely suffer from diseases or pests, although aphids are occasionally found on the soft trailing stems of *H. carnosa* before leaves develop. Most failures are caused by incorrect cultivation.

Hydrangea macrophylla (mixed hortensias)

Hydrangea macrophylla (lacecap)

Hydrangea
(Saxifragaceae)

Hortensias, hybrids of *H. macrophylla*, are marketed in large numbers from spring and through the summer. They are small deciduous shrubs with large mop heads of bloom, up to 8 in across, made up of numerous small, star-shaped florets.

Hydrangea flowers may be white or in shades of pink, red, blue or purple. The degree of acidity in the compost affects the colouring of the flowers considerably.

The midgreen leaves are oval with lightly toothed edges; they fall in autumn. Partly because of their deciduous growth habit and partly because they are not easy to bring into bloom again in the home, hydrangeas are usually grown as temporary house plants. They are fully hardy and can be planted out in the garden when past their best.

Buying hints Choose plants with flowers showing some green colouring to indicate that they are just beginning to open. Widely sold by most types of plant outlets, hydrangeas vary considerably. Some are offered as single-stemmed plants topped with one huge flower head, others are planted two or three together in one pot. Prices vary accordingly, but none are cheap. In other instances, the plants have been encouraged to form several branches, each with a smaller flower head. These are probably the best if most expensive buys as they will continue to bloom over a long period.

General care Hydrangeas can grow for their short indoor lives in the compost and pots in which they were bought.

Light Place in bright, indirect light, shaded from hot sun.

Temperature Kept as cool as possible and away from heating appliances, blooms will last for several weeks.

Humidity A high level of humidity helps to extend the flowering period. Stand pots on trays of moist pebbles and spray unopened flower buds with tepid water.

Watering and feeding Keep the compost thoroughly moist at all times or the plants will collapse. Should this happen soak the pots in a bowl or bucket of water. Such neglect, though, will shorten their lives. Overwatering can be equally fatal.

Feed every two weeks with dilute liquid fertiliser.

Propagation Although cuttings taken in late spring or summer will root readily they are unlikely ever to reach flowering size in the home.

Disorders Aphids may attack young growing tips, and red spider mites may appear at too dry an atmosphere.

Impatiens wallerana (mixed hybrids)

Impatiens
(Balsaminaceae)

Popularly known as busy Lizzie, the hybrid strains developed from *I. wallerana* are extremely easy to grow. Many compact-growing strains are readily available, and these have replaced the lanky-stemmed type species with its shocking-pink flowers.

Busy Lizzies grow 6-12 in high with a similar spread; the elliptic leaves are light green or bronzy-red and set on succulent stems. Flat-faced, 2 in flowers with a long spur on the lower petals are produced almost continuously. They may be white, in shades of pink, red or orange, or striped with any of these colours.

Most hybrid plants are discarded before winter when they are past their best. Grown on for a second year, they are seldom as good.

Buying hints Young seedling plants are freely available at most types of shops from spring onwards. They are cheap and will begin flowering when only a few inches high.
General care Grow in John Innes No. 1 or 2 or a peat-based compost. Pot on as required, to a final 5 in pot size.

Light Place in bright light, ideally in a position with 2 or 3 hours of direct sunlight early or late in the day.
Temperature A minimum temperature of 55° F is necessary for continuous flowers.
Humidity During hot weather especially, increased humidity is essential. Stand pots on trays of moist pebbles, but do not spray the foliage.
Watering and feeding Water generously while the plants are in active growth; never allow the compost to dry out completely or the leaves will drop. If retained over winter, keep the compost just moist.

Feed every two weeks, from May to September, with a high-potash liquid fertiliser to encourage flowers.
Propagation Tip cuttings, taken at any time, root easily at room temperature, in plain water or a rooting compost. Seed may be sown in early spring, preferably in a propagator at 70° F. Ensure that seedlings are grown in bright light at all times or they will become leggy.
Disorders Watch out for aphids on young shoots. Red spider mites may occur at low humidity. Wash the mites off under gently running tepid water and repeat if necessary.

Jasminum polyanthum

Jasminum
(Oleaceae)

Jasmine is valued for its sweetly fragrant flowers and graceful foliage. It is a vigorous climber from China, and comparatively easy as a pot plant. *J. polyanthum* (jasmine) can grow as much as 6 ft in a year, but is generally kept smaller by judicious pruning. The slender stems bear leaves composed of five or seven pointed leaflets.

The flowers, which appear from December to April, are borne in loose clusters from the leaf axils. They are narrowly tubular, opening into five rounded petals, pink on the outside, pure white inside.

Buying hints Small plants are available from most types of plant shops. They are often sold already in flower, in 3½ in pots, and these are the best buys, at inexpensive to medium prices.

Check that plants have plenty of unopened flower buds.
General care Grow in John Innes No. 2 and pot on annually in early summer until in final 8-10 in pots.

Train the slender stem round a wire hoop or several 3-4 ft long canes, lashed together at the top.

Keep plants at manageable sizes by regular pruning immediately after flowering. Cut back old growth by up to two-thirds. During summer and autumn, nip out the growing tips at regular intervals.
Light Place in bright light in a position that receives 3 or 4 hours of early

morning or late afternoon sun. Move to brightest possible light in late autumn when flower buds are forming.

Temperature Keep cool at all times and away from heating appliances. Jasmines are almost frost-hardy; they do not thrive at temperatures above 60° F and tolerate winter temperatures down to 40° F.

Humidity Fairly tolerant of dry air, some degree of air moisture is necessary for flower production. Stand pots on trays of moist pebbles to help counteract dry air in heated rooms during winter. Spray the foliage regularly during summer.

Watering and feeding Water sparingly for a few weeks after flowering has ceased to induce a short rest period. Gradually increase the amount of water after pruning and potting on. From late summer and until flowers fade, keep the compost moist.

Feed with a liquid fertiliser every two weeks from August to Christmas.

Propagation Increase from 3-4 in heel cuttings taken in summer. Root in a propagator at 60° F or under a polythene bag in a warm room.

Disorders Aphids may collect on the soft young growing tips and developing flower buds.

Pelargonium domesticum (mixed)

Pelargonium
(Geraniaceae)

Almost invariably called geraniums – a quite different genus – and universally popular for outdoor summer bedding, some pelargoniums also make excellent long-flowering house plants.

P. domesticum hybrids are known as regal pelargoniums and grown for their showy clusters of open trumpet or funnel-shaped flowers produced from May throughout the summer months.

Regal pelargoniums are bushy plants, growing and spreading 12-18 in. The green oval leaves, slightly rough or finely hairy, have lightly scalloped and wavy edges.

The 2 in wide flowers are borne near the tips of the shoots; they open in succession and each lasts for up to a week. The colours include pink, red, mauve and white, often marked at the throat with fine veining or bold streaks of a deeper colouring. Plants remain very decorative for between three and four months.

Many named cultivars are readily available from specialist growers, and many are sold unnamed by florists.

'Aztec', pale-pink, white and bronze markings; 'Black Knight', deep purple, white edging to the petals.

'Carisbrooke', rose-pink, frilled edges and veined with maroon; 'Grand Slam', scarlet and crimson; 'House and Garden', turkey-red with mauve-pink throat and maroon upper petals.

'Lavender Grand Slam', bright lavender-purple; 'Princess of Wales', strawberry-pink, white throat and white edges; and 'Victoria Regina', white with deep purple blotches.

Buying hints Specialist growers dispatch young plants in early spring, and these are the best buys. Flowering plants in 5 in pots are available from garden centres, florists and other plant shops from May onwards and give an immediate effect. Depending on area and quality, they are in the inexpensive to medium price range.

Choose plants with few open flowers and plenty of buds. Avoid those with yellowing foliage.

General care Grow in John Innes No. 2 or 3, potting on or repotting in early spring into 5-7 in pots for mature plants. Two, or at the most three years' growth is normally the maximum recommended; young plants flower more profusely than older ones.

Many people discard pelargoniums when flowering is over, but provided they can be grown in full sun they can be retained for subsequent years. Cut down all stems by half and water sparingly for four or five weeks, before starting into new growth.

Light It is imperative that pelargoniums be given all sun possible.

With this they will succeed, without it fail. Move outdoors if possible during late summer and autumn.

Temperature During late spring and summer they thrive at normal room temperatures; they will tolerate heat, although this will shorten the life of the flowers. During winter they are best kept at 50-55° F for a semi-rest period, with sparse watering.

Humidity Pelargoniums like dry air and should be stood on saucers filled with dry sand. Do not spray the foliage.

Watering and feeding Water plentifully during the growing period, but allow the compost to dry out almost completely between applications. During the rest period give just enough water to prevent the compost from drying out.

Feed every two weeks from March through to September.

Propagation Take tip cuttings in July or August and root, uncovered, at 60° F or more. Cuttings dislike the humid atmosphere of a propagator or plastic bag. Move rooted cuttings into 3½ in pots by the beginning of October and into 5 in pots in late February.

Disorders Whitefly can be troublesome and should be tackled in the early stages. Black leg is caused by a fungus and kills soft fleshy growth at compost level. Cuttings kept in too wet compost and fluctuating temperatures are particularly vulnerable to attack.

Primula
(Primulaceae)

Primula obconica

Three tender primulas are popular small flowering pot plants from late autumn until spring. Their slightly hairy, ovate leaves are arranged in symmetrical rosettes, with the dainty flowers held on 8-12 in stalks well clear of the foliage.

Primulas are best treated as temporary plants and discarded after flowering, although one, *P. obconica*, often blooms for several months.

P. × kewensis originated in Kew Gardens as a chance hybrid. The light green leaves are 6-8 in long with slightly toothed edges. Young leaves and flower stalks are sprinkled with a white meal. Buttercup-yellow flowers, fragrant and bell-shaped, are borne in loose whorls on erect stalks.

P. malacoides (fairy primrose) is native to China. The wavy-edged, green leaves are dusted with white meal. The scented, star-like flowers, up to ½ in across, are arranged in graceful tiers; they range from mauve, brick-red and cherry to lilac and white. Double-flowered forms are available.

P. obconica, also from China, has more circular leaves, 3-4 in across, with notched edges. The fine hairs on the undersides may cause skin irritation. Funnel-shaped, flattened flowers, up to 1 in across, are borne in large clusters and may be white, pink, pale orange, lilac, red or blue-purple, all with a yellow eye. They are long-lasting and suitable for cutting.

Buying hints Primulas are readily available from all types of plant shops, usually at 6-10 in high and in 3½ in pots. They are generally cheap. For most economic buys, choose those with plenty of unopened buds and few fully developed flowers. Avoid any with yellowing leaves.

General care If *P. obconica* is bought in a 3-4 in pot, this is likely to be filled with roots, and the plant is best moved into a 5 in pot of John Innes No. 3. Other primulas can stay in their pots.

Remove any yellowing leaves and pinch off individual flowers as they fade. Cut off at the base completely spent flower stalks, to tidy the plants and encourage more flowers.

Light As these plants flower when light is at a minimum level, give them as bright a position as possible.

Temperature Primulas prefer cool conditions and will stay in bloom longest if kept between 55 and 60° F.

Humidity A good level of air moisture prolongs the plants' lives. Group several pots on wide pebble trays.

Watering and feeding Keep the compost moist, though not waterlogged at all times. Feed weekly with a high-potash fertiliser.

Propagation Primulas are raised annually from fresh seed.

Disorders Aphids may disfigure flower stalks and petals.

Rhododendron simsii (azalea hybrid)

Rhododendron
(Ericaceae)

The almost hardy, low-growing and shrubby plants, botanically included in the *Rhododendron* genus but commonly called florists' or Indian azaleas, are grown for their showy flowers in winter and early spring.

They produce a short, spectacular display followed by a comparatively long period out of bloom. They are usually disposed of or transferred to a garden frame or greenhouse when the flowers have faded. Azaleas resent dry air, and only if they can be stood outdoors from late April to September are they likely to flower indoors the following year.

Two kinds are popularly grown: hybrids derived from the Asiatic *R. simsii*, with large, $2\frac{1}{2}$ in wide, broadly funnel-like flowers, and hybrids of the Japanese *R. obtusum*, with smaller flowers up to 1 in across.

The leaves of both types are oval-pointed, 1-2 in long, leathery and dark green. Some plants are of spreading habit and no taller than 9 in, others are globe-shaped, up to 12-15 in high.

Some azaleas are trained as low standards, with a 12-18 in woody stem, topped with a spreading head of foliage and flowers. They are only practical if they can spend the summer outdoors.

Azalea flowers may be white, in shades of pink or red, mauve or purple; they may have many or few petals, some with frilled or crimped edges and in more than one colour.

Buying hints Widely sold in 5 in pots by florists and garden centres, azaleas vary greatly in quality. They are in the medium to expensive price range. If it is intended to keep them for another year, larger plants are the better buys as they will usually have been growing in their pots for some time and have adapted to that form for cultivation.

Smaller plants are often potted immediately prior to sale and may have had their roots pruned. Standard-trained azaleas are very expensive.

Choose plants with few open flowers and many buds; avoid any with dry, browning and dropping leaves.

General care Azaleas belong to the so-called lime-haters, and it is essential that they are grown in an acid peat-based compost. Plants purchased in bloom will not need potting on until they are placed outdoors in April. At the same time, prune any long shoots back by up to half. Stand the plants in a sheltered and shaded position where they will not be forgotten. Bring them back indoors before the first frosts.

Light Indoors place azaleas in bright, but filtered light.

Temperature These plants are almost hardy and prefer cool growing conditions where their flowers will remain attractive for longer. Avoid positions near heating appliances. The ideal day temperature is 55-60°F; at night this can fall appreciably lower.

Humidity High humidity is vital. Stand the pots on trays of moist pebbles and spray the foliage and the papery bracts daily with tepid water; avoid moistening the open flowers as this can cause spots.

Watering and feeding Water with rain or soft water whenever possible. Azaleas need to be kept permanently moist at the roots, and the pots may need dunking every few days in a bucket of tepid water for 20 minutes. Remember to water plants in the open.

Feed outdoor plants every month, from April until flowering begins, with a lime-free liquid fertiliser.

Propagation Impossible indoors.

Disorders Aphids may infect young growing tips.

Saintpaulia ionantha (mixed)

Saintpaulia
(Gesneriaceae)

Hundreds of named cultivars of African violets are grown, with little resemblance to one of the original species *(S. ionantha)* from East Africa. The typical plant is a handsome flattish rosette shape of round or oval, hairy leaves on 2-4 in long stalks, with clusters of 1-2 in flowers on fleshy stems.

There are, however, many variations. Some have trailing stems; some are miniature or semi-miniature. There are types with single, semi-double or fully double blooms, and others with velvety or smooth, crinkly-edged or variegated foliage.

The flowers may be white, pink, red, blue, purple or bicoloured, and they may be ruffle-edged or star-shaped with pointed petals.

The African violets favoured by commercial growers are invariably those of compact habit, which are easy to grow and which flower most easily. Beginners are recommended to start with these easier kinds before moving on to more specialised plants. Two strains, Ballet and Rhapsodie, are popular and readily available.

Ballet: 'Anna', single, frilled, pale pink; 'Erica', single or semi-double, dark fuchsia-red, quilted and ruffled leaves; 'Eva', semi-double, medium blue; and 'Heidi', single, bright pink.

'Lisa', single, frilled, bright salmon-pink; 'Marta', single or semi-double, orchid-pink and lavender; 'Meta', single, ruffled, deep violet-blue; and 'Ulrike', single, frilled, dark blue.

Rhapsodie: 'Birgit', single, bright pink; 'Candy', single, white with pink blush; 'Elfriede', single, bright blue; 'Gigi', semi-double, white with blue stripes; 'Gloria', single, pale pink; and 'Neptune', single, star, medium blue.

Miniature saintpaulias under 6 in in diameter include: 'Davy Crockett', single, star, light blue; 'Edith's Toy', single, star, pink; and 'Window Blue', double, dark blue.

Semi-miniatures, such as 'Little Red', single, red; and 'Window Lace', double, orchid-pink with darker edges, are under 8 in across.

Among the rarer trailing saintpaulias, with small flowers along their lengths, are 'Mysterium', semi-double, pale pink; 'Trail Along', miniature, double, star, bright pink; and 'Violet Trail', single, star, amethyst-mauve, red-backed leaves.

Buying hints Young rooted plantlets not yet showing flower buds are the most economical buys. They are only obtainable from specialist nurseries.

Plants from florists, garden centres and other sources are invariably flowering-sized plants. They vary considerably in quality; usually sold in 3 or 4 in pots they are inexpensive.

Choose plants with few open flowers and plenty of unopened buds. Avoid those with torn or damaged leaves and any which have stood outdoors.

General care Peat-based potting composts are ideal provided that the plants are properly fed. Small pots are better than large ones as saintpaulias are shallow-rooted and flower best when the roots are restricted; 4 in pots are generally the maximum size needed. Repot in spring only when necessary, probably every other year.

Well-grown saintpaulias flower over a surprisingly long period. Encourage plants that have flowered for most of the year to take a short winter rest.

Young plants that come into bloom in autumn for the first time should be given the best possible growing conditions, perhaps with supplementary artificial light, so that they will open all their buds in winter and spring.

Remove spent flowers and older and damaged leaves cleanly from the base of the crown.

Light At least 12 hours of good bright light daily is essential for steady and continued flowering; ideally the plants should receive 3-4 hours of direct sun, though not at midday in summer. Alternatively, provide 12-14 hours under fluorescent light.

Saintpaulias will not initiate flower buds in winter, but if the natural day is extended by 4-6 hours under artificial light, flowering will continue.

Temperature A year-round temperature of around 65° F is ideal. Prolonged periods much above this result in flower bud drop, and below 60° F flowering will cease. Do not attempt saintpaulias below a day or night temperature of 55° F. Avoid draughts.

Humidity Good humidity is essential. Stand plants on trays of moist pebbles or use the double-pot method, filling the gap with moist peat. Do not normally spray the foliage.

Watering and feeding From spring to mid-autumn keep the compost moderately moist at all times, but never sodden. During any rest period give only enough water to keep it from drying out; a four to six weeks dry spell sparks off a flowering period when normal watering should be resumed.

Avoid wetting the foliage as water can mark the hairy leaves.

During the growing and flowering periods give a liquid fertiliser every two weeks, choosing one high in potash – a tomato fertiliser will do. Standard house-plant feeds encourage leaves at the expense of flowers.

Propagation Increase in spring or early summer by dividing overcrowded clumps, or by cutting off and re-rooting a prized rosette that has developed a long thick stem. Or take leaf cuttings and root in water or compost in a propagator at 70° F.

Disorders Aphids and mealy bugs can be troublesome. Grey mould, and powdery mildew are both encouraged by very high humidity, low temperatures and draughts.

Senecio × hybridus (cineraria)

Senecio
(Compositae)

The plants commonly called cinerarias are now classified as *S. × hybridus*. They are of mixed parentage and far removed from the original species, *S. cruentus*, from the Canary Islands.

Cinerarias serve as temporary house plants only and are discarded when the flowers have faded. Their outstanding feature is the broad heads of daisy-like flowers in brilliant, sometimes garish colours during late winter and early spring. The clusters are often 6-8 in across and made up of several 1 in blooms, single, semi-double or double, in blue, purple, red, pink, white or bicolours.

Cinerarias may reach a height and spread of 1-2 ft. The dark green leaves are covered with fine hairs and roughly heart-shaped, up to 9 in across. Some leaves and stems have a purplish hue.

Buying hints Widely and inexpensively sold by most types of plant shops, cinerarias range in quality from poor to excellent. Choose plants with few opened flowers and many tight buds. Reject those with damaged leaves or signs of aphids. Take great care during transportation as the leaves are easily damaged.

General care Usually sold in 5 in pots, cinerarias can stay in these for their short lives. Young plants in 3½ in pots can be potted on, using John Innes No. 2.

Remove wilting leaves and individual flowers as they fade.

Light Place in bright light, ideally close to a window; winter sun will not harm them.

Temperature Keep at a cool temperature around 55-60° F and away from heating appliances. At night this can drop to 46-50° F.

Humidity Stand the pots on trays of moist pebbles.

Watering and feeding Cinerarias are often potbound when bought and quickly droop if the rootball is allowed to dry out. Keep thoroughly moist at all times, soaking the pots if necessary in a bowl or bucket of water. Feeding is not normally necessary.

Propagation Raise from seeds sown between late spring and summer.

Disorders Aphids are liable to attack cinerarias, concentrating on growing tips and flower buds.

Sinningia speciosa (gloxinia hybrid)

Sinningia
(Gesneriaceae)

This genus includes the popular florists' gloxinias (botanically *S. speciosa*) and a species which until recently was listed as *Rechsteineria cardinalis*.

Both species, originating in Brazil, have tuberous roots and grow to a height of 9-10 in and a spread of about 12 in. They are perennials, losing their top growth in late autumn, with a limited lifespan of two or three years.

S. cardinalis has oval, light green and softly hairy leaves set closely together in tiers. The scarlet, tubular flowers, 2 in long and with a protruding upper lip, appear from June onwards. They are borne in loose clusters at the tops of the shoots and open in succession over a period of three months.

S. speciosa hybrids and cultivars are almost stemless, with large and oval, fleshy overlapping leaves. In summer clusters of upright, bell-shaped blooms, 2-3 in across, appear from the centre of the plants. The flowers may be red, purple, pink or white, single or double, with smooth or frilled petals.

The following are a few of the most popular cultivars: 'Emperor Frederick', scarlet with white edges; 'Emperor William', dark violet-blue with white borders; and 'Tiger Red', dark red with frilled edges. The Tigrina strain has white flowers spotted with red, blue or purple.

Buying hints These plants are most cheaply purchased as dried tubers from bulb merchants and garden centres. Florists offer potted growing plants from spring onwards, usually at reasonable prices. Check that there are plenty of flower buds and that the foliage is unmarked.

General care In early spring start dried tubers into growth at a temperature of around 70° F, potting them singly in 4-5 in pots with a peat-based compost. Set the tops of the tubers just level with the compost surface.

At the end of the growing season, when the leaves turn yellow and wither, clear the tubers of all top growth. Remove them from the pots and let them dry thoroughly before storing them in dry peat over winter. Discard tubers more than three years old if they have lost vigour.

Light Place in bright but filtered light, out of hot direct sun.

Temperature Normal room temperatures suit these plants. A minimum of 60° F is needed for healthy growth.

Humidity Provide high humidity by standing the pots on trays of moist pebbles. A very fine misting of the foliage is beneficial, but avoid spraying the flowers which mark easily.

Watering and feeding Water sparingly after potting and until roots are established. Thereafter keep the compost moist but not soggy. As the flowers fade, gradually reduce the amount of water, ceasing altogether when the leaves begin to wither.

Feed every two weeks once growths are 2 or 3 in tall, with a dilute liquid fertiliser. Stop feeding when the last flowers have opened.

Propagation Sinningias are not easily increased in the home; leaf cuttings rooted in a propagator at 70° F are, however, usually successful.

Disorders Fungus diseases may occur if leaves are damaged or moisture remains on them.

Solanum
(Solanaceae)

These small shrubby plants are called by the common names of winter or Jerusalem cherries after the highly decorative red, orange-red or, rarely, yellow berries in winter. Solanums are often grown as annuals and discarded when the berries have shrivelled. They may be kept for another year if they can spend the summer in the open.

Solanums flower in June and July with insignificant white, star-shaped flowers along the twiggy branches and almost hidden by the dense, dark-

Solanum pseudocapsicum

green, lance-shaped leaves. The round, ½-1 in berries that follow, ripen gradually from green.

S. capsicastrum, from Brazil, grows to about 18 in tall and 12 in across. The 2-3 in softly hairy leaves are set thickly along the branches.

S. pseudocapsicum, from Madeira, is a more robust and taller-growing plant, with undulating glossy leaves on short stalks, and poisonous berries. The two species are very similar.

The most popular cultivars are dwarf types, such as 'Tom Thumb', or spreading plants such as 'Pattersonii', both of which take up little room but bear a profusion of berries.

Buying hints Offered in late autumn and winter by florists, garden centres and many department stores, solanums are inexpensive. Large plants are in the medium price range, but these are not necessarily the best buys.

Choose plants with few coloured berries and many green ones. Avoid any which show signs of shrivelled leaves, which indicate dryness at the roots at some stage.

General care Most plants can stay for their relatively short indoor life in the pots in which they were purchased. Young plants, however, and any that are obviously potbound, will do better in 5 in pots with John Innes No. 2.

Unless the plants are discarded in spring, cut all stems back by half.

Move into the next pot size and stand the pots outdoors in sun and shelter. Keep them watered and fed. As growth progresses, pinch out the growing tips to force side-branching.

When the flowers appear, spray them with tepid water to help production of fruit. Move plants indoors again before frosts.

Light Stand in the brightest possible position. Good light, ideally sun, is necessary for the flowers to set and the berries to colour fully.

Temperature Solanums are best kept cool to ensure the longest possible life. The ideal temperature is 55° F, but if humidity is high, warmer though not hot conditions are tolerated.

Humidity At ordinary room temperatures maintain a high level of humidity by standing the pots on trays of moist pebbles and spraying the foliage daily with a fine mist.

Watering and feeding The compost should be kept moist at all times. Newly bought plants will almost have filled the pots with roots and need regular watering, without flooding, or moving into larger pots.

Give fortnightly feeds of a dilute liquid fertiliser if plants are to be retained for another year.

Propagation Commercially solanums are grown from seed; this is hardly practical indoors.

Disorders Yellowing and dropping leaves are due to overwatering.

Spathiphyllum
(*Araceae*)

Closely related to anthuriums, these Columbian plants, sometimes called white sails, are outstanding for their sail-like spathes backing up a creamy-white spadix.

The main flowering season is from late spring to late summer, but odd flowers are produced at other times.

S. wallisii is the best known species. It grows to a height and spread of about 12 in. The glossy, green 6 in long leaves rise on long stalks from a rhizome.

The 3-4 in spathes are held well clear of the foliage on stiff, dark green, 18 in long stems. They are pure white and often age to a pleasant greenish shade.

The cultivar 'Mauna Loa' is taller, up to 2 ft high in ideal conditions, with 4-6 in spathes and longer leaves.

Buying hints Spathiphyllums are specialist plants, found at good florists and garden centres. They are generally expensive. Buy plants in late spring when they will have summer and autumn to adapt to indoor conditions before the onset of winter.

Spathiphyllum wallisii 'Mauna Loa'

General care Grow in John Innes No. 2, potting on or repotting as necessary in spring in final 5 in pot sizes. 'Mauna Loa' will need a 7 in pot. The spathes remain attractive for a couple of months; when they are past their best, remove them, with the stalks, from the base.

Light Place in bright but filtered light in spring and summer. In winter move the plants close to a sunny window to encourage early flowers.

Temperature Normal room temperature is suitable. In winter this should preferably be above 60° F and at night not fall below 55° F.

Humidity A high level of air moisture is essential. Provide this by standing the pots on trays of moist pebbles; spray the leaves daily during the summer months.

Watering and feeding From April to September water generously, flooding the pots and then allowing the compost to almost dry out before the next application. During the rest period give just enough water to moisten the compost.

Give fortnightly feeds of liquid fertiliser from April to September.

Propagation Divide crowded clumps in April or May. Take care not to damage the roots more than necessary. Ideally establish the divisions in a propagator at 65-70° F.

Disorders Brown or black patches on the leaves are caused by low temperatures or saturated soil.

Stephanotis floribunda

Stephanotis
(Asclepiadaceae)

The heady fragrance of stephanotis flowers is enough to tempt any house plant grower although this native of Madagascar is not the easiest plant to keep regularly in flower. The waxy blooms are much used by florists for buttonholes and in bridal bouquets.

S. floribunda is the only species in general cultivation. It is an evergreen climber of slow growth, whose stems may reach many feet in length; they are normally trained around hoops of wire or cane or allowed to twine round several upright supports. The oblong, 4 in leaves are leathery, glossy and dark green and arranged in opposite pairs.

Scented, waxy, white flowers, made up of a narrow tube flaring into five petals, appear in clusters of six to ten from late spring to mid-autumn.

Buying hints Because of their relatively slow growth rate and the initial care needed stephanotis are expensive and usually only offered by florists and garden centres.

Choose young plants with unblemished leaves and at least one truss of bloom about to open. Spring is the best time for buying.

General care Grow in 2 parts of John Innes No. 2 and 1 part of coarse leafmould. Pot on or repot annually in April or May until in final 6-8 in pots.

Train the stems round supports as they grow. The plants tend to produce more flowers if the shoots are trained horizontally and spaced at regular intervals. Cut away completely any short straggly growth in early spring and prune drastically if shoots become too long or dense.

Light Stephanotis will not flower without sufficient bright light. During the summer place them in bright but filtered light. For the rest of the year move them near a window that admits as much good light as possible.

Temperature Ordinary living-room temperatures are suitable as long as these do not fall below 65° F during spring and summer. A minimum of 55° F must be provided in winter. Avoid draughts at all times.

Humidity Maintain a steady level of humidity by standing the pots on trays of moist pebbles. Mist spray the foliage frequently in warm weather.

Watering and feeding From April to September keep the compost moist at all times. During the winter rest period give enough water to prevent it from drying out.

Regular feeding is essential for flower production. Every two weeks during the growing period give a dilute liquid fertiliser.

Propagation Increase during summer from 4 in cuttings of non-flowering side shoots. Root in peat and sand in a propagator kept at 65-70° F.

Disorders Scale insects and mealy bugs may cluster on the undersides of leaves and in the leaf axils. Bud drop is caused by insufficient water, fluctuating temperatures, draughts and poor light.

Streptocarpus hybrid

Streptocarpus
(Gesneriaceae)

The common name of these plants is Cape primrose which describes their natural habitat of South Africa and their large, wrinkled and coarse-textured, strap-shaped leaves.

In 1946 a hybrid, 'Constant Nymph', was introduced which had most of the good attributes of its ancestors and few of the faults. It proved to be an excellent house plant, flowering for most of the year. Since then many new cultivars, with an extended colour range, have been introduced, mainly from the John Innes Institute.

S. 'Constant Nymph' has wrinkled green leaves up to 12 in. Several flower stems, 8-10 in long, branch near the top and bear loose clusters of violet-blue flowers. They are five-lobed, 2 in across, with yellow to white throats and fine violet veining on the three lower segments.

The John Innes hybrids are similar to the 'Constant Nymph' and even more floriferous: 'Diana', deep cerise, white throat; 'Fiona', clear pink, wavy-edged; 'Karen', magenta-pink, with darker veining; and 'Louise', deep violet-blue, faint white stripes.

'Margaret', small but continuous, with purple-blue flowers; 'Marie', dusky purple, white throat; 'Paula', reddish-purple, darker veins, yellow throat; 'Tina', pale pink and bright magenta.

White-flowered cultivars are also available, such as 'Albatross', large-flowered, yellow eye; 'Maasen's White', a white mutant of 'Constant Nymph'; and 'Snow White', freesia-like, compact with continuous flowers.

Buying hints The John Innes cultivars are rarely available in florists' shops, but can be ordered as collections from specialist nurseries by mail order. They are by far the best types and comparatively inexpensive considering their long season of bloom.

General care Young plants can spend their first year in $3\frac{1}{2}$ in pots filled with equal parts of John Innes No. 2 and leaf-mould or coarse peat. Move overgrown plants in the spring of the second year into 5 in pots or half-pots.

Remove individual flowers as they fade, and the stalks to the base as flowering is finished.

Light Place in bright light, but shade from hot strong sun in summer. Artificial lighting at other times of the year extends the flowering season.

Temperature Ordinary room temperature is sufficient. Induce a short winter rest by keeping the plants at a steady 50° F from late November until February.

Humidity During the growing season from March to November stand the pots on trays of damp shingle.

Watering and feeding Water freely, but allow the compost to dry out slightly before the next application. At the rest period, keep the plants on the dry side. Feed fortnightly from March to September, alternating a standard liquid fertiliser with one high in potash.

Propagation Increase in spring or early summer by breaking up overcrowded clumps and repotting the younger sections. Alternatively, use leaf cuttings, cut crossways into 3 in wedge-shaped sections. Root at a temperature of 70° F.

Disorders Aphids may attack flower stalks and flowers.

119

INDOOR FLOWERING BULBS

Bulbs and corms grown as house plants fall into two categories. Most belong to the short-lived group and include hyacinths and daffodils, usually specially treated by professional bulb growers for indoor cultivation. Once they have flowered they can be planted in the garden, at once or in the autumn, or simply discarded.

The second – and smaller – group comprises bulbous plants of tropical origin, such as the popular hippeastrums or amaryllis. These can be flowered for several years running, but being perennial they need a cool and dry rest period.

Pots of hyacinths, daffodils and tulips are widely offered for sale at Christmas and early in the year. Most will show colouring flower buds which, disappointingly, sometimes fail to open in the home. The explanation is that these are hardy plants and react to the sudden change from low to high temperatures by drying up and ceasing further growth.

The successful cultivation of indoor bulbs, whether short or comparatively long-lived, depends on closely related, initial factors of light and temperature. Once rooted, inadequate light results in drawn, leafy plants with poor blooms. Too much warmth inhibits or curtails flowering. For detailed growing instructions of indoor bulbs, see pages 161-163.

To many people a bulb is a bulb, but botanically bulbous plants comprise the true bulbs, corms and tubers. Bulbs and corms contain storage organs, in a bulb composed of fleshy leaf bases, in a corm of a stem base. However, a bulb contains an embryo plant, unlike the corm which develops stems and roots from the small upper bud. Tubers are thickened fleshy roots from which leaf and flower stems rise. Their cultivation differs slightly from that of bulbs and corms. Tuberous house plants include caladiums, cyclamen and some begonias.

Propagation

Bulbs and corms reproduce from offsets, bulbs by forming bulbils at the sides of the parent bulb, corms by tiny cormlets at the base plate. The offsets can be removed and grown on, but will take several years to reach flowering size. Home propagation of bulbs grown for one indoor display only is hardly a practical proposition, and new bulbs are in any case inexpensive, healthy and of flowering size.

In addition, bulbs grown in fibre or pure water exhaust themselves in producing flowers and are unlikely ever to form offsets. Long-term bulbs such as the hippeastrums can, however, be successfully increased from bulbils which will flower after a few years.

Disorders

Given correct conditions of light and heat, few troubles affect indoor bulbs. In too warm and humid surroundings, aphids may cripple shoots and flower buds.

Crocus chrysanthus cultivar

Crocus
(Iridaceae)

Crocuses are popular and easily grown corms, particularly the early spring-flowering cultivars of *C. chrysanthus*. These have smaller blooms than the large-flowered Dutch types. Flowers grow directly from the top of the corm and reach a height of 3-4 in.

There are numerous, readily available cultivars, including the following: 'Blue Pearl', light blue; 'Cream Beauty', ivory-white with deep orange stigmas and brown petal bases; 'E.P. Bowles', bright yellow, brown at the base; 'Lady Killer', purple with broad white edges; 'Princess Beatrix', clear blue with gold bases and orange stigmas; 'Snowbunting', pure white with orange-yellow stigmas; and 'Zwanen-burg Bronze', deep yellow with bronze shading.

The large-flowered Dutch cultivars have goblet-shaped blooms, 4-5 in high. The striped, blue and white cultivars are generally the best for indoor culture, especially 'Flower Record', blue-violet; and 'Kathleen Parlow', pure white.

Other cultivars include 'Little Dorrit', silvery-blue; 'Paulus Potter', deep purple; 'Pickwick', pale lilac with deeper stripes; and 'Remembrance', purple-blue.

Buying hints Crocuses can sometimes be bought, from florists and garden centres, already potted and started into growth. They are generally inexpensive though those in special crocus pots, with several lipped planting holes round the sides, are slightly more expensive. Make sure the shoots are not too far advanced: ideally about 1 in of growth should be visible, with unblemished shoots.

When buying corms for planting make sure they are firm, dry and undamaged and not starting to grow. Most garden shops stock dry corms at cheap to inexpensive prices.

Buy the largest corms available. The Dutch cultivars are graded into sizes, and the best buys are corms with a $2\frac{3}{4}$-$3\frac{1}{2}$ in circumference. Each will produce three or more flowers.

General care Pot in September or October, using John Innes No. 1, a proprietary loam-less potting compost or bulb fibre. A standard crocus pot will take about eight corms round the sides and four at the top.

A 6 in bowl will accommodate about eight corms. Just cover the tops of the corms with compost or fibre.

After flowering, gradually cease watering until the foliage has died down, then dry off the corms and store them until autumn when they can be planted in the garden.

Light After potting, place the containers in total darkness, at a temperature of 43-48° F, until the shoots are $\frac{1}{2}$ in high. Move to subdued light indoors, in a cool room. Seven to ten days later, provide full light.

Temperature Do not try to force crocuses into flower too quickly. Keep them at 50° F until the colours begin to show. They can then be moved into a warmer room by day, but benefit from a cooler night temperature.

Watering and feeding Keep the compost moist at all times. Decorative containers with no drainage holes can be tilted after watering to drain off excess water.

Feeding is unnecessary, but one or two liquid feeds could be given after flowering to help build up the new corms for outdoor planting.

Gloriosa
(Liliaceae)

These tuberous-rooted, climbing lilies from tropical Africa are known as glory lilies after their handsome flowers. They bloom readily in the home if given adequate heat and humidity during the growing season and a complete winter rest in a warm place.

The stems, at least 4 ft tall, bear glossy, green and elliptic leaves equipped with tendrils by which the plants attach themselves to supports.

The lily-like flowers, with reflexed, wavy petals, are borne in summer through to early autumn.

G. rothschildiana, the most popular species, has 3-4 in, crimson flowers edged with pale yellow. They are favourites for florists' bouquets.

G. superba, which will grow to 6 ft tall, has deeply waved petals in deep orange and red.

Buying hints Less widely available than other bulbs, and consequently more expensive, gloriosas are worth seeking out from bulb specialists and good garden centres. The elongated tubers should feel firm to the touch and be wholly or partly enclosed in a brown tunic or skin.

Make sure that each tuber has a dark rounded bud at one end as only this will produce a shoot.

General care Pot the tubers in February or early March, setting one tuber in a 6-8 in pot, with plenty of crocks to ensure good drainage. John Innes No. 1 is a suitable compost; the tubers should be potted lengthways, with the buds just visible.

As growth progresses, train the stems up trellis or tall bamboo canes. After flowering, the stems gradually die back. Cut them out at soil level and store the pots, on their sides, for the winter rest.

In early spring repot the tubers in fresh compost, taking care not to damage the brittle roots.

Light Provide bright light from the time of potting and until growth has

Gloriosa rothschildiana

died down in autumn. Light is not necessary when the tubers are resting.

Temperature Maintain a steady temperature of 70° F throughout the growing period. During dormancy, store the tubers at 55-60° F.

Humidity During the growing season when high temperatures are essential, provide a moist atmosphere. Stand the pots on moist pebble trays and spray the foliage daily with water.

Watering and feeding After potting keep the compost barely moist until growth is under way. Thereafter ensure a permanently moist compost by watering whenever the surface shows signs of drying out.

After flowering, reduce watering, and when the stems have died down keep the tubers completely dry over winter. Feeding is not essential, but a dilute liquid fertiliser may be given at two-week intervals while the plants are in flower.

Propagation Remove offsets at the time of repotting. Potted up and grown on as mature plants, they may reach flowering size after a couple of years.

Hippeastrum cultivar

Hippeastrum
(*Amaryllidaceae*)

Bulbs of hippeastrum, popularly but incorrectly known as amaryllis, can be kept for many years and are easily flowered. They bloom naturally in spring or early summer, but specially prepared bulbs are sometimes available for Christmas and winter flowering. Most hippeastrums are of hybrid origin, with several 4 in or more, trumpet-shaped flowers on 18-24 in stems. The thick-textured, strap-shaped leaves grow 18-24 in long and appear after the flowers.

Named cultivars, some of which are available for early flowering, include 'Appleblossom', pale pink; 'Belinda', deep red; 'Excelsior', orange; 'Fiery Diamond', orange-red; 'Glorious Victory', salmon-orange; 'Hecuba', salmon; 'Minerva', red and white; 'Mont Blanc', white with green throat; 'Parsifal', orange-scarlet; 'Picotee', white with red edges to the petals; and 'Rembrandt', dark red.

Buying hints Purchase firm and large bulbs, 3-3½ in in circumference, from garden centres, horticultural shops and specialist bulb merchants. Generally available from November onwards, hippeastrums can sometimes be bought as flowering pot plants.

General care Pot untreated and prepared bulbs soon after purchase in autumn. Set one bulb in a well crocked 6 in pot with John Innes No. 2, leaving the top half of the bulb uncovered. Keep the bulbs at a temperature of 60° F, and begin watering only when growth is obvious.

After flowers and leaves have withered, store the pots, on their sides, in a dry, frost-free place for about three months. Restart into growth in February, replacing the top 1 or 2 in with fresh compost. Repot only every three or four years as hippeastrums resent disturbance of the roots.

Light Place hippeastrums in the brightest position available, from the time growth begins and until it ceases.

Temperature During the growing period maintain a temperature not rising above 60° F. Prepared bulbs for Christmas flowering need 70° F; they will revert to the normal flowering season in subsequent years.

Watering and feeding Start watering when growth begins and increase this gradually as the plants develop, to keep the compost just moist. After flowering, when the leaves have developed, feed the plants fortnightly with a liquid fertiliser and place them in a sunny spot to build up the bulbs.

In autumn, when the leaves turn yellow, reduce watering and cease this altogether when the foliage has died.

Propagation Increase, at the time of repotting, from the bulbils attached to the parent plant. Pot these singly in 3 in pots of compost and treat as mature bulbs. Pot them on progressively.

Hyacinthus
(Liliaceae)

Hyacinthus 'Blue Haze'

Undoubtedly the most popular indoor bulbs, hyacinths are easy to grow, even in pure water. Many cultivars, raised by Dutch breeders, are prepared for early forcing to flower at Christmas and early in the year. Untreated bulbs flower later, the timing depending on the cultivar.

Hyacinths prepared for early flowering have large, tight spikes of very fragrant, long-lasting blooms, generally one spike to a bulb. Popular cultivars include, 'Blue Haze', pale blue; 'Delft Blue', bright blue; 'Jan Bos', red; 'King of the Blues', indigo-blue.

'Lady Derby', pale mauve-pink; 'L'Innocence', white; 'Myosotis', sky-blue; 'Ostara', dark blue; 'Pink Pearl', deep pink; 'Princess Margaret', pale pink; 'Salmonetta', apricot-salmon; and 'Yellow Hammer', creamy-yellow.

The Roman hyacinths, *H. orientalis*, are early-flowering, with fragrant white, pink or blue flowers from November to January. There are generally several spikes to each bulb with looser florets than in the large-flowered Dutch cultivars.

Buying hints Bulbs can be bought from most garden centres and shops, and bulb specialists list a wide range of cultivars. Choose large-flowered prepared bulbs $6\frac{1}{2}$-$6\frac{3}{4}$ in in circumference and $4\frac{3}{4}$-$5\frac{1}{2}$ in Roman hyacinths. Unprepared bulbs of top-size hyacinths, the so-called exhibition hyacinths, are 7-$7\frac{1}{2}$ in in circumference.

All bulbs should feel firm and heavy for their size, and be dry, undamaged and dormant. Hyacinths can also be bought potted and started into growth, with flower buds developing.

General care Plant bulbs in September, using a loam-less compost or bulb fibre. Set three large or two exhibition bulbs to a 6 in bowl and leave the top third of the bulbs uncovered. Plant only one cultivar in each bowl to ensure all will flower simultaneously.

Support the developing flower spikes with thin canes. After flowering plant the bulbs in the garden.

Single bulbs are often grown in hyacinth glasses, filled with water to just below the constricted necks. The bulb fits snugly in the neck, and roots grow down into the water.

Light Provide total darkness and a temperature of 43-48° F until the shoots are 2 in high, after five to eight weeks. Move into subdued light for seven to ten days, then to full light.

Temperature When the bulbs have rooted and shoots are growing, keep them at 50° F. When the flower buds are well formed and clear of the bulb necks, move to a temperature of 60° F. After flowering, return the bulbs to cool or unheated quarters.

Watering and feeding Keep the compost or fibre moist at all times, but avoid waterlogging. After flowering, continue watering until the leaves have died down. The water level in glasses should be kept just below the bulbs.

Bulbs intended for planting out in the garden later may be given one or two liquid feeds after flowering.

Lilium
(Liliaceae)

A few lilies are suited to indoor pot culture although they need large pots and plenty of space. Occasionally treated bulbs for flowering in February and March can be found, headed more often than not by the attractive cultivar 'Enchantment', with beautiful orange-red flowers on erect 3 ft stems.

Other early-flowering cultivars include 'Harmony' (3 ft), wide-petalled, rich orange flowers spotted with dark brown; 'Paprika' (2-$2\frac{1}{2}$ ft), crimson; and 'Prosperity' (3 ft), pale yellow.

Untreated bulbs, which flower in summer, include *L. auratum*, with white and fragrant, trumpet-shaped flowers, as much as 12 in long, spotted and banded with gold. As a pot plant it grows 4 ft high.

123

Lilium auratum cultivar

The Easter lily, *L. longiflorum*, has trumpet-shaped, white, fragrant flowers, about 6 in long, on 3 ft stems. Particularly outstanding are the cultivars 'White Queen', with pure white blooms, and 'Mount Everest', with even larger, waxy-white blooms on straight 6 ft tall stems.

The popular *L. regale* attains a height of 3 ft and bears 5 in, trumpet-shaped flowers of white suffused with gold, purplish on the outside.

Buying hints Lilies are chiefly offered by garden centres and bulb merchants, in the medium to expensive price range. The bulbs are delicate as they have no outer tunics to protect them. They are often supplied in polythene bags and packed in moist peat. Make sure the fleshy roots have not shrivelled or show signs of mildew, other suspicious patches or rotting. The scales should be succulent and plump.

General care It is essential to plant lilies as soon as possible after purchase or delivery in autumn. A 6 in pot will hold only one bulb; an 8 in pot will take two, and a 9 in pot will accommodate three bulbs. A well-drained compost is vital. Use John Innes No. 2, adding an extra third part of leaf-mould or coarse peat. Place a layer of crocks in each pot for good drainage.

Fill each pot two-thirds with compost, setting the bulbs so that the tips are just below the surface. When the stems are about 8 in tall, fill with more compost to leave a 1 in space below the rim for watering. Bulbs can be started into growth in an outdoor cold frame and taken indoors when 3 in high.

Pot lilies kept for a second year should be repotted in fresh compost at the beginning of the dormant season.

Light Provide bright, but filtered light at all times. Where this is not possible, augment daylight with artificial light from fluorescent tubes during the growing period.

Temperature Pot lilies will not tolerate temperatures above 50° F at any stage of growth. Prepared bulbs, however, need 68° F if they are to flower in early spring.

Watering and feeding Keep the compost moist, but never wet, throughout the growing season. When flower buds are visible, apply a standard liquid fertiliser every two weeks. As the leaves turn yellow in autumn, cease feeding, reduce watering and let the compost dry out slightly before the next application.

Once the stems have died down completely, the bulbs are best planted out in the garden as flowering is seldom successful in subsequent years.

Narcissus
(Amaryllidaceae)

Narcissus 'Craigford'

Narcissi or daffodils are among the most easily grown bulbs, and several are well suited to indoor culture in bowls, pots or shallow dishes of pebbles and water, where they will flower long before the garden types.

A number of popular cultivars are specially prepared for forced flowering early in the year. Among the best are 'Golden Harvest', a golden-yellow trumpet type; 'Jack Snipe', a dwarf hybrid with white reflexed petals and an orange-yellow cup; and 'Peeping Tom', also reflexed, but golden-yellow and with a long trumpet.

'Texas' has cream, yellow and orange double flowers. The bunch-flowered tazetta and poetaz cultivars are ideal for indoor cultivation, particularly the fragrant, deep yellow 'Grand Soleil d'Or', with an orange cup; and the popular white-flowered, orange-cupped 'Craigford'.

Buying hints Daffodils are often sold according to size and number of growing points per bulb. The best buys for indoor flowering, at inexpensive to medium prices, are the socalled mother bulbs, each with two or three growing points which will generally produce up to six blooms. Bulbs with two growing points are cheaper and equally good.

All bulbs should feel firm and dry and be free of cuts, dents, bruises and mould. Avoid any with soft patches or showing signs of premature sprouting.

General care Pot in September or early October, using bulb fibre or a loam-less potting compost, and setting the bulbs so that the tips just show above the compost level. A 6 in bowl will take two bulbs, an 8 in bowl, three; a 10 in bowl, five bulbs; and a 12 in container, six bulbs.

Daffodils may also be planted in two layers in a deep and large, well-crocked pot for a mass of flowers. Set the upper bulbs in the spaces between the lower ones, separated by a thin layer of compost or fibre.

After flowering, narcissi are best planted out in the garden as they are not successfully forced a second time. Most Tazetta cultivars, however, are not generally hardy and are usually discarded after flowering.

Light Start potted bulbs into growth in a dark place at a temperature below 48° F. When the shoots are 1-1½ in high, move them to subdued light and about a week later to full light.

Temperature After the initial rooting process, a temperature of 50° F is needed for steady growth. When the flower buds are well formed, raise this to 60° F. After flowering move the plants back to cool conditions until the foliage has withered.

Watering and feeding Keep the fibre or compost moist at all times, but not saturated. Take care to tip out excess water from decorative bowls without drainage holes.

After flowering a liquid fertiliser may be applied once or twice to bulbs that will be kept for outdoor displays.

Tulipa
(Liliaceae)

While tulips are less popular than daffodils as indoor plants, they are just as easy to grow if the choice remains with the early-flowering types. In addition to these, specialist bulb breeders offer cultivars prepared for flowering around Christmas.

The most popular indoor tulips include the scarlet 'Brilliant Star', carmine 'Christmas Marvel', the yellow 'Marshal Joffre', and the pink 'Princess Margaret', all single. 'Scarlet Cardinal' is double-flowered.

Buying hints Tulips are readily available from garden shops and centres, at inexpensive prices. They are often sold according to circumference, the best buys for forcing being 4½-5½ in. Choose firm and dry bulbs, but do not necessarily reject those which have lost their brown outer skins; these easily rub off during lifting and marketing. However, avoid bulbs with sunken or damaged areas.

General care Pot the bulbs as soon as possible, before mid-September for flowering by Christmas. Bulb fibre and loam-less compost are equally suitable. A 6 in bowl will comfortably hold five, and a 12 in bowl, 12 bulbs. Leave the tips of the bulbs exposed above compost level.

After flowering, let the top growth die down naturally, then take up the bulbs, dry them off and store in a cool place until autumn when they can be planted out in the garden. They cannot be forced a second time.

Light As with narcissi, keep the bulbs in darkness, below 48° F for several weeks to initiate the growth process. When the flower buds are clear of the bulbs, move the pots into subdued light for about a week, then provide full daylight.

Temperature When the plants are exposed to full light, they need a temperature of 68° F for early blooms. After flowering return the bulbs to cool conditions if they are to be saved for outdoor planting.

Watering Keep the fibre or compost evenly moist throughout the growing period, from potting time until the leaves have died down, or until the plants are discarded.

Tulipa 'Christmas Marvel'

ORCHIDS

The family *Orchidaceae* is thought to be the largest family of plants, containing more than 20,000 different species distributed throughout the world, and probably many yet to be found. Orchids have been sought by botanists and other plant hunters over the centuries. Where nature has failed to yield new and exciting plants, professional breeders have crossed and re-crossed known species and genera to produce what are known as bi-, tri- and quadrigeneric hybrids. Man-made hybrids now outnumber known species at the rate of 3:1.

An aura of mystery and awe surrounds the cultivation of the exotic orchids, and while it is true that they largely need controlled greenhouse culture, a number of the less demanding types can be successfully grown in the home.

In broad terms all orchids, whether naturally occurring or of hybrid origin, fall into two categories: the epiphytes and the terrestrials. Epiphytic orchids, which form the larger group, are native to the Tropics where they grow on trees and shrubs, taking support only from their hosts.

Terrestrial orchids are mainly confined to temperate regions though some are native to the Tropics. In the British Isles about 50 species of orchids grow wild.

The make up of an orchid is unique in the plant world and differs to some extent between epiphytic and terrestrial types. Terrestrial orchids, such as paphiopedilums, grow from clumps of fleshy underground roots, while epiphytes develop from rhizomes at or just below soil level. From the rhizome grow one – or more often – several stems, known as pseudobulbs from the swollen bulb-like bases.

The pseudobulbs produce the leaves, which vary greatly in shape, size, texture, colour and arrangement, from strap-shaped to oblong, papery to leathery, light green to blue-grey, and from singles and pairs to large fans.

The construction of the orchid flower is unlike that of any other. It consists in every case of three sepals and three petals surrounding the reproductive organs, collectively called the column. Male and female organs are found together, unlike other plants which usually have separate sexual organs. At the top of the column is the male pollen and below that the female ovary from which the seed pod eventually develops.

Petals and sepals are generally symmetrically arranged; petals tend to be larger than the sepals, and the third and lower petal is often the largest. It is transformed into a spectacular lip, often spurred, pouched or frilled, and usually in a different colour to the other petals.

The flowers, which are sometimes sweetly fragrant, in other cases scentless, may be borne singly or in groups on the flower stalks, and can be of erect or pendulous habit. They are long-lasting, for several weeks or even months on the plants, and almost as long as cut blooms.

Buying hints

Orchids are best bought from specialist nurseries, when they are in or just about to flower. They are comparatively expensive, but the blooms last for several months at a time. The seemingly high cost is due to the fact that orchids have been nursed under controlled laboratory conditions for anything from 5 to 15 years before they are offered for sale as flowering plants.

The best buys are named hybrids of proven origin. Species orchids are the most expensive, but seedlings are in a cheaper price range. These can be expected to perform well if purchased from reputable orchid nurseries.

General care

The cultivation of orchids is related to their natural habitats. Most popular orchids are epiphytic and need different treatment to the terrestrial types, though the prerequisite for both is adequate humidity and an open soil mixture.

The growing compost must essentially be free-draining. Orchid nurseries usually supply the correct mixture suitable for the plants. Epiphytic orchids are grown in a compost made up of equal parts of ground bark, of varying degrees of coarseness, peat, sphagnum moss and vermiculite. Osmunda fibre, from the osmunda fern, mixed with sphagnum moss was for long the preferred growing medium, but it is expensive and difficult to obtain. Most commercial orchid composts have dried fir bark as a substitute for osmunda fibre, and sometimes shredded plastic waste.

Terrestrial orchids can be grown in a similar bark-based compost. Some do better in a more loamy compost, such as equal parts of fine bark, loam, sand, sphagnum moss, and leaf-mould or moss peat. All components must be sterile.

Pots and containers

Terrestrial orchids can be grown in conventional clay or plastic pots. These may also be used for the epiphytes, though special containers are better. These are available from orchid nurseries and some garden centres and come as perforated clay pots, slatted wooden baskets or wire baskets.

Many epiphytic orchids are also ideal for growing on slabs of bark, tree fern or osmunda fibre. The roots are wrapped in moist sphagnum moss and wired to the bark slab with thin copper wire or nylon fishing line.

Repotting
Potting on and repotting become necessary when the orchids outgrow their containers, after flowering or at the beginning of the growing season. Young plants will probably need to be potted on every year, but mature plants should only need to be repotted or potted on every other year.

Knock the plant from its container, and tease away the old exhausted compost until the roots are exposed. Trim off dead and damaged roots with a sharp sterilised knife and pack fresh compost round the feeding roots.

Set the oldest part of the rhizome towards the back of the pot, with the crown level with the pot rim, and the new growth towards the middle. Build the compost up in a small mound around the plant.

Do not water newly potted plants for the first two weeks, but mist spray the foliage. For the next fortnight give only moderate amounts of water, until new top growth makes it obvious that the roots are re-established.

Growing and rest periods
Some orchids, like cattleyas and odontoglossums, may grow throughout the year, though they slow down in autumn and winter. Others, such as laelias, have a resting phase when they need less water, warmth and humidity.

Tall-growing orchids will need the support of canes pushed into the pots. Fragile flower stems with several blooms may also need to be tied to canes. Remove individual flowers as they fade, and the flower stem at the base when all flowers have finished.

Keep the foliage clean and free from dust by sponging the leaves frequently on both sides.

Light
Epiphytic orchids grow naturally in diffused sunlight. In the home they can be placed in bright light if this is filtered by a net curtain or blinds during the hottest part of summer days. Window sills facing east or west are the ideal positions for here the plants will receive 3-4 hours of filtered sun a day.

In winter, epiphytic orchids should be moved closer to good light. Flower bud initiation is most successful where the plants receive not less than 10 and not more than 12 hours of light a day; ideally supplement existing daylight with artificial light.

Terrestrial orchids, as well as the epiphytic miltonias, need filtered light at all times of the year. Never expose them to direct sun.

Temperature
The amount of heat required by orchids is related to their origins. The temperature ranges are usually defined as warm, intermediate and cool and refer to night temperatures. Day temperatures should be 10-15° F higher.

Warm:
   65° F (winter); 75° F (summer)
Intermediate:
   55° F (winter); 65° F (summer)
Cool:
   45° F (winter); 55° F (summer)
Orchids that require warm temperatures include some brassavolas, cattleyas, laelias and some paphiopedilums. Intermediate temperatures are suitable for some cymbidiums, miltonias and paphiopedilums.

Cool temperatures are adequate for most odontoglossums, and for some types of cymbidium, miltonia and paphiopedilum.

Humidity
All orchids, whether epiphytic or terrestrial, need a high degree of air moisture and only slightly lower in the rest period.

Supply the essential humidity by standing the pots on trays of pebbles or peat kept permanently moist. In addition, mist spray the foliage once a day during the growing season, more frequently for orchids grown at warm temperatures and for those on bark slabs and hanging containers.

Watering and feeding
Overwatering is a common mistake, and again the needs vary from epiphytic to terrestrial types.

During the growing season, give epiphytic orchids a thorough watering whenever the compost begins to dry out. From November to March, when some orchids are resting, water sparingly, enough to prevent the compost and pseudobulbs from drying out.

Terrestrial orchids should be watered more freely while in growth; keep the compost moist at all times, and do not wait for it to dry out. In the rest period, reduce watering as for epiphytic orchids.

Plants grown on bark and in hanging baskets are easiest watered by immersing them, complete with bark or container, in a bucket of tepid water for about 5 minutes. Do this twice a week in spring and summer, once every 10 days for the rest of the year or whenever the moss or compost feels dry to the touch. Drain thoroughly before returning plants to their positions.

Feeding is essential for all orchids in a peat or bark-based compost. Fertilisers, for use during the growing season, are specially formulated for (1) young plants, (2) adult plants, and (3) plants approaching flowering. These feeds are sold by orchid nurseries, with full instructions. Occasional foliar feeds are also beneficial.

Propagation

Division of the rhizomes is the most suitable method for home propagation. This is best carried out at the time of potting-on or repotting. Cut well established plants clean through the rhizome so that each division contains two or three healthy pseudobulbs.

Pot the divisions separately in the usual growing medium. Water sparingly and keep the divisions slightly warmer than previously until new growth is obvious.

Disorders

Given good cultural conditions, orchids are surprisingly free from pest and disease attacks. Aphids, mealy bugs, red spider mites and scale insects may sometimes cluster on the undersides of leaves. A weekly sponging of the foliage should prevent colonies forming.

Certain virus diseases may infect the foliage, usually causing yellow to brown pits, mottling or streaks. Virus diseases cannot be cured, and the plants must be burnt.

Hybrids and species

The following orchid species are a small selection from several genera that can be grown in the home. Named hybrids are often more readily available; they have the same growing needs as the species.

In addition to those described, species and hybrids of *Brassia*, *Lycaste*, *Oncidium* and, marginally, *Dendrobium* usually succeed. Recently hybrids of the moth orchid, *Phalaenopsis*, have grown in popularity as window-sill plants.

× *Brassolaeliocattleya* hybrid

× *Brassocattleya* hybrid

Brassavola

This is an epiphytic genus from the West Indies, Mexico and Brazil, needing slightly more than warm temperatures and plenty of water during the growing season. Best mounted on bark slabs or grown in hanging baskets.

This genus has been crossed with *Cattleya* to produce the hybrid race × *Brassocattleya*, and with *Laelia* and *Cattleya* to give yet another attractive orchid race, the easy-grown × *Brassolaeliocattleya*.

B. digbyana grows compactly to 6 in high, each pseudobulb carrying but a single leaf covered with a persistent white bloom. The 6 in wide, pale green flowers are produced singly during spring and summer. They have a heady fragrance at night, and are outstanding for their large, creamy-white, purple-tinged and frilled lips.

B. nodosa has stem-like, often pendent pseudobulbs, each with a single, 12 in long cylindrical leaf. Up to six blooms, 4 in across, are borne in a 6 in spike at any time of year. They pale from light green through yellow to pure white and release their scent at night.

Cattleya

This large and popular epiphytic genus is distributed throughout Central and South America. It is allied to and interbreeds freely with such genera as *Brassavola*, *Epidendrum*, *Laelia* and *Sophronitis*, and has been used in the raising of thousands of hybrids.

Cattleyas are divided into two groups: the labiate species and hybrids with a single leaf from each pseudobulb, and the bifoliate group with a pair of leaves.

Outstanding labiate cattleyas, suitable as house plants, include *C. maxima*, with club-shaped stems 12-18 in long. The flower spikes which appear in autumn and winter, bear up to ten bright rose flowers, the lip marked with dark crimson veins.

C. mossiae, up to 12 in, is extremely free-flowering, in early summer. The 8 in blooms, in spikes of four or five, vary from deep blush to pale pink, crimson, purple and white according to variety. These two species need intermediate temperatures.

The bifoliate division includes the dwarf, 6 in high *C. aclandiae*. This bears flowers in pairs or singly, $4\frac{1}{2}$ in wide, olive-green and blotched with purple; the lip is magenta-purple. It flowers in summer and autumn as does *C. aurantiaca*, with five to ten, $1\frac{1}{2}$ in wide orange blooms. Both are best grown in rafts or baskets, close to good light, in warm temperatures.

C. bicolor has $1\frac{1}{2}$-2 ft slender stems and bears one to ten flowers with pale

Cymbidium 'Balkis' hybrid

Miltonia 'Red Knight'

Miltonia hybrid

green, copper-tinged petals and sepals. The flowering season is autumn onwards. This species needs intermediate temperatures.

C. loddigesii, 12 in, flowers in late summer, with long-lasting, fragrant blooms. Each spike has four or more waxy flowers, $4\frac{1}{2}$ in across, and white to blush pink. Grow at intermediate to warm temperature, in bright light.

Cymbidium

Terrestrial and epiphytic species are found in this genus from the Far East and Australia. Cymbidiums for home cultivation are all epiphytic and need cool to intermediate temperatures.

Most species grow too large for average rooms, but a number of excellent miniatures have been bred from dwarf species.

C. devonianum, which blooms in the spring, bears a pendent spike with several, $1-1\frac{1}{2}$ in blooms, usually olive-green spotted with crimson, and a purple-crimson lip.

C. pumilum is tiny, with 1 in high pseudobulbs and erect flower spikes, carrying numerous $1\frac{1}{2}$ in flowers. They are borne in August and September and are reddish-brown with yellow edges and white lips.

Numerous hybrids have been raised between the miniature and standard cymbidiums, including 'Brook Street', large, mauve-red flowers, late spring; 'Miss Muffet', a compact cross between the two species, yellow and green flowers in autumn and winter; 'Nonina', bright green, 2 in wide, autumn; and 'Tom Thumb', bronze-red, autumn and winter.

Laelia

This epiphytic genus from Mexico, Central America and Brazil is related to *Cattleya,* and the two hybridise readily. *L. anceps* bears a single leaf at the top of the 2-3 in pseudobulb, and a 2-4 ft flower spike with up to five blooms, 4 in wide. The rose-coloured flowers appear in December and January. Grow at intermediate to warm temperatures.

L. pumila is similar, but has a short 8 in flower spike with a single, rose-coloured bloom, mottled with purple, and a white throat. Flowering is in autumn, and temperatures can be cool to intermediate.

L. purpurata is called the King of Orchids and is the national flower of Brazil. It grows 2 ft high, each pseudobulb producing one thick and leathery leaf. The flower spike, in spring and early summer, carries up to seven flowers, 8 in across, in a wide range of colours.

A large number of hybrids have been bred from this and related genera.

Miltonia

All epiphytes, the species in this genus, popularly known as pansy orchids, fall into two groups: those from Colombia with blue-green leaves, and those from Brazil with yellow-green leaves. Intermediate temperatures.

M. roezlii, a Colombian species, has blue-green, 12 in long leaves and a slightly shorter flower spike with up to five, 4 in wide blooms. Appearing in autumn, the flowers are pure white, with purple blotches on the petals and an orange-yellow disc on the lip.

M. spectabilis, a Brazilian, yellow-leaved species, bears a single, 3 in wide flower at the top of a 12 in stem. Flowering in summer, the long-lasting blooms are creamy-white tinged with rose; the large lip is burgundy-red with heavy veining.

Odontoglossum hybrid

Paphiopedilum hybrid

Paphiopedilum hybrid

M. vexillaria is probably the most striking of the Colombian species. The flower spikes, up to 20 in, carry in spring and early summer five or more flowers, almost 4 in wide and of a uniform pale rose colour.

Hybrids flowering in late spring and early summer include 'Knight Errant', deep red, crimson mask to the lip; 'Piccadilly', light to deep red: and 'Red Knight', pale to deep rose, darker at the base of the lip.

Odontoglossum

One of the largest orchid genera, *Odontoglossum* is found throughout Central and South America. They are high-altitude plants, needing cooler conditions than can be achieved in the average home. There are, however, a large number of natural varieties and even more man-made hybrids which will grow at cool, intermediate or warm temperatures.

Intergeneric hybrids bred from this genus and *Cochlioda*, *Miltonia* and *Oncidium* will probably become popular house plants in the future.

O. grande is the largest and most striking species and ideal for growing as a house plant. Each 4 in pseudobulb, with one to three leaves, produces a 12 in spike of four to eight flowers, each as much as 7 in wide. They appear from late autumn to spring, and both sepals and the broader petals are bright yellow and cinnamon-brown; the lip is white or pale yellow.

Paphiopedilum

These orchids differ in appearance and structure from other genera. Distributed throughout the Far East and mainly growing in the foothills of the Himalayas, these terrestrial or soil-dwelling orchids grow from rhizomes, without pseudobulbs. The leaves are held in tufts and are often mottled with purple or maroon.

A single flower rises on an erect stem from the centre of the leaves and is distinguished by a large dorsal sepal, two narrow petals and a prominent, shoe-shaped lip from which the plants take the name of slipper orchids.

The following paphiopedilums are easily obtained, at reasonable prices, and suitable as house plans given cool or intermediate temperatures, light shade and a moist compost.

P. bellatulum is a dwarf species and remarkable for its 3 in flowers which grow low down among the mottled foliage. They are yellow, with purple spots and a large, egg-shaped lip. Flowering is in spring.

P. callosum is outstanding for its flowers in which the dorsal, heart-shaped sepals are fluted and 3 in wide. They are pure white with impressive green to purple vertical veins; the green petals are tinted pale rose-purple. It flowers in winter and spring.

P. fairieanum, which flowers in summer and autumn, is one of the best for house culture. The single flower on a 5-6 in stem, has a white dorsal sepal veined with purple and stained yellow-green at the base. The narrow petals are curved like buffalo's horns.

P. spicerianum is spring-flowering, with purple-spotted leaves and 3 in wide flowers. The dorsal sepals are white with crimson-purple bands, and the petals are yellow-green and red-spotted with wavy edges. The lips are brown and crimson.

P. villosum is taller than the other species, to $1\frac{1}{2}$ ft, with a tall hairy flower spike carrying one glossy bloom, 5-6 in across. This has a green, brown and white, hairy dorsal sepal, yellow and brown-purple petals and lip.

The range of hybrids is wide, with flowers in any imaginable colour except blue. They are generally larger than the species. Most are autumn to spring flowering. The large, white-flowered hybrids of Miller's Daughter are extremely popular.

CACTI AND OTHER SUCCULENTS

All succulent plants arouse interest, sometimes admiration and sometimes genuine dislike. This no doubt stems from their curious appearance which, compared to ordinary garden plants, seems all wrong. Yet in spite of their exotic, often bizarre look, most succulents are not difficult to grow, and thousands of species can be obtained.

The term succulent is used for any plant which stores water in its tissues above ground. In cacti the stems are the water reservoirs, while in most other succulents it is the leaves which have adapted. This adaptation is one of nature's marvels and a testimony to the plants' durability in face of the long dry spells they experience in their natural semi-desert habitats.

True cacti, with only one or two exceptions, are native to the Americas. Typically, the stems are the swollen, water-holding parts, leaves being almost or completely non-existent. The stems themselves are usually reduced to globular or cylindrical shapes which expose the smallest surface area possible, and consequently suffer less loss of water from evaporation. The exceptions are the few genera of epiphytic cacti from the tropical rain forests.

One feature is unique to the true cacti: all members of the *Cactaceae* family have areoles. These are the equivalent in other plants of short side branches, but are reduced to no more than a tiny swelling of tissue. They usually carry two minute buds, one of which is an incipient flower bud, the other carrying spines or hairs.

In the prickly pear and its allies (*Opuntia* species), the areoles have sharply barbed tips known as glochids. Many cactus species bear large, colourful flowers, and most will bloom regularly.

The majority of succulent plants from other families have fleshy leaves, though a few notable exceptions, such as *Euphorbia obesa*, have swollen stems. Few bear spines, and many belong to genera with non-succulent members.

Most succulents, including cacti, have practically identical growing needs, determined by their original habitats. In the plant descriptions, which start on page 132, cultural advice is referred to the following general instructions, for desert and forest species.

DESERT SPECIES
General care
A free draining compost is essential, and a loam-based one is easier to handle than one based on peat. Add about one third by bulk of fine grit or coarse sand. Plastic and clay pots are equally suitable and can be set inside decorative waterproof containers.

Pot on or repot as for other house plants, usually in spring. Handle spiny stems and plant bodies with a sling of rolled newspaper.

Like other indoor plants, succulents collect dust. Clean smooth-stemmed species with a moist pad of cotton wool, spiny types by syringing gently.

Light
Plenty of light and direct sun is required throughout the year and particularly in winter. For cacti, a window shelf is essential; a south exposure is the ideal position. Give the pots a quarter turn at regular intervals so that all plants receive an equal amount of light and sun.

Temperature
During the growing season, from spring until autumn, most succulents thrive in full sun and as high a temperature as is likely to occur.

They do, however, need a definite resting period in winter. From October to March they are best kept in a room with a temperature not normally above 50° F; they will survive at 37° F for long spells.

Humidity
Extra humidity is not necessary.

Watering and feeding
In the growth period and particularly while flowering, succulents need plenty of water. In late March or April bring them back into a warm room and water thoroughly, preferably by soaking. After this, let the compost become just dry before watering again.

In September or October reduce the frequencies of watering and by early November, move the plants to a cool room. In a warm room they may show signs of shrivelling. If this happens, soak the pots once, then let them dry out again. Some natural shrinkage occurs during the rest period as stored water is used up.

Apply dilute liquid feed every two to three weeks during the growing period. Choose a fertiliser high in potassium.

FOREST SPECIES
General care
Identical to desert species, but best in a peat-based compost mixed with one third part of fine grit or coarse sand.

Light
Subdued or filtered light is required; from spring to autumn, keep the plants away from direct sun which will scorch the leaves. In winter, move close to good light.

Temperature
Normal room temperatures of 65-74° F are suitable throughout sum-

mer and until flowering is over. For the winter rest period, keep them between 45 and 50° F.

Humidity
Being forest plants they prefer extra humidity in dry rooms. Stand the pots on moist pebble trays or mist spray frequently.

Watering and feeding
Allow the compost to become almost dry before watering, throughout the year. Water will be needed less often if the plants are kept cool at the rest period.

Apply a dilute liquid feed every two or three weeks while the plants are growing.

Buying hints
Garden centres, and to a lesser extent supermarkets, offer the more common succulents. Best buys are often plants from local nurseries where size, quality and price compare favourably with those at supermarkets.

Succulents of particular interest are best obtained from specialist nurserymen who have a wider selection at cheaper prices.

Propagation
Desert and forest succulents, including cacti, are increased from stem or leaf cuttings, division, seeds and grafting. Cutting and division are the most practical for home propagation.

Newly potted divisions should be kept on the dry side for a week or two, then watered sparingly until new growth starts. Taking cuttings needs some courage, not just because of the spines but in selecting the right material. It is easy enough to sever complete pads of *Opuntia* or the leaf-like sections of *Epiphyllum*, more daunting to behead a treasured *Echinopsis*. However, a cut surface soon heals and produces one or several shoots which can be taken as cuttings.

It is important that fleshy cuttings are left to dry for several days before being inserted in the rooting medium. This ensures that the raw wet surface of the cut does not come into contact with moist soil which may cause rotting.

Disorders
With proper care, succulents are generally trouble-free. Mealy bugs and root mealy bugs occasionally occur, but rotting is the most commonly encountered problem.

Rot may set in where a stem or pad has been damaged and will quickly spread unless the bruised section is cut right back to clean healthy tissue.

Rotting at the base and the roots, is due to overwatering.

Agave americana 'Medio-picta'

Agave
(Agavaceae)

A large genus of slow-growing succulents from the warmer part of America, with rosettes of sword-shaped leaves, often toothed and striped. In the wild, mature plants bear flowers, but these are not produced on pot-grown plants. *A. americana* (century plant) is the most commonly grown species. The narrow, grey-green leaves are edged and tipped with spines and may grow 5 ft long under ideal conditions. As pot plants, they rarely exceed 12 in.

Several cultivars are available, including 'Marginata', with bold leaf margins of creamy-yellow; and 'Medio-picta', with yellow stripes. *A. filifera* is smaller, with 10 in long, stiff leaves edged with white, thread-like fibres.

Buying hints Agaves are available from florists and garden centres; 3-4 in plants in 3-3½ in pots are cheap to inexpensive. Larger specimens, above 10 in, are very expensive.
Cultivation As desert species. Keep almost dry in winter.

Aloe
(Liliaceae)

These easy, slow-growing succulents vary from small, stemless rosettes to large, tree-like plants. They are native to arid and semi-desert regions of Africa and have tough, narrow leaves often with spiny or horny edges. They flower readily, with red, yellow or orange spikes resembling those of red hot pokers.

Unlike the similar, but unrelated agaves, the rosettes do not die after flowering. The plants spread by offsets and can also be grown from seeds. A number of species are sometimes offered by specialist growers, but the two described are the most popular.

A. aristata is called lace aloe from the

Aloe aristata

thread-like bristles at the tips of the leaves. It is a stemless plant, eventually forming clumps of dense rosettes. The leaves are about 4 in long, tapering to a point, mid to dark green and white-edged and covered with white, wart-like spines or tubercles. Orange-red, 1½ in long flowers are carried in loose spikes, 20 in tall, in summer.

A. variegata (partridge-breasted aloe) is the most widely grown species. It grows to a height of 8 in or more, in an elongated rosette. The closely over-lapping leaves are 2-5 in long, narrowly triangular and spreading at the tips. They are dark green, with pale horny margins and a contrasting pattern of white bars and spots.

Flower spikes, 10 in high, appear from the top of the plant in spring, bearing nodding, pink to dull scarlet flowers, 1½ in long. It often flowers when only 4 in high and reproduces readily from basal offsets.

Buying hints Purchase these plants, like most other succulents, in late spring or early summer rather than in the winter rest period. Obtainable from florists and garden centres, aloes are usually offered as quite small plants in 2-3½ in pots; they are generally in the inexpensive range.

Cultivation As desert species. Shade from strong sun in summer and water sparingly in winter.

Aporocactus mallisonii

Aporocactus
(Cactaceae)

A small genus of epiphytic cacti from Mexico where they trail from tree branches and rocks. The long stems are shallowly ribbed along their entire length and have numerous spine-bearing areoles and aerial roots.

A. flagelliformis (rat's tail cactus) is easy and rapid-growing. The slender, branched stems eventually reach a length of 3-6 ft, and it makes a striking plant for a hanging basket or perched on a pedestal. Each stem has 10-14 ribs edged with numerous tiny areoles and equally small, white spines. The crim-

son, trumpet-shaped flowers, 3½ in long, appear in profusion on older stems in spring and summer.

A hybrid of this species and an unspecified *Heliocereus* is sometimes listed as *A. mallisonii*. It resembles the rat's tail cactus, but is of more robust and stiffer growth, with larger, bright orange flowers.

Buying hints Mainly obtainable from specialist nurseries, in the medium price range. Choose plants with bright green, evenly distributed stems.

Cultivation As forest species. Place in brighter light and give only occasional water in winter.

Chamaecereus silvestrii

Chamaecereus
(Cactaceae)

This genus contains only one species, native to Argentina. As its Latin name indicates, it is related to *Cereus*, but the stems lack the rigidity of the latter, and it grows flat on the ground. The funnel-shaped flowers are large and in common with those of many other cacti almost out of proportion

C. silvestrii (Cereus silvestrii) is sometimes known as peanut cactus. It is one of the most familiar of window cacti, extremely easy to grow and propagate.

It has cylindrical, branched stems made up of short, peanut-shaped sections. Well-grown plants spread rapidly to 12 in or more. The areoles are small, with bristly, white spines that form tiny stars. From spring to summer, 2-2¾ in long, orange to scarlet flowers open, often in profusion.

Buying hints Available from florists and garden centres, 3 in plants are cheap but good buys.

Cultivation As desert species. Plenty of water and bright sun are necessary during the growing period.

Crassula portulacea

Crassula
(*Crassulaceae*)

This diverse genus contains tiny annuals at one extreme and large evergreen shrubs at the other. Crassulas occur in all parts of the world, but the greatest concentrations are found in South Africa. Almost all are succulent, and several make easy and slow-growing house plants, some grown for the attraction of their fleshy leaves, others for their showy clusters of wide open, starry flowers.

C. arborescens may reach shrub-like proportions of 3 ft after many years in a large container, but is easily kept at around 12 in in a smaller pot. The stem bears opposite pairs of oval, $1\frac{1}{4}$-$2\frac{3}{4}$ in long, grey leaves margined with red. Large specimens may produce clusters of white to pink flowers in spring and summer. They are, however, seldom seen on pot plants.

C. falcata grows as a lanky, usually single-stemmed plant to 3 ft or more. It is best cut back by half each year in spring or regularly propagated by cuttings. The $2\frac{1}{4}$-4 in long leaves are deep grey-green and broadly sickle-shaped; they are arranged in pairs twisted like a ship's propeller. Showy

red flowers are readily borne in 3-4 in wide clusters during summer.

C. lycopodioides has slender, branching stems, erect to reclining, which eventually form a shrublet 6-12 in tall. The tiny triangular leaves overlap like the teeth in a zip. The tiny yellow flowers are insignificant.

C. portulacea (*C. argentea*) is the popular, almost indestructible jade tree. It resembles *C. arborescens*, but branches more freely with narrower, glossy green and often red-edged leaves. It rarely flowers as a pot plant.

C. schmidtii, sometimes and erroneously listed as *C. schmidtiana*, is highly colourful. It forms a tufted hummock with crowded, narrow leaves, dark pitted above and red beneath. For much of the year and particularly from autumn to spring, long-lasting carmine flowers open in succession. For a reliable winter display, a minimum temperature of 45-50° F is necessary.

Buying hints Crassulas are easily obtained from florists and other plant shops. Most are offered as 3-5 in plants and are generally cheap.

Cultivation As desert species, with periodic watering in winter.

Echeveria gibbiflora

Echeveria
(*Crassulaceae*)

These evergreen succulents grow wild from the southern parts of the United States to Argentina, but occur chiefly in Mexico. The majority form rosettes of various patterns, from loose and long-stemmed to tight, stemless and ground-hugging. In some species the leaves are velvety, in others smooth and hairless. The tubular, bell-shaped flowers, with five fleshy petals, are often showy and an additional bonus.

E. gibbiflora produces a slowly extending stem eventually 2 ft or more tall and sometimes branching. The stem terminates in a 10-24 in wide rosette of paddle-shaped, grey-green leaves flushed with red. Flowering stems rise

up to 2 ft above the rosettes, with clusters of 1 in bright red flowers, from autumn to winter.

'Carunculata' is an outstanding cultivar, with a metallic pink-lavender patina and wart-like protuberances on the leaves.

E. glauca is probably the best known species. The 4 in wide, neat and dense rosettes of blue-grey leaves were formerly used for carpet bedding. Nodding spikes of red and yellow bells open from late spring to summer.

E. harmsii (*Oliveranthus elegans*) grows slowly as a branching, soft-stemmed shrublet to 12 in. Each stem is tipped with a cluster of narrow, bright green leaves covered with fine hairs and faintly edged with red. From spring to summer, yellow, red-tipped flower bells, about 1 in long, open in succession. The species is distinguished for its branching habit and its attractive flowers.

Buying hints Most echeverias sold by florists and garden centres are 2 in plants in thumb pots. They are good, cheap buys, generally of good quality.
Cultivation As desert species. *E. gibbiflora* and *E. harmsii* are best overwintered at a minimum temperature of 45° F or slightly above. All echeverias should be watered sparingly in winter.

Echinocactus
(*Cactaceae*)

The socalled barrel cacti from North America contain a few species suitable as house plants and impressive for their shapes and fierce spines. Many are almost perfectly globular when young, sometimes broadening with age and sometimes elongating to cylindrical stems. The plant bodies are divided by wide ribs which bear the areoles from which sprout long and short spines.

At the top of the plants the areoles become woolly. The funnel-shaped flowers also grow at the top, but they are rarely or ever seen on pot-grown plants. Echinocacti are comparatively easy and relatively slow-growing.
E. grusonii is aptly named golden barrel cactus. It is one of the most striking of all cacti, forming a solitary globular body, flattened on top and with about 20 ribs closely set with yellow to grey woolly areoles. Each areole bears 10-15 golden-yellow spines, the longest up to 2 in. It is slow-growing and long-lived, and if potted on regularly can eventually reach a height of 12 in or more.
E. ingens is globular when young, but eventually elongates to a height of 2 ft or more. Young plants have five to eight ribs which multiply to about 50 with age. The areoles are well spaced and thickly woolly.

Buying hints Buy these plants from florists of repute. They are marketed at 2 in high, in small pots, and though cheap it is difficult to assess quality from the miniature sizes.
Cultivation As desert species.

Echinocactus grusonii

Echinocereus
(*Cactaceae*)

These easy, slow-growing plants from southern United States and Mexico are among the most popular cacti, combining fascinating shapes with attractive flowers, readily produced at an early age. They are clump-forming cacti with oval or shortly cylindrical stems. The showy, funnel-shaped and many-petalled flowers are usually in shades of pink and red. They bloom from the top of the stems in summer.
E. baileyi has cylindrical stems, 4 in tall and 1½-2 in thick, with about 15 ribs. The elongated areoles carry up to 16 white or yellow radiating spines, the longest about 1 in. In summer pink flowers, up to 2½ in long, appear.
E. cinerascens is erect to semi-procumbent with 8 in long stems bearing six to eight ribs. The white or yellow areoles bear slender white spines and red-purple flowers.
E. pectinatus branches from the base with oval to cylindrical stems, 4-8 in tall and up to 2½ in thick. It has about 20 ribs thickly covered with pink to white spines in star shapes. The pink, 3 in long flowers are fragrant.
E. pentalophus has thin, sprawling and near prostrate stems, about 6 in long and 1 in thick. They have four or five ribs, with short but sharp white spines. The brilliant violet flowers, 4 in long, are borne at the tips of the stems.

Buying hints Large garden centres are most likely to stock these cacti. Plants offered rarely exceed a height of 4 in, but many will begin to flower at this size. They are generally cheap.
Cultivation As desert species.

Echinocereus cinerascens

135

Echinopsis rhodotricha

Echinopsis
(Cactaceae)

These South American cacti include a number of globular species which make adaptable, easily grown and rewarding flowering plants. The stems may be solitary or clump-forming, with radial and central spines. The trumpet-shaped flowers, which appear in summer, are notable for their long tubes; they are white or pink, the white-flowered species opening their blooms only after dusk.

E. bridgesii (*E. salmiana*) forms groups of cylindrical to club-shaped stems, eventually to a height of 12 in. Each stem has 11-14 deeply notched, glossy dark to grey-green ribs with a large, brown areole in each notch. The brown to grey spines rise in groups of 10-14. White flowers are up to 7 in long.

E. multiflex is the most popular species. The globular stems, 4-6 in tall, readily form offsets from the base and sides. Each stem has 12-14 ribs, with well-spaced, woolly areoles bearing awl-shaped brown spines, the central ones $1\frac{1}{2}$ in long. The 7-8 in pink flowers, with tubes as long as 8 in, are sweetly fragrant.

E. rhodotricha is also clump-forming, but grows slowly to $2\frac{1}{2}$ ft, with oval to cylindrical stems. Each has 8-13 ribs and grey areoles with yellow-brown spines. It flowers when only 6-8 in tall, with 6 in white flowers.

Buying hints These cacti are stocked by specialist nurseries and some florists and garden centres. The plants offered are cheap and small, but avoid any shorter than 2 in.

Cultivation As desert species.

Epiphyllum 'Celestine'

Epiphyllum
(Cactaceae)

These epiphytic cacti from the rain forests of Central and South America are unlike most other members of the *Cactaceae* family. Their branched stems are flattened and resemble long, narrow and notched leaves. They bear tiny, mainly spineless areoles which demonstrate their true nature by producing flowers on two-year and older stem sections.

The cup-shaped, brightly coloured flowers appear in summer.

Epiphyllums are often sold as phyllocacti or orchid cacti; they are of moderate vigour and easy to grow and care for. The plants offered are usually hybrids with other epiphytic cacti, or named cultivars, with flowers in white, yellow, pink or red.

The white and yellow-flowered types often produce their blooms at the base of the current year's stems, less freely than pink-flowered kinds.

The following popular cultivars grow 2-3 ft tall, with flattened to winged, triangular leaf-like stems, and 4-6 in bell to trumpet-shaped flowers: 'Celestine', bright pink; 'Cooperi', creamy-white; 'Curt Backeberg', orange-yellow and red; 'Golden Gleam', yellow with purple eye; 'Kismet', white; 'Lady Irene', orchid-pink; 'Red Velvet', deep red.

Buying hints Epiphyllums are often confused with the Christmas cacti (*Schlumbergera*), but can be recognised by their erect stems. Young plants, about 6 in high and of flowering size, are in the medium price range.

Cultivation As forest species.

Euphorbia
(Euphorbiaceae)

This remarkable genus of more than 2000 extremely varied species is distributed throughout the world. They include annuals and perennials, small succulents and large shrubs and trees.

The true succulents are largely from South Africa, many of them stem succulents with a cactus-like appearance. Euphorbias are not related to

Euphorbia milii

cacti, but have adapted to similar arid terrains; some have spiny ribs, but lack the characteristic areoles of true cacti.

Almost all euphorbias contain a milky-white latex which is poisonous and can irritate the skin. The greenish-yellow flowers are inconspicuous, having no petals, but in some species, notably the non-succulent poinsettia (*E. pulcherrima*), they are surrounded by brightly coloured bracts.

E. milii (*E. splendens*) is popularly known as crown of thorns. It is a sprawling, semi-evergreen shrub, 1-2 ft tall, with stout, deeply grooved, spiny stems. The light green, oval leaves, $\frac{3}{4}$-4 in long, are arranged in clusters near the tips. They drop off during the rest period, and young leaves appear only on new growth.

Throughout the year, and particularly in winter and spring, small, flat-topped clusters of tiny flowers and larger bright crimson bracts unfold.

E. obesa is quite different and probably the most unique of all euphorbias. The solitary unbranched stem is reduced to a grey-green globe of succulent tissue, prominently netted with red-purple lines. Sometimes called Hottentot hut, it takes many years to attain $2\frac{1}{2}$ in in height. Thereafter it elongates.

Tiny yellow-green flowers appear in summer. Male and female flowers are borne on separate plants.

Buying plants *E. milii* is the most readily available species, usually sold by garden centres and florists as 6-8 in, flowering-sized plants, in the inexpensive to medium price range. *E. obesa* is rarer, but worth seeking out.

Cultivation As desert species. For a good show of flowers on *E. milii*, maintain a minimum winter temperature of 50° F and water occasionally.

Haworthia
(Liliaceae)

These small, clump-forming succulents from South Africa are long-lived and tolerant house plants, grown for their highly decorative leaves. The rosettes are made up of a number of fleshy, triangular leaves clustered on short stems. In many species the leaves are marked with small, wart-like tubercles which give them a variegated appearance.

The tubular, green and white-striped flowers, carried in loose clusters at the top of slender, wiry stems, are insignificant.

H. attenuata has rosettes of tapering, pointed leaves, $2\frac{1}{2}$-3 in long, and dark green with bands of white warts.

H. cuspidata is representative of those

Haworthia attenuata

haworthias which in the wild are almost buried in sand, with only the leaf tips showing above ground. In order to assimilate sufficient light for continued growth, the tips have transparent "windows".

The species forms hummocks or clusters of 3 in wide rosettes. The 1 in long, pale green leaves are broad, thick and fleshy and taper to a small point.

H. planifolia is similar to *H. cuspidata*, but the leaves are less fleshy, and the "windows" are smaller or missing.

Buying hints Best purchased from specialist cactus nurseries, haworthias are offered as $1\frac{1}{2}$-2 in plants in thumb pots; they are generally inexpensive.

Cultivation As desert species. Give *H. attenuata* an occasional watering during the rest period.

Kalanchoe
(Crassulaceae)

These succulent perennials and shrubs are widespread throughout the Tropics, though the species commonly cultivated chiefly originate in Malagasy. They are extremely varied, of erect or prostrate habit. Some are grown for their attractive fleshy leaves which may be velvety-hairy or smooth, shiny and waxy.

Kalanchoe blossfeldiana

Others are grown for their freely borne clusters of bright, tubular to bell-shaped flowers. All are vigorous and easy, and most are long-lived.

K. blossfeldiana is the most popular species, and many cultivars are available with red, orange or yellow blooms. It is a bushy plant, eventually woody at the base, and shrub-like to 12 in or more. The oval, rich glossy green, red-edged leaves are $1\frac{1}{2}$-$2\frac{3}{4}$ in long and provide an excellent foil for the scarlet flowers freely borne in dense clusters. They are long-lasting, opening from winter to early summer.

Flowering plants bought around Christmas may not bloom again for more than a year as they were specially forced for the market. But in subsequent years they will flower regularly in spring.

K. daigremontiana (Bryophyllum daigremontianum) forms an erect sheaf of stems, 2-3 ft tall, clad with opposite pairs of narrowly triangular leaves, 4-10 in long. They are spotted with light reddish-brown and bear numerous tiny plantlets along the margins. The pendent, purple flowers are about $\frac{3}{4}$ in long and carried in large clusters during winter and spring.

K. fedtschenkoi has reclining to erect stems, supported by aerial roots, and eventually up to 12 in. The broadly oval leaves are blue-green with darker, boldly scalloped margins. In spring, loose terminal clusters of orange-red flowers develop.

Buying hints *K. blossfeldiana* is the most widely seen, offered as a flowering pot plant by most sources around Christmas, in the inexpensive to medium price range. The other species are sold by good florists and garden centres and are somewhat dearer.

Cultivation As desert species. Ideally provide a minimum winter temperature of 45-50° F, and water the plants occasionally.

Lithops
(Aizoaceae)

Lithops aucampiae

These extraordinary South African succulents are called living stones, perfect descriptions of the short plant bodies composed of two fleshy, greatly swollen leaves. They are fused together from the base and look like pebbles split down the middle. In the wild, the leaves expose only the flat tips. During the winter rest period, the leaves shrivel, but a new pair develops between them; after flowering two pairs may appear.

The surprisingly large, daisy-like flowers grow from the minute stems below the leaves and push their way through the central slit. They appear on two or three year old plants in autumn and are about 1 in wide.

Lithops make good house plants provided they are placed in a sunny window and kept dry and cool during the winter rest.

L. aucampiae is clump-forming with plant bodies about $\frac{3}{4}$ in tall. The convex tops are tinted olive-green and brown. The flowers are yellow.

L. karasmontana is taller, with clumps of plant bodies 1-$1\frac{1}{2}$ in high. They have flattened to convex tops, light grey to bluish-yellow with brown wrinkled pits. White flowers.

L. lesliei is often solitary, but may also form clumps. Each plant body is 1-$1\frac{3}{4}$ in tall, with a flat, light red-brown top, spotted and pitted dark green-brown. The flowers are golden-yellow.

L. schwantesii has plant bodies 1-$1\frac{1}{2}$ in tall, with flattened to convex tops. It usually forms clumps. The overall colour is grey, patterned with red lines and dots and with a border of rusty yellow. Yellow flowers.

Buying hints Rarely seen at the normal plant sources, lithops are increasingly offered by mail-order nurseries as unspecified, cheap collections of unnamed species.

Cultivation As desert species. Water sparingly during growth and not at all from late October to April.

Lobivia species

Lobivia
(Cactaceae)

Some of the most rewarding and undemanding cacti, valued for their ease of flowering, are found in this genus. They are of South American origin, especially from Bolivia which, in anagram form, has given the genus its name.

Most species are globular, others become cylindrical with age. They are attractive plants with conspicuous spines as well as large, brightly coloured flowers in summer.

L. aurea (Echinopsis aurea) has globular to shortly cylindrical, 2-4 in stems. Each has 12-15 prominent ribs and brown areoles bearing 10-14 spines, the central ones yellow-tipped and 1 in long. The lemon-yellow, widely bell-shaped flowers are up to $3\frac{1}{2}$ in long.

L. backebergii (Echinopsis backebergii) is globular to oval, up to 4 in tall. The 14-16 angular and notched ribs are usually arranged in a spiral. The areoles are woolly when young and bear several brown, hooked spines. The carmine flowers are 4 in long.

L. famatimensis has oval to cylindrical, dark green stems up to 6 in tall, with numerous shallow ribs and small dense areoles with light brown spines. The white, red or yellow flowers are almost as large as the plants.

Buying hints Best purchased in late spring from florists and garden centres, lobivias are offered as 2 in plants which should flower the same or the following year. Cheap and of good quality.

Cultivation As desert species.

Mammillaria bocasana

Mammillaria
(Cactaceae)

This is the largest and possibly the most popular cactus genus. In the wild the 300 species inhabit semi-deserts of the south-western States of America, down through Central America.

Most mammillarias are fast-growing but small, clustering plants with round to cylindrical stems bearing prominent tubercles crowned with short spines and variable amounts of hair. The funnel to bell-shaped flowers, mainly in shades of red, are borne in a circle round the upper part of the stems. Some species also have ornamental club-shaped fruits.

Mammillarias are easy to grow and repay good care and bright sun with an abundant display of flowers during summer.

M. bocasana has $1\frac{1}{2}$-2 in, clustering and globular stems which elongate with age. The cylindrical tubercles bear numerous white, bristle-like radial spines tipped with silky hairs, and a few central hooked spines. The straw-yellow flowers, about $\frac{1}{2}$ in long, are marked with red veins.

M. hahniana is known as old-woman cactus from the long silky hairs that cover the stems. Eventually clump-forming, the stems may stay solitary for several years. Mature stems are globular, $3\frac{1}{2}$ in thick, and flattened on top. They bear conical tubercles and are densely covered with white spines and hairs. The purple-red flowers, $\frac{3}{4}$ in long, appear in a neat ring near the top of the plants.

M. prolifera (M. pusilla) has globular to cylindrical, $1\frac{1}{2}$-2 in stems in spreading clumps. The tubercles are dark green, and the areoles bear numerous, bristle-like, white to yellow spines. Yellow flowers, $\frac{1}{2}$ in long, are followed in autumn by coral-red, strawberry-flavoured fruits.

M. rhodantha is one of the larger species, with branching, cylindrical to club-shaped stems eventually growing 12 in tall and forming large clumps. The tubercles are conical; the rounded areoles bear many needle-like spines, white or yellow, red or brown. Bright carmine flowers, $\frac{3}{4}$ in long, are followed by similarly coloured fruits.

M. zeilmanniana is sometimes known as the rose pincushion from its hooked spines and reddish flowers. Usually solitary, mature plants sometimes form offsets. The stems are oval to shortly cylindrical, about $2\frac{1}{2}$ in tall and glossy green, with oval tubercles. The woolly areoles bear many slender spines, the outer ones white, the inner red-brown and hooked. The flowers, $\frac{3}{4}$ in wide, are freely produced and range from pale violet to red-purple and white.

Buying hints Mammillarias are sold by florists, garden centres and some large department stores. Offered as 2 in plants, quality varies according to source, and costs range from cheap to medium priced. Few are offered as named species or cultivars.
Cultivation As desert species.

Notocactus
(Cactaceae)

Notocactus leninghausii

Easy to grow in a sunny window, these small, usually globular cacti from South America are valued for their handsome spines and large flowers which appear on plants only three years old. They are often known as ball cacti though some species become oval in shape as they age. The stems may be solitary or clump-forming, always with numerous ribs and closely set areoles.

The large flowers are funnel-shaped and $1\frac{1}{2}$ in long; they appear in abundance in summer.

N. leninghausii is larger than most other notocacti. The cylindrical stems are solitary until they reach flowering size when they produce branches at the base. The plants may reach a height of 3 ft, but growth is extremely slow. There are about 30 ribs on each stem, with areoles bearing 15 bristle-like and pale yellow radial spines, and several longer and reflexed central spines. The species flowers less readily than others, with yellow blooms.

N. ottonis may be solitary or clump-forming. Each globular, dark green and $2\text{-}4\frac{1}{2}$ in wide stem has 10-13, often spiralling ribs. The areoles bear 10-18 yellow and brown spines, up to 1 in long. The flowers are shiny yellow and as much as 4 in long.

N. scopa has solitary globular and pale green stems and gradually elongates to 6 in. The numerous ribs are low and notched, with areoles producing up to 40 small white and bristle-like spines. Several canary-yellow flowers open simultaneously.

Buying hints Florists and garden centres are the best outlets for these small cacti. Sold as 1-3 in young plants, they are cheap and good value for money. Sometimes two or three plants are potted together for greater effect; these are obviously expensive but not necessarily better buys.
Cultivation As desert species.

Opuntia
(Cactaceae)

Opuntia microdasys

This large genus from North and South America includes the edible prickly pears grown as food plants in Mexico and parts of South America. Opuntias are distinguished by flattened or cylindrical stems, jointed into sections known as pads. These can be rounded or pear-shaped and are produced end to end, often at different angles to each other.

The pads may be with or without spines, but are usually covered with barbed bristles, known as glochids, which easily embed themselves in the skin and are difficult to remove.

Flowers are produced at the edges of young pads and are followed by pear-shaped fruit which are edible in some species. However, flowers are only borne on mature plants, and rarely or never occur on pot-grown opuntias which are primarily cultivated for their interesting shapes.

O. ficus-indica has naturalised itself in many parts of the world and will reach shrub-like proportions. As a pot plant it is considerably smaller. The oblong, bright green pads are 12 in or more long, with few spines.

O. microdasys, the most popular species, is sometimes known as bunny ears after the shape and texture of the pads. It is a shrubby species capable of reaching a height of 3 ft or more, but is extremely slow-growing. The oval, yellow-green and downy pads, $3\frac{1}{4}$-6 in long, are spineless, but the numerous areoles are covered with dense tufts of golden glochids. The cultivar 'Albispina' has smaller pads and silvery-white glochids.

O. scheerii is of spreading habit and grows slowly to 1-3 ft. The pads are rounded to oblong, 6-8 in long, grey to blue-green and densely set with areoles. These bear yellow short spines and yellow glochids.

Buying hints *O. microdasys* is the most readily available, from florists and garden centres; 3 in plants are cheap, but 6 in specimens, a little more expensive, are the better buys. Other species are chiefly obtainable from specialist nurseries, but are still inexpensive.

Cultivation As desert species. *O. scheerii* is best kept at a minimum winter temperature of 50-55° F.

Rebutia
(Cactaceae)

Rebutia violaciflora

This is one of the most attractive cactus genera prized for its dainty appearance and free-flowering habit. Native to arid regions of Bolivia and Argentina, rebutias have globular or sometimes cylindrical, ribless stems, closely covered with tubercles, areoles and starry clusters of spines. Some have solitary stems, others cluster freely.

The trumpet-shaped flowers, which open flat, appear several at a time at the base of the plants in summer, often forming complete circles.

R. chrysacantha is a clustering species with globular to shortly cylindrical stems, 2-2$\frac{1}{2}$ in tall. The tubercles are spirally arranged, with dense tufts of bristle-like, white to yellow spines. The flowers, $\frac{3}{4}$ in long, are brick-red and orange-yellow.

R. deminuta also forms clumps of globular stems, 2-2$\frac{1}{4}$ in tall. The tubercles are borne in spirals, each with a star of short, white, brown-tipped spines. The orange-red flowers are 1$\frac{1}{4}$ in long.

R. senilis is known as fire-crown cactus from the carmine-red, 2 in flowers set among the large clusters of glossy white spines. The globular, 2$\frac{3}{4}$ in high, pale green stems form clumps and have twisting rows of tubercles.

R. violaciflora is clump-forming, with 2-3 in tall, globular stems bearing rows of tubercles and numerous short, white to yellow spines and grey or yellow wool. The lilac-rose, 1$\frac{1}{2}$ in long flowers are freely produced.

Buying hints Best purchased from specialist nurseries, some florists also market rebutias, usually as 2 in plants in thumb pots. They are cheap and generally of good quality.

Cultivation As desert species.

Rhipsalidopsis
(Cactaceae)

There are only two species in this epiphytic genus from Brazil. Both have flat, jointed stem sections, dark green in colour and sometimes suffused with red. They lack spines, but the areoles produce hairy bristles. The plants are of arching habit and best displayed in hanging baskets.

The many-petalled flowers are funnel-shaped and carried in profusion on even small and young plants.

A number of named cultivars are available; these and the species are fast-growing, reaching maturity in a few years. They are easy to grow.

R. gaertneri (Schlumbergera gaertneri), the Easter cactus, reaches 8-12 in in height, with numerous arching and spreading chains of stem sections.

Rhipsalidopsis gaertneri

They are oblong, with purple, scalloped margins. Scarlet flowers, $2\frac{1}{2}$-$3\frac{1}{2}$ in long, open in spring from the areoles at the tops of the stems.

Several hybrids have been raised from this species and *R. rosea*, with flowers in shades of red and pink. They are somtimes listed as *R. × graeseri*. *R. rosea* resembles a dwarf Easter cactus, smaller in all parts and with low, arching branches pendulous at the tips. The rose-pink flowers expand to $1\frac{1}{2}$-$1\frac{3}{4}$ in and appear slightly later. Dark red and white cultivars also exist.

Buying hints Small plants, 4-6 in, are the best buys and are quite cheap. Avoid purchasing plants in bud or flower as they dislike disturbance at this time and easily drop their blooms at the slightest touch.

Cultivation As forest species. Ideally at a minimum temperature of 55-61° F, though 50° F is adequate.

Schlumbergera × buckleyi

Schlumbergera
(Cactaceae)

These easily grown forest cacti are epiphytes from southern Brazil. The flattened, leaf-like jointed stems are spineless and arch gracefully. Well-grown specimens are attractive plants for hanging baskets.

S. × buckleyi (S. × bridgesii) is the popular Christmas cactus, a hybrid between *S. russelliana* and *S. truncata*. It has freely borne, rose-purple to magenta flowers, up to $2\frac{1}{2}$ in long, during winter. Individual blooms last for only a few days, but they usually open in succession.

S. russelliana has arching stems spreading to 3 ft when mature. They consist of $1\frac{1}{2}$ in long, narrowly oblong stem sections. These are brownish-green with one or two notches at the margins. In late winter, the tubular, magenta flowers appear.

S. truncata (Zygocactus truncatus) is called crab or lobster cactus from the shape of its light green stem sections.

It is similar in growth habit to *S. russelliana*, but eventually reaches a height of 12 in. The stem sections have two to four pointed teeth on each side.

Flowering begins in late autumn and continues well into winter. Each bloom is about 3 in long, with a white tube and rose-pink, sharply reflexed petals.

Buying hints Most schlumbergeras are simply sold as Christmas cacti, often labelled *Zygocactus*. The best, inexpensive or medium-priced buys are 6-8 in plants in 4 in pots.

Cultivation As forest species. Ideally maintain a minimum winter temperature of 55-61° F.

Sedum morganianum

Sedum
(Crassulaceae)

Collectively known as stonecrops, most sedums are hardy garden plants, but a few tender species make attractive, trouble-free indoor pot plants. They are valued for their fleshy, bean-shaped or flattened, often colourful leaves, and small starry flowers.

Sedums are of world-wide distribution, but most of the tender species come from Mexico and Central America. They grow fairly rapidly, but deteriorate after a few years; new plants are easily raised from cuttings.

S. morganianum is an epiphyte, probably from Mexico. It is known as burro's or donkey's tail after the 2 ft long stems densely clothed with blue-white, cylindrical and slightly incurving leaves, 1 in long. In spring, a few small clusters of red flowers sometimes appear at the stem tips. The plant is most effective in a hanging basket.

S. rubrotinctum is an erect or semi-erect shrub-like plant, about 8 in tall. The small club-shaped leaves are lustrous green, strongly flushed with red and crowded along the stems. It rarely flowers as a pot plant.

S. sieboldii is of tufted habit with

prostrate and arching, slender stems bearing almost circular, blue-grey leaves in clusters of three. In autumn it bears 2-3 in flat clusters of pink flowers and is known as October plant.

Buying hints Readily available from florists and garden centres, most sedums are cheap buys as 2-3 in plants in small pots, and generally of excellent quality. Handle the plants carefully as the leaves are brittle and easily knocked off during transportation.

Cultivation As desert species. *S. sieboldii* dies back in autumn and is best plunged outside in a cold frame for the winter or kept in a similar cold, but frost-free place.

Senecio rowleyanus

Senecio
(Compositae)

This is one of the largest genera of flowering plants containing almost every plant form, from tiny annuals to trees, and including some diverse stem and leaf succulents, formerly included in the genus *Kleinia*.

S. articulatus (Kleinia articulatus) is an erect, shrubby plant, 1-2 ft tall whose growing period occurs in winter. The fleshy, glaucous stems are cylindrical and jointed into candle-like sections, covered with a white, waxy patina which easily rubs off.

The plant is peculiar in being leafless for the greater part of the year. In late summer the long-stalked, 1 in leaves appear; they are usually three-lobed and dark to blue-green. In spring, when the rest period begins, the leaves shrivel and drop. The plant often sheds stem sections which provide a ready means of increase.

S. rowleyanus has been in cultivation for only a few years, but has quickly become a favourite basket plant. It is prostrate with slender stems trailing to 2 ft or more. They bear round, light grey-green leaves, hence the common name of string-of-beads. Each leaf has a vertical, semi-translucent zone down one side. Solitary white and purple, fragrant flowers appear during autumn.

Buying hints *S. articulatas* is cheap and often ignored if come upon during its leafless stage. *S. rowleyanus*, offered by most good florists, is in the medium price range, for 2-6 in plants.

Cultivation As desert species. Give occasional watering in winter. *S. rowleyanus* will tolerate partial shade.

Yucca aloifolia

Yucca
(Agavaceae)

Although yuccas, from North America, are not true succulents, they have an overall appearance of arid-region plants, with their long, narrow and stiff, slightly fleshy leaves. They are carried in a short-stemmed or almost stemless rosette, on rough stems.

Outdoors, yuccas bear huge clusters of bell-shaped, white or cream flowers, but these are not produced on pot plants. Indoors, yuccas are extremely slow-growing, excellent as specimen or feature plants.

Y. aloifolia is a recent, but very popular newcomer to house plant collections. It grows as an unbranched woody stem, eventually to 3-4 ft, topped with rosettes of rigid, blue-green leaves as much as 2 ft long. They terminate in sharp dagger points.

Y. elephantipes resembles *Y. aloifolia*, but the stem is often swollen at the base, and the arching dark green leaves are flexible and lacking the sharp tips.

Buying hints These plants have topped the popularity list in recent years and are widely sold by florists and garden centres, in spite of steep prices. *Y. aloifolia*, usually sold unnamed, is the most frequently offered, with 9 in plants in the medium price range; 3-4 ft plants are very expensive.

Cultivation As desert species. Continue watering through winter.

Quick Guide to 126 house plants

The following charts provide a ready reference to the chief characteristics of the plant genera described and illustrated on pages 50-143. It is advisable to check each individual genus for detailed information as the requirements of one species may differ from that of another.

Botanical names refer to the Latin nomenclature by which all plants are classified. Plant type identifies the growth habit commonly associated with a given plant, such as tree-like or rosette-forming, climbing or trailing, fern or cactus.

Growth rate and height are those that can be expected under good growing conditions, from infancy to maturity. Flowering seasons vary slightly, depending on growth, and mainly concern plants of regular flowering habit. Light needs – full sun, bright, filtered, shade – should be considered in conjunction with the essay on natural and artificial light (page 22) and with individual plant descriptions.

Temperatures refer to winter night temperatures which, with the exceptions of cacti and succulents, are the minimum acceptable. Humidity requirements indicate the amount of air moisture necessary to maintain and encourage healthy and steady growth.

BOTANICAL NAME	PLANT TYPE	GROWTH RATE/HEIGHT	FLOWERING SEASON	LIGHT	TEMPERATURE/HUMIDITY
Achimenes	Bushy; trailing	Moderate/10 in	Summer to autumn	Bright	65°F/moderate
Adiantum	Fern	Moderate/2-3 ft	—	Filtered	55-60°F/high
Aechmea	Bromeliad	Moderate/18 in	Summer	Bright	60°F/high
Agave	Succulent	Slow/12 in	—	Full sun	50°F/low
Aglaonema	Bushy	Slow/2 ft	—	Shade	55°F/high
Aloe	Succulent	Slow/8 in	Spring to summer	Bright to filtered	50°F/low
Ananas	Bromeliad	Slow/3 ft	—	Full sun	60°F/high
Anthurium	Bushy to upright	Moderate/18 in	Spring to autumn	Filtered	60°F/high
Aphelandra	Bushy	Moderate/18 in	Any season	Bright	60°F/high
Aporocactus	Cactus	Fast/3-6 ft long	Spring to summer	Bright	45-50°F/low
Araucaria	Tree	Slow/6 ft	—	Shade	45°F/high
Asparagus	Trailing	Fast/4 ft	—	Shade	40-55°F/moderate to high
Aspidistra	Clump	Slow/12 in	—	Poor to shade	40-50°F/low
Asplenium	Fern	Slow/1½-2 ft	—	Filtered to light shade	55-60°F/low to moderate

BOTANICAL NAME	PLANT TYPE	GROWTH RATE/HEIGHT	FLOWERING SEASON	LIGHT	TEMPERATURE/HUMIDITY
Begonia (foliage)	Rosette	Moderate/12 in	—	Filtered	50°F/moderate
Begonia (flowering)	Shrubby; bushy; upright	Fast to moderate/9 in-4 ft	Any season, depending on type	Bright	50-60°F/moderate
Beloperone	Bushy	Fast/18 in	Spring to winter	Bright	50°F/moderate
Billbergia	Bromeliad	Moderate/12-18 in	Spring to summer	Bright	45-60°F/moderate
Brassavola	Orchid	Slow/6 in	Spring to autumn	Filtered to bright	65°F/high
Caladium	Clump	Fast/15 in	—	Bright to filtered	55-65°F/high
Calathea	Upright	Slow/2 ft	—	Filtered to shade	50°F/high
Calceolaria	Bushy	Temporary/9-12 in	Summer	Filtered to bright	65°F/moderate
Campanula	Trailing	Fast/12 in	Summer to autumn	Bright	45°F/moderate
Capsicum	Bushy	Temporary/15 in	Winter berries	Bright	55°F/moderate
Cattleya	Orchid	Moderate/18 in	Any season	Filtered to bright	65°F/high
Ceropegia	Trailing	Fast/3 ft	—	Full sun	50°F/low
Chamaecereus	Cactus	Fast/12 in	Spring to summer	Full sun	50°F/low
Chamaedorea	Palm	Fast/4 ft	—	Moderate	50-55°F/high
Chlorophytum	Grassy	Fast/3 ft	—	Bright to filtered	45°F/moderate
Chrysan-themum	Bushy	Temporary/9-12 in	Any season	Bright to filtered	55°F/moderate
Cissus	Climbing	Fast/8 ft	—	Moderate to shade	40-50°F/moderate
Citrus	Shrubby	Slow/1½-3 ft	Spring to summer	Bright to filtered	55°F/moderate
Clivia	Arching	Moderate/2 ft	Spring	Filtered	50°F/low
Crassula	Succulent	Slow/1-3 ft	Summer; autumn; spring	Full sun	50°F/low
Codiaeum	Upright	Moderate/2 ft	—	Bright to filtered	60°F/high
Coleus	Bushy annual	Fast/18 in	—	Bright	55°F/moderate
Cordyline	Shrubby	Slow/3 ft	—	Bright	50-55°F/high
Crocus	Flowering bulb	Temporary/4 in	Winter and spring	Bright	50°F/low
Cryptanthus	Bromeliad	Slow/prostrate/12 in	—	Filtered	50°F/high
Cuphea	Bushy	Moderate/12 in	Spring to autumn	Full sun	45°F/high
Cyclamen	Rosette to bushy	Temporary/12 in	Autumn to spring	Bright	55°F/high
Cymbidium	Orchid	Moderate/12 in	Any season	Filtered to bright	55°F/high
Cyperus	Grassy	Moderate/2 ft	Summer	Full sun	50°F/high

BOTANICAL NAME	PLANT TYPE	GROWTH RATE/HEIGHT	FLOWERING SEASON	LIGHT	TEMPERATURE/HUMIDITY
Cyrtomium	Fern	Slow/2 ft	—	Bright	50°F/moderate
Davallia	Fern	Fast/12 in	—	Bright to full sun	50-60°F/high
Dieffenbachia	Upright	Fast/1½-4 ft	—	Filtered	60°F/high
Dizygotheca	Palm-like	Slow/4-5 ft	—	Bright to filtered	55-60°F/high
Dracaena	Upright; bushy	Fast/2-4 ft	—	Bright to filtered	50-55°F/high
Echeveria	Succulent	Slow to fast/4 in-2 ft	Any season	Full sun	45-50°F/low
Echinocactus	Cactus	Slow/2 ft	—	Full sun	50°F/low
Echinocereus	Cactus	Slow/8 in	Summer	Full sun	50°F/low
Echinopsis	Cactus	Slow to moderate/4 in-2½ ft	Summer	Full sun	50°F/low
Epiphyllum	Cactus	Moderate/3 ft	Summer	Bright to filtered	45-50°F/low
Euphorbia	Succulent	Slow to moderate/2½ in-2 ft	Any season	Full sun	50°F/low
Euphorbia (poinsettia)	Shrubby	Moderate/2-4 ft	Autumn to spring	Bright	55-60°F/low
× **Fatshedera**	Climbing	Fast/4-6 ft	—	Light shade	40-50°F/low
Fatsia	Shrubby	Fast/4 ft	—	Shade to filtered	40°F/low
Ficus	Tree; shrubby; climbing; trailing	Moderate to fast/2-6 ft	—	Filtered to shade	45-60°F/moderate to high
Fittonia	Creeping	Fast/4 in	—	Shade	55°F/high
Gloriosa	Climber	Fast/4-6 ft	Summer to autumn	Bright	70°F/high
Guzmania	Bromeliad	Slow/12-16 in	Summer to autumn	Filtered	65°F/high
Gynura	Bushy; trailing	Fast/1½-3 ft	Spring to summer	Bright	50°F/low
Haworthia	Succulent	Slow/3 in	—	Full sun	50°F/low
Hedera	Climbing; trailing	Fast/indefinite	—	Filtered to shade	35-40°F/moderate
Heptapleurum	Tree	Fast/6 ft	—	Bright to filtered	50°F/moderate
Hibiscus	Shrubby	Moderate/3 ft	Summer to autumn	Bright	55°F/moderate
Hippeastrum	Flowering bulb	Fast/2 ft	Winter to summer	Bright	60-70°F/low
Howea	Palm	Slow/8 ft	—	Filtered to light shade	55°F/moderate to high
Hoya	Shrubby; climbing	Fast/9 in-6 ft	Summer	Bright	50°F/high
Hyacinthus	Flowering bulb	Temporary/8-10 in	Winter to spring	Bright	55-60°F/low
Hydrangea	Deciduous shrub	Temporary/1½-2 ft	Spring to autumn	Bright to filtered	Cool/moderate
Impatiens	Bushy	Fast/12 in	Spring to winter	Bright	55°F/moderate

146

BOTANICAL NAME	PLANT TYPE	GROWTH RATE/HEIGHT	FLOWERING SEASON	LIGHT	TEMPERATURE/HUMIDITY
Jasminum	Climbing	Fast/6 ft	Winter to spring	Bright	40°F/moderate
Kalanchoe	Succulent	Fast/1-3 ft	Winter to summer	Full sun	45-50°F/low
Laelia	Orchid	Fast/2-4 ft	Spring to autumn	Filtered to bright	45-65°F/high
Lilium	Flowering bulb	Temporary/3-6 ft	Spring to summer	Bright to filtered	50°F/low
Lithops	Succulent	Slow/1¾ in	Autumn	Full sun	50°F/low
Lobivia	Cactus	Slow/6 in	Summer	Full sun	50°F/low
Mammillaria	Cactus	Fast/1½-12 in	Summer	Full sun	50°F/low
Maranta	Bushy	Moderate/8 in	—	Filtered to light shade	50°F/high to moderate
Miltonia	Orchid	Moderate/20 in	Any season	Filtered to bright	55°F/high
Monstera	Climber	Fast/indefinite	—	Filtered	50°F/high
Narcissus	Flowering bulb	Temporary/12 in	Winter to spring	Bright	55-60°F/low
Neoregelia	Bromeliad	Slow to moderate/ 12-15 in	Any season	Full sun	60°F/high
Nephrolepis	Fern	Fast/1½-6 ft	—	Bright	55°F/moderate
Nidularium	Bromeliad	Moderate to slow/ 12-18 in	Any season	Bright to filtered	65°F/high
Notocactus	Cactus	Slow/6 in-3 ft	Summer	Full sun	50°F/low
Odontoglossum	Orchid	Moderate/12 in	Autumn to spring	Filtered to bright	45-65°F/high
Opuntia	Cactus	Slow/3 ft	—	Full sun	50-55°F/low
Pandanus	Upright; palm-like	Slow/4 ft	—	Bright	65°F/high
Paphiopedilum	Orchid	Moderate to slow/ 4-18 in	Any season	Light shade	45-55°F/moderate to high
Pelargonium	Shrubby	Moderate/18 in	Summer to autumn	Full sun	50°F/low
Pellaea	Fern	Moderate/12 in	—	Filtered to light shade	50-55°F/low to moderate
Peperomia	Rosette; clump	Slow/6-9 in	Any season	Filtered to light shade	60°F/high
Philodendron	Shrubby; climbing; trailing	Fast/6 ft	—	Filtered to shade	55°F/moderate to high
Pilea	Bushy	Fast/8-10 in	—	Light shade	50°F/moderate
Platycerium	Fern	Slow to moderate/2 ft	—	Filtered to light shade	50-60°F/moderate to high
Plectranthus	Trailing	Fast/2 ft	—	Bright to light shade	45°F/low to moderate
Primula	Rosette	Temporary/10 in	Autumn to spring	Bright	55-60°F/moderate

BOTANICAL NAME	PLANT TYPE	GROWTH RATE/HEIGHT	FLOWERING SEASON	LIGHT	TEMPERATURE/HUMIDITY
Pteris	Fern	Moderate to fast/10 in-3 ft	—	Filtered to light shade	60°F/high
Rebutia	Cactus	Slow/3 in	Summer	Full sun	50°F/low
Rhipsalidopsis	Cactus	Fast/12 in	Spring	Bright to filtered	55-60°F/low
Rhododendron (azalea)	Shrubby; upright	Slow to moderate/9-18 in	Winter to spring	Bright to filtered	55-60°F/high
Rhoeo	Rosette	Slow/14 in	—	Light shade	55°F/high
Saintpaulia	Rosette	Slow/6 in	Any season	Bright	55°F/high
Sansevieria	Upright; rosette	Slow/6 in-4 ft	—	Full sun to light shade	50°F/low
Saxifraga	Trailing	Fast/9 in	Summer	Filtered to light shade	35-40°F/low to moderate
Schefflera	Tree-like	Slow/6 ft	—	Bright to filtered	50°F/moderate
Schlumbergera	Cactus	Moderate to fast/trailing to 3 ft	Autumn to spring	Bright to filtered	55-61°F/low
Scindapsus	Climbing; trailing	Fast/4-6 ft	—	Light shade	60°F/moderate
Sedum	Succulent	Fast/8-24 in	Spring; autumn	Full sun	50°F/low
Selaginella	Creeping	Fast/6 in	—	Shade	50°F/high
Senecio (cineraria)	Bushy	Temporary/2 ft	Winter to spring	Bright	50°F/moderate
Senecio	Succulent	Moderate to fast/2 ft	Autumn	Full sun to light shade	50°F/low
Sinningia	Herbaceous rosette	Moderate/10 in	Summer	Filtered	60°F/high
Solanum	Bushy	Temporary/12-18 in	Summer; winter berries	Full sun	55°F/moderate
Sonerila	Clump	Slow/6 in	—	Filtered to light shade	65°F/high
Spathiphyllum	Compact; erect	Moderate/12-24 in	Spring to autumn	Filtered to bright	60°F/high
Stephanotis	Climbing	Slow/4 ft	Spring to autumn	Filtered to bright	55°F/high
Streptocarpus	Rosette	Moderate/10 in	Spring to autumn	Bright to filtered	50°F/moderate
Syngonium	Climbing	Fast/2-4 ft	—	Light shade	60°F/moderate
Tradescantia	Trailing	Fast/1-3 ft	—	Bright	50°F/low
Tulipa	Flowering bulb	Temporary/12 in	Winter to spring	Bright	68°F/low
Vriesea	Bromeliad	Moderate/1½ ft	Summer to autumn	Bright to filtered	64°F/high
Yucca	Succulent	Slow/4 ft	—	Full sun	50°F/low
Zebrina	Trailing	Fast/3 ft	—	Bright	50°F/low

Part Three

Arranging Plants Indoors

Plant Displays

Plants used in interior designs add life and colour, emphasise or diminish room proportions, conceal awkward features and complement furnishings

The beginner to indoor gardening may well feel bemused at the vast number of house plants available, with such variety of form, habit and colouring, and of cultural needs. It is advisable, therefore, to begin with a few of the easier kinds and get the 'feel' of how to grow them. Initially, match their cultural requirements with what you can offer in the way of temperature, humidity and light.

As you gain experience and confidence in handling these plants, you can add to your collection others with more specific requirements or of a specific type – bromeliads, for example.

The successful choice and decorative use of house plants requires time, thought and planning – in the home. You will often find that plants bought on impulse may be impossible to grow in the conditions you can provide, or do not fit into your existing schemes.

Pinpoint first of all the areas you want to decorate with plants, then the types you would prefer and finally decide if the two can be combined in your home.

You can now move on to the more aesthetic and imaginative aspects of indoor gardening and consider the visual effects of plants in individual pots, small or large group arrangements, plant troughs and hanging baskets.

Most people will start with a number of plants placed individually around a room. The decorative value of a single plant is heightened by setting the pot in an attractive outer container, be it plastic, ceramic or basket work, large enough to conceal the rim of the plant pot.

Group arrangements

Too many separate plants, however, not only make for more work, but can create a restless effect. The creative arrangement of indoor plants starts when they are grouped or strategically placed as single focal points.

The use of a large container for a plant arrangement is usually easier and tidier than grouping a number of separate plants, even though it permits less flexibility.

All containers, whatever their shape and size should be waterproof, and preferably large and deep enough for peat to be packed round the pots.

The most important factor for any group arrangement is plant compatibility. This means in effect that the plants should have similar needs in respect of water, humidity, heat and light. You can often cheat a little where light is concerned and mix plants with different needs by placing shade lovers near taller, large-leaved plants.

You can create an informal group arrangement simply by assembling a number of individual plants, in identical pot-holders. Ideally, such a group should have a central theme, based for example, on contrasting or harmonising leaf textures, shapes or colours.

Alternatively, you could make a fascinating display round a single plant genus. *Ficus* or *Philodendron* species, for example, grouped to emphasise the diversity of their leaves, can make stunning floor groups for spacious areas. An equally dramatic effect can be achieved by grouping together on a table two or three low-growing plants, such as species of *Peperomia,* or African violets *(Saintpaulia)* of different colours.

Shapes and forms

Most house plants fall roughly into a few distinct categories of shape and growth habit. Some are more or less tree-like, with a single upright, usually woody stem and a number of branches, as found in some *Ficus* species and *Araucaria*, for example.

Other upright forms include the climbers, whose lax stems need supports of some kind, and single-stemmed, non-branching plants like *Dieffenbachia*. The sansevierias, or sword plants, are also termed upright. Although lacking a stem, their long narrow leaves rise almost vertically from the soil level, and they are particularly valuable as contrasts to plants with a mass of smaller leaves.

Bushy types are mainly small-leaved plants, of rounded outline and composed of several stems rising from a central growing point or crown. Most are of small to medium height, but many upright plants can be induced to become bushy and branching by pinching out the growing tips.

Variable in size, rosette plants have leaves radiating from a central point. The leaf rosette is sometimes flat, as in saintpaulias and primulas, and sometimes radiating upwards. Notable among these are the bromeliads where the leaf rosettes are sheathed at the base to form an inner vase.

Trailing and sprawling plants are invaluable for hanging baskets, for covering the edges of containers and troughs and for filling in between foreground plants. Young plants of many climbing species can also be allowed to trail.

Colours and patterns

House plants are generally of permanent character, and for the majority of them their decorative value lies in their leaves. We tend to think of foliage plants as green, but this basic colour runs through numerous shades, and in many the leaves have a pattern picked out in a different colour.

Leaf variegations are frequently white or cream, yellow, golden or silver, but red, bronze and purple are also common. These contrasting colours may occur as clearly defined margins or stripes, follow the network of the veins or be scattered irregularly over the green leaf surface.

In some instances, notably the crotons, several brilliant colours are mixed on some or all of the leaves, ranging from yellow through gold, orange, red and purple to near black. In others,

such as the rex begonias, the various colours are so intense that they practically obliterate the green background.

Add to this gamut of colours a virtually inexhaustible variation in leaf size, shape and texture, and the house plant arranger has a palette, as it were, as full of possibilities as that of a painter.

With such a vast choice of different components, much depends on personal taste, but in general a successful arrangement will include one or more variations of all the possible characters.

You may, for example, highlight an all-green group with a variegated plant, contrast corrugated or wrinkled foliage with a smooth and glossy-leaved species, or relieve the solidity of a compact grower with the airy grace of an arching, narrow-leaved plant.

Plants which rely solely on the beauty of their flowers are usually best displayed as single units. Many flowering pot plants are in any case annuals which are discarded when the flowers have faded, and others need a cool resting period to initiate flower buds for the following year. But the

HANGING BASKETS AND POTS

Ordinary garden baskets may be used indoors provided they are concealed, after planting, in an outer waterproof container. Polythene, with punched drainage holes, is used as a liner before trailing plants are bedded in compost. Ready-made hanging pots, in light-weight plastic, usually come complete with drip saucers.

positive colours of flowering plants can often be included to advantage in permanent foliage groupings.

The most suitable plants for mixed groups are those that flower over a long period. If you sink the pot among foliage plants it is easily removed and replaced when past its best. For a temporary arrangement and table centre-piece, a small pot of flowering primulas or begonias can add instant colour to a foliage group.

African violets are particularly suitable for low groups, partly because of their frequent and extended flowering periods, and partly because they are attractive plants even when not in bloom.

In larger group arrangements bromeliads become invaluable adjuncts. Their beautifully patterned leaf rosettes are focal points in themselves, and the flower bracts persist for months.

Alternatively, if you build up a large-scale floor grouping of several containers of different size, the lower containers at the front can be devoted to temporary displays of short-lived flowering plants.

Keen flower arrangers can extend their talents to house plants, in the socalled *pot-et-fleur* arrangements. Group pot plants in a container and push one or two metal or plastic flower tubes (available from florists) into the peat. Fill them with water and insert a few fresh-cut flowers to tone or contrast with the foliage plants. The flowers can be easily removed or replaced as necessary.

Group patterns

If the group is to be placed against a wall, set taller plants at the back, with lower and trailing types towards the front. A free-standing group to be seen from all sides should be taller in the centre, with lower plants around the rim. Compose a table group of all low-growing plants, perhaps with one erect or taller, gracefully arching plant set off-centre for contrast. Avoid trailers in tall arrangements.

A rectangular plant box or trough is most decorative in a triangular outline. Set tall plants at the left or right and grade others gradually down towards the opposite side. You can also arrange one tall plant in the centre of the trough and grade down towards both sides. Such triangular shapes are visually pleasing and create a better effect than a straight row of plants of similar height.

Put the plants into the trough and move them around until you are satisfied with the effect. You can now add a drainage layer of pebbles and bed the plants down in peat. Pack more peat round the pots to keep them stable, ideally also covering the pot rims. You can add a few artistic touches to the planted trough, strategically placed stones, perhaps, a weathered chunk of contorted driftwood or a piece of statuary.

Never be tempted to knock plants out of their separate pots and plant them directly in the growing medium. Their roots will eventually intermingle, making repotting or replacement of an unsatisfactory individual virtually impossible. When watering a group arrangement do make sure that each plant gets an adequate drink in its individual pot.

Ready-made group arrangements, purchased from florists' shops and presented as expensive gifts on festive occasions, can prove to be potential death traps for the plants. They are usually

PLANT TROUGHS AND TABLE GROUPS

Conceal individual pots in a plant trough with peat kept moist for extra humidity. Allow room for growth

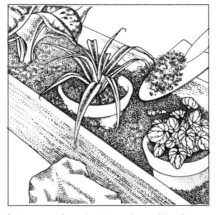

between the plants and avoid mixing fast and slow growers. Use creepers for edges, tall plants for accents. Ring

the changes in small table groups, temporarily replacing a foliage plant with one in full bloom.

bare-rooted, potted together in a shallow container, with insufficient compost. Quite often they are grouped for their eye-catching appeal only, with total disregard for individual growing needs.

Your best plan of campaign in this situation, after a short interlude for appreciation, is to dismantle the whole arrangement and carefully pot the plants up individually. You can then incorporate them in existing arrangements, grow them on as specimen plants or build up compatible arrangements round them.

Table groups

One of the easiest starting points from which to gain experience is a bowl of foliage plants as a semi-permanent group for a dinner or coffee table setting. Using young plants in small pots and aiming for effective variation, you might, for example, combine the spear-shaped *Syngonium podophyllum* with the small leaved, trailing or climbing *Ficus pumila* and a silvery *Pilea cadierei*. A small ivy or two, green or variegated, as contrast to the feathery stems of *Asparagus setaceus* would heighten the decorative effect.

Groups of different cultivars of one plant species can also look attractive: for instance, a basket of different forms of *Begonia rex* or *Pilea* hybrids.

Floor displays

Very large displays are only suitable in spacious surroundings where they constitute a real indoor garden. One possible grouping could consist of a *Chamaedorea* palm for height, red-edged *Cordyline terminalis* for colour, a *Vriesea splendens* rosette as a focal point, surrounded with the low-growing colourful *Maranta leuconeura* and furry, purple *Gynura aurantiaca*.

Over the edges of the container you could trail green-striped *Tradescantia fluminensis* or a small-leaved variegated ivy.

The dead areas

An arrangement for an awkward, fairly dimly lit corner could be a mixed group of ferns, with their infinite variety in shape, habit and colour. A particularly decorative idea, to simulate a forest lake, would be a group of pots, sunk in peat on a waterproof tray on the floor, round a shallow dish of water or mirror, the edges concealed with pebbles and moss.

A disused fireplace, which may appear an eyesore, can be transformed into a handsome background for a skilfully arranged collection of plants, set in a deep box or basket or merely consisting of pots grouped on a tray. Remember to choose plants that are natural shade lovers. If the fireplace is never used, fix a mirror, cut to fit, behind the plants. The effect can be even more dramatic if you can install concealed lighting.

However you decorate a room with plants, individually or in groups, avoid siting highly coloured or strongly patterned types near a boldy patterned wallpaper; the result will be restless and unattractive. Most plants look best against a plain background and are particularly striking when reflected in a mirror.

Single-plant displays

Although plant groups provide maximum visual effect, the single, uncluttered specimen plant also plays an important role and can make an impressive focal point in any room. For this purpose choose a perfectly grown plant and select a handsome container to complement the other furnishings.

Depending on the room size, a

POT-IN-POT DISPLAYS

Small trailing or arching plants can be grouped vertically in three pots — unusual and space-saving.

Fill the largest pot with compost and insert plants round the edges. Set the second pot in the centre.

Use the same plants throughout to form a green pyramid or top with a plant of contrasting shape and texture.

focal plant can be as large as a rubber plant, *Ficus elastica*, grown to tree-like proportions, or an elegant weeping fig, *Ficus benjamina*. On a smaller scale, try a handsome bromeliad, such as the urn plant, *Aechmea*, or a large pot of trailing *Tradescantia* – even a bowl of bulbs can act as an instant if temporary eye-catcher.

A single plant display is not confined to a pot on the floor or a table. It may be suspended in a hanging basket, trailing from a holder fixed on a wall or perched on a pedestal, resplendent in a Victorian ceramic jardinière.

Epiphytes, such as bromeliads and some orchids, as well as the staghorn fern *(Platycerium)*, can be attached to a picturesquely gnarled dead tree branch or bark-covered log (see page 21). Wedged in heavy containers or fixed to baseboards such displays add a touch of the exotic.

A simple yet effective display feature, most attractive when planted with *Chlorophytum, Asparagus* or *Saxifraga*, can be made by using pots-within-pots. You will need three pots, each at least 1 in narrower in diameter than the other, which will fit snugly into each other. Fill the largest pot with compost and set the chosen plants around the rim; place the next pot in the centre and repeat the process. Finally set the smallest pot in the second pot and fill with compost and plants. In time this arrangement will produce a cascade of greenery.

A large area of plain wall can be broken up effectively with trailing plants. There are several designs of wall pot-holders; the most suitable have built-in drip saucers.

Dish gardens

Miniature or dish gardens are fun to create and particularly popular with children. They are basically composed of small slow-growing plants arranged to simulate a miniature landscape, with gravel chippings, ceramic figures, bridges, mirror pools and pagodas. The idea lends itself particularly to slow-growing cacti and other succulents (see page 159).

Room dividers

Many modern houses have combined living and dining areas which need separating visually at some point. You may already have shelves or a room-divider unit with books and ornaments. A few well-chosen plants, such as a trailing or climbing *Philodendron scandens,* an elegantly arching *Chlorophytum* or a flowering plant or two will add life to a functional unit.

Room dividers or screens of living growing plants are immensely decorative, and several climbing plants are suitable.

Ideally, a plant room divider should be started at floor level, in large and deep, waterproof troughs so that the plants will have plenty of root room. You will also have to erect some kind of support for the plants to climb on. Conventional trellis can be fixed to upright supports at each end of the trough, or you can tack netting or cords to a wooden framework or attach them to the ceiling.

A less permanent and movable divider can be achieved by standing pots of climbing plants along a shelf unit or cupboard.

Where light is good, either natural or artificial, *Cissus antarctica* and × *Fatshedera* give quick and dense cover in cool rooms; ivies *(Hedera helix)* will do just as well in moderate light. In warmer conditions, *Cissus discolor,* scindapsus, philodendrons and syngonium are among the best climbers for quick screening purposes.

Window displays

Climbing plants can create problems when they outgrow the supports in their pots. When they reach this stage you will either have to discard them or give them yet more room in which to scramble.

Climbers with low light requirements, such as philodendrons and scindapsus, can be grown up a wall on unobtrusively fixed cords or fine wire. More light-demanding types can be similarly trained round the frame of a window or patio doors. The plants can be grown in large pots, on floor or sill level, or at either end of a plant trough, with lower-growing and trailing plants in the centre.

Plant windows

The most perfect way of growing plants indoors is in a plant window. This is in effect a miniature greenhouse created between an external window, which should be double-glazed for winter insulation, and an internal sheet of glass, preferably in the form of sliding overlapped panels for easy access. The base of the window has a waterproof lining, a deep drainage layer of pebbles and a peat bed in which the plant pots are buried.

In such an enclosed environment, air humidity, essential for specialised tender plants like orchids, is constant. The window can also be installed with a heating unit beneath the planting bed, and automatic lighting and watering devices can be incorporated.

A modified version of a plant window can be created in a deep bay window, spanned by well supported metal shelves for planting beds or troughs. Double glazing of the window is essential, but the niche can be open to the room within. If the plants are bedded in peat, a high degree of humidity is created within this micro-climate.

Plant cases and bottle gardens

Jam jars and fish bowls, fern cases and demijohns make potential greenhouses for miniature tropical gardens

A number of plants require a higher degree of humidity and a greater evenness of temperature than can be provided in the home. Nearly all these are foliage plants, in particular the tender delicate-leaved ferns, which in the wild flourish in the dappled sunlight and steamy heat of tropical forests.

On a large scale, such warm and humid conditions are created in the hothouses of botanical gardens; in the home closed plant cases can provide similar micro-climates. A plant case, whatever its shape and size, is in effect a miniature glass-house – clear so that essential light can be admitted and closed so that humidity and temperature can remain constant.

Wardian fern cases

The first popular plant case was the brainwave of one Dr. Nathaniel Ward, whose absorbing interest in the life cycle of the moth led him, accidentally, to the conclusion that plant life could be sustained in a closed glass container.

In this instance, the container was a laboratory closed test tube, and the plant a seedling fern. This obviously developed from a spore in the bit of moist soil beneath the chrysalis whose metamorphosis into a moth the doctor was intent on studying. Instead of a moth – or perhaps as well as – a small fern appeared in the tube.

The cultivation of ferns was another of Dr. Ward's hobbies, so far without any notable success. The closed glass tube provided a solution to this problem. After a number of experiments, closed plant cases were launched, to become an instant success. By 1840 almost every Victorian parlour boasted, in addition to a pot of aspidistras, an ornate fern case. Many of these were huge and elaborate display cases which are now collectors' items.

In Victorian days, closed plant cases made possible the cultivation of delicate plants which would otherwise quickly perish in the fume-laden atmosphere of rooms

A SELECTION OF GLASSWARE

The Wardian case (far left) is the prototype for an indoor garden under glass, but almost any type of glass container can be used. Close-fitting lids or stoppers are essential, and tinted glass should be avoided.

155

lit and heated by paraffin or coal-gas fires.

Today the indoor atmosphere is free of such impurities, but central heating while solving one problem has created another in the form of dry air. So plant cases come into their own again, even to the extent of replicas of Dr. Ward's fern cases being marketed as novelties, at exceedingly high costs.

Glass containers

In theory, the plant community in a sealed case should be self-supporting. Once the case has been planted, correct temperature and moisture established, and the container sealed, moisture from the compost and transpiration from the plants condense on the sides and roof of the case and trickle back to perpetuate the cycle.

In practice, condensation may become so heavy that the glass clouds, and the lid must be removed to improve ventilation.

Any kind of container can be used provided it has clear glass sides – ideally, choose a case with rounded or sloping sides and a domed top; in a straight-sided container, condensation tends to collect and fall in drops which may spot the foliage below.

Coloured and non-transparent glass should be avoided as it does not admit sufficient light. Plastic may be used if it is truly transparent, but it clouds rapidly and becomes ingrained with dust as it ages. It also lacks the crystal clearness of glass.

Wardian cases, converted aquariums, fish bowls and tanks, brandy snifters and apothecary and confectionery jars are all suitable as plant cases if they are equipped with lids or stoppers to exclude air.

An easy plant case can be made with a group planting in a shallow dish, covered with a bell jar, glass cheese cover or one of the antique glass domes once used to house dried flower arrangements.

Somewhat more difficult, but highly decorative is a glass-topped coffee table, specially made or adapted, with a deep waterproof tray to hold a collection of small plants beneath the glass.

The most expensive, but effective plant case is a large plant window, purpose-built and affixed to an inner or outer room wall. It might, for instance, house a large collection of exotic orchids or a miniature tropical garden. Ideally, it should be equipped with sliding glass panels, concealed lights and temperature, humidity and ventilation thermostats.

On the other hand, a plant case may be as simple as a small lidded jam jar holding a miniature fern or a prized saintpaulia.

Bottle gardens

Wardian and fern cases, terrariums, vivariums and bottle gardens are all alternate descriptive names for closed plant cases. A bottle garden more often than not refers to a carboy.

Ready-planted bottle gardens are popular if expensive florists' gifts. Unfortunately most of these attractive-looking plant displays are contained in large bottles of thick green glass, quite inadequate for the light needs of most plants. Condensation sometimes forms during the first few days after a bought bottle garden has been moved to the warmer surroundings of the home. If this happens, remove the stopper until the glass has cleared completely.

Filling a plant case

The size of the container determines the size and number of the plants. Avoid small cases for plant groups which will outgrow their allotted space too quickly, and consider, too, the opening of the case. It is a good idea to try your hand at a simple plant case before attempting the more complicated task of planting a large, narrow-necked carboy or bottle.

Having chosen a suitable container, wash and dry it thoroughly, then prepare the compost. A drainage layer of small stones or pebbles is sometimes recommended, but this tends to collect stagnant water and easily becomes smelly.

Use preferably an all-peat compost mixed with a few pieces of charcoal to keep it sweet. Put in enough compost to give an overall depth of 3 in, though in very shallow containers 1 in is adequate. A deeper compost layer may be used in large plant cases, but the more root run the plants are given, the more vigorously even slow growers will spread.

Moisten the compost well, through a fine rose on the watering can, until only a drop or two of water oozes out when a handful is squeezed between the fingers.

Planting in containers wide enough for hands to be used is no different to planting in pots or pans. Special tools are needed for a bottle garden.

Some florists and large garden centres sell sets of tools for planting and maintaining a bottle garden. However, a trowel and fork can be fashioned from kitchen utensils tied to bamboo canes of suitable length. An empty cotton reel fixed on the end of another cane is handy for firming plants and compost.

Before planting any case, work out a plan for the positioning of the plants. Avoid a flat look by shaping the compost into gentle hills, slopes and valleys. If the case is to be viewed from one side only, bank up the compost at the rear and set the tallest plants there. For an all-round view, mound the compost in the centre and position the tallest plant here.

You can add small stones or pebbles, pieces of bark or driftwood to the finished planting so as to imitate a natural landscape. Cleverly arranged strips of foil can simulate rivers and waterfalls.

Always use small plants, ideally rooted cuttings or young divisions. Knock them from their pots and gently shake most of the soil from the roots.

Make a small hole in the compost with a long-handled spoon and carefully drop the plant into the bottle. Manoeuvre it into place with two canes used like chopsticks or with a spoon and fork. Scuff the compost over the roots and firm it with the cotton reel, sufficiently to prevent the plant from falling over. When all the plants are in position, wipe any smears from the glass with a piece of sponge or pad of cottonwool fixed to a cane.

Cover the planted case with an airtight lid – cork stoppers can be used for bottles. Place it out of direct sun; the best position is by a north-facing window.

Alternatively, use a plant case as a feature point for a dull corner by providing artificial light. For a bottle garden a table lamp may be enough, for larger cases, install fluorescent tubes.

Surplus condensation may prove a major problem in a newly planted case or bottle garden. Once the plants are established and correct humidity is present, the atmosphere inside the case will be balanced, with carbon dioxide and oxygen and hence water being continually recycled.

It usually takes a short while to achieve the perfect conditions, so for a day or two after planting, leave the case uncovered. If condensation forms after the lid has been positioned, remove it again until the glass has cleared. Condensation may form on an established case or bottle if moved to a cold place. Left alone it will soon return to normal once back in its former place.

Choosing the plants
Any plant which enjoys extra humidity is theoretically suitable, but there is little point in using plants which thrive outside it.

PLANTING A BOTTLE GARDEN

Use a spoon tied to a cane to shape the compost and to take out shallow planting holes at suitable distances.

Position the first plant with the aid of two 'chopsticks' Work from the sides of the bottle towards the centre.

As planting progresses, firm with a cotton reel. Clean the inside of the glass and stopper the bottle.

157

Vigorous-growing plants should always be avoided. Tradescantias, zebrinas and *Ficus pumila* are some-times recommended or included in bought bottle gardens, but all grow fast and will need frequent pruning if they are not to swamp slower-growing types. For small containers use plants of a rosette or tufted growth habit. Flowering plants are not recommended for bottle gardens with restricted necks. Faded flowers must be constantly removed to avoid fungal infections.

All plants must have identical temperature and humidity needs. Heat is not easy to regulate, but is largely a matter of maintaining a constant room temperature.

At a temperature of 65-70° F many small, colourful plants can be used in bottle gardens or small cases. *Fittonia* species and *Peperomia argyreia* do well, but the real gems are less common, though worth seeking out. *Bertolonia marmorata*, also known as jewel plant, has bright green, heart-shaped leaves spangled and striped with silvery-white, and rich purple beneath. The leaves are erect in contrast to those of the green earth star *(Cryptanthus acaulis)*, a bromeliad with flat rosettes of leathery, glossy green leaves.

Brown spiderwort, *Siderasis fuscata*, grows in a solid rosette of brown, velvety-textured leaves. As a further contrast to growth habits and leaf textures, such a small collection would be enhanced with a baby rubber plant. Correctly *Peperomia obtusifolia* it has a superficial resemblance to its popular namesake, but bears fleshy leaves. *P. rubella* is also recommended, being a bushy little plant with tiny silvery-veined, green leaves.

Bottle gardens with comparatively wide necks might well accommodate *Chameranthemum igneum*, with beautiful dark brown, velvety leaves strongly veined with red; it also has small, bright yellow flowers. *Sonerila margaritacea*, with pearly spotted, coppery-green leaves, and rosy-pink flowers, could also be tried.

For larger, equally warm containers, two creeping, fairly slow-growing pellionias are outstanding. Both have small, attractively marbled leaves, *P. daveauana* in purple-brown with pale grey centres, and *P. pulchra* with a pale greeny-grey back-ground to the darker markings.

The dainty *Episcia dianthiflora*, its lacy-fringed, white flowers set off by dark green, velvety leaves, and *Scindapsus pictus* 'Argyraeus', with dark satiny leaves flecked with silvery dots, also come into this category.

For narrow-necked bottles and small cases where the temperature is likely to fall to around 55-65° F, the following are suitable: *Peperomia caperata* and the button fern, *Pellaea rotundifolia*, have good shape; small hardy ferns, such as *Cystopteris*, can also be used. The dwarf mossy cultivar of *Selaginella kraussiana*, known as 'Brownii', is ideal for ground cover and contrast.

In more easily accessible containers, try the tiny eye-lash begonia, *Begonia boweri*, with its shell-pink flowers above glossy green, brown-marked leaves, or the bright green, mossy bead plant, *Nertera depressa (N. granadensis)* which is covered in early autumn with orange-red berries.

For large containers there are a number of extremely attractive plants even though they eventually grow too large and must be propagated and replaced. A seedling of that elegant palm, *Chamaedorea elegans*, makes a delightful centre-piece. Young plants of *Maranta* *leuconeura* and the two calatheas, *C. lancifolia* and *C. ornata*, both with slightly broader, pale green leaves banded with pinky cream, are also most decorative.

As ground cover for large plant cases, the fern-like selaginellas are recommended though they tend to be fast-growing; *S. kraussiana* is probably the most effective.

Maintenance of plant cases

Strict hygiene is important in all types of plant cases. Remove dead leaves and flowers as soon as they are seen, in a bottle with chop-sticks, or with a pin fixed to a cane. If a dead leaf is still attached to the plant, cut it off with a razor blade tied to a cane. This tool is also handy for pruning plants which throw out long stems.

After several months, depending on the growth of the plants, check the compost and health of the plants to see if water is needed. Once the original small plants are growing and have more foliage to maintain, water must generally be given once or twice a year. Mist spray plants and compost lightly and clean the glass. Replace the lid or stopper and deal with any condensation that may occur.

Do not feed plants in closed cases where the growth rate should be kept as slow as possible. It may be possible to remove from a large case a plant which has outgrown its space, but in a bottle garden this is impossible.

Prune hard whenever possible, and when the garden eventually becomes too much of a jungle, start afresh. It is not nearly as easy to remove plants from a bottle as it was putting them in, and it is rarely possible to save any plants. Usually the plants are cut into pieces with a razor blade, and it may be easier to abandon the garden altogether and start with a new bottle.

Dish gardens

Tiny and slow-growing plants are ideal for miniature compositions of arid deserts, shady forest glades and mountain landscapes

The terms dish and miniature gardens are used somewhat loosely and often convey the same concept. Miniature gardens are properly scaled-down versions of outdoor garden features and are generally based on certain patterns, such as rose or water gardens, mountain or desert landscapes or austere Japanese gardens composed mainly of stones and rocks.

Often these miniature gardens are embellished with paths and lawns, arbours and benches, wells and pools, pergolas and terraces.

Dish gardens, too, and especially those bought as florists' gifts, are sometimes decorated with artistically arranged pieces of wood, and a surface covering of polished pebbles or coloured stone chips.

Plants alone make the difference between dish and miniature gardens. The latter – and most of these are suited solely for outdoor purposes – often contain dwarf and/or slow-growing plants, trees and shrubs which take many years to outgrow their containers.

A dish garden, on the other hand, is merely a group arrangement of house plants in miniature. Very few house plants remain small, and, with the exception of cacti and succulents, dish garden displays must be considered of temporary duration.

Small plant arrangements
In spite of their limited lifespan, dish gardens of foliage and flowering house plants have a delicate charm. They should be in scale with their surroundings and are best used as centre-pieces, placed on small low tables or on ledges and niches where they can be seen from above or at eye level.

Any kind of shallow dish that will hold soil is suitable, pottery and china being favourites. Ideally the dish should be 3-4 in deep, waterproof and lined with a drainage layer of crocks or gravel beneath the compost.

The composition of a dish garden is similar to that of any other group arrangement. It should be based on similar requirements for compost, water, temperature and

MINIATURE PLANTS FOR MINIATURE GARDENS

A shallow, earth-coloured container is a natural setting for low-growing rosette plants. The small-leaved ivy mutes the striking colours of cryptanthus, the quilted peperomia leaves and the bright saintpaulia flowers.

light. Knock the chosen plants from their pots and set them in holes in the compost.

Whichever plants you choose, select young and slow growers, such as dracaenas, pileas, peperomias, small-leaved philodendrons, variegated hederas, most of the ferns, and a bromeliad such as the small cryptanthus.

Among flowering plants, *Begonia semperflorens*, *Kalanchoe blossfeldiana* and saintpaulias have the longest flowering season and smallest root systems.

Depending on rate of growth, but usually within 9–12 months, plants in a dish garden become crowded and starved. At that stage, dismantle the arrangement and grow the best subjects on in individual pots.

Cacti and succulent gardens

The most successful plants for dish gardens are the slow-growing and shallow-rooted cacti and other succulents. They make attractive features in decorative bowls, preferably less than 2 in deep which need no drainage layer.

Use a proprietary potting compost, peat or loam-based, mixed with one third part of coarse sand or fine grit.

Avoid using too many plants in one dish, allowing each as much room as it would occupy when fully grown. Cacti of the *Mammillaria* type, for example, have a tendency to rot at the base if they are denied free air circulation round them.

Err on the side of too few plants rather than too many, and concentrate on composition instead of numbers. A collection of opuntias, for instance, can illustrate the diverse shapes of a couple of species. Or you might choose a theme of columnar, spiny cacti like chamaecereus, or globes like the echinocereus and the easy-flowered mammillarias.

It is important that all the plants have the same watering regimen and rest period. It is also best to avoid mixing cacti and succulents unless the latter are small, single-bodied or tufted plants which will not dominate the others and which will accept being kept dry in winter. The small *Lithops*, *Euphorbia obesa*, and some of the haworthias are all suitable.

Planting a dish garden of cacti is no different to ordinary pot plant-ing, and that, too, should be placed in good bright light.

The surface of the bowl is often covered with coarse grit or stones to give a desert-like appearance to the planting. From the cultural point of view, though, this has its drawbacks.

The major problem with the otherwise easy cacti is knowing when to water. If the compost surface is covered with stones it is doubly difficult to gauge the moisture in the compost beneath. Some stones will have to be moved aside so that the soil can be checked with a finger.

Overwatering is fatal to a succulent dish garden and leads to rotting which quickly spreads from one plant to another. Water the bowl in accordance with its contents, and allow it a rest period in a cool place.

A dish garden of cacti or small succulents will last for several years without the need for disturbance or alteration if the plants are chosen with care, placed a good distance apart and watered carefully. If quick-growing succulents are used, frequent pruning may be necessary to control them.

DISH GARDENS OF FLESHY SUCCULENTS AND SPINY CACTI

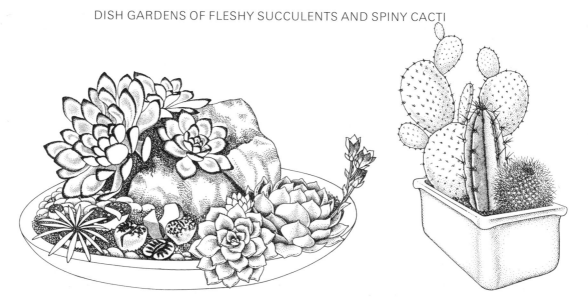

Winter and spring flowering bulbs

On their own or against a backdrop of foliage plants, spring bulbs bring colour and new life to the indoor garden

Early-flowering bulbs are among the easiest and most thankful plants for growing in the home. Little experience or care is needed to produce a brief but colourful display of blooms to brighten the dullest days of the year.

Many of these indoor bulbs are regarded as short-term plants. After flowering they are either discarded or planted in the garden because they cannot be successfully flowered indoors a second time. Examples are crocus, hyacinths, lilies and narcissi.

The most suitable bulbs for indoor cultivation are those which have been specially prepared by professional growers for forcing into early bloom around Christmas and the New Year. Before such bulbs are offered for sale, from September onwards, they have been subjected to a cool winter period by refrigeration at controlled temperatures.

Once marketed, treated bulbs are ready for bursting into rapid growth and must be planted as soon as possible before the effects of the treatment wear off.

Composts and containers

The growing medium for treated bulbs can be a proprietary loamless compost or the loam-based John Innes No. 1 or 2. However, many people prefer to use bulb fibre, a mixture of sphagnum moss, crushed charcoal and oyster shell. This is available, prepackaged, from horticultural shops and garden centres, and is lightweight, easy and clean to handle.

Several mail order firms offer package deals of treated bulbs, containers and bulb fibre.

Bulb fibre contains few nutrients, and the bulbs have to draw on their stored reserves. They recover less quickly in the garden than bulbs grown in a potting compost, but if they are in any case to be thrown out after flowering this is of little importance.

The most popular containers are decorative pottery or plastic bulb bowls which have no drainage holes. Place two or three small pieces of charcoal in the bottom, before adding the growing medium, to prevent stagnant conditions. Ordinary flower pots, clay or plastic, can also be used, with a drainage layer of broken crocks beneath the compost. In fact, any waterproof container is suitable, from a tea cup to a soup tureen.

Potting up

Bulb fibre is bought in the dry state and must be thoroughly moistened before use. This is easiest done by punching a number of holes in the plastic bag and immersing this in a bucket of water until the fibre is wet. Squeeze it almost dry through the fingers. If potting compost is used, moisten this through a fine-rosed watering can and let it drain thoroughly before planting the bulbs.

Place a layer of compost or damp bulb fibre in the container, firm it lightly and position the bulbs so that the tops are level with or just above the rim of the bowl. Set them close together, without touching. Refrain from twisting the bulbs into position which may easily damage the root bases.

Add more fibre or compost between and around the bulbs and again firm this lightly. Leave a space of $\frac{1}{2}$ in between the compost surface and the rim of the container for watering.

After planting, bulbs for forcing need a period in complete darkness and cool conditions, below 48° F, to encourage root growth. Enclose the containers in black polythene bags and stand them in the coolest place possible, a cellar, dry shed or

POTTING BULBS FOR FORCING

Pot treated bulbs as soon as available. Half fill a shallow bowl with compost or bulb fibre and firm lightly.

Set the bulbs as close as possible, at a depth that will bring the tips level with the rim. Add more compost.

Cover small bulbs completely; leave the tips of large bulbs exposed. In both cases, allow room for watering.

spare room. Better still, if you have a garden, bury them 4-6 in deep in a bed of ashes or sand in a cool, shady corner.

Check the bowls from time to time to see that the compost is moist but not wet. If necessary, water the bowls and let them drain thoroughly.

Within 5-8 weeks the bulbs will show top shoots, and when these are about 1 in high, remove the polythene covering and transfer the containers to a position in subdued light for 7-10 days before exposing them to full bright light.

At this stage the temperature should not exceed 50° F. An unused spare room, cool but well-lit, is a suitable place. It is important not to force the growth too much otherwise flower buds will fail to develop or go blind and refuse to open. Increase the temperature to 60° F only when flower buds are well formed.

When the leaves have fully developed, and the flower buds are showing colour, move the bowls to living room conditions, in good light. Prolong the flowering period by returning the bowls to a cooler position overnight.

Pay particular attention to watering: the compost or fibre should never be allowed to dry out, nor should it be saturated. Watering causes no problems with bulbs in ordinary pots, but in bowls with no drainage holes, excess water must be removed by tilting the bowls on one side.

After flowering, you can throw out the contents of the bowls and start afresh the following autumn. If, however, you intend to keep the bulbs for planting in the garden, keep them watered until the leaves, too, have withered. Knock them out of the containers and leave the bulbs to dry. Remove the compost and faded foliage and store the bulbs in a cool, dry place until planting time.

Hyacinth glasses and crocus pots
Other kinds of containers for indoor bulb culture include glasses shaped to fit a single hyacinth, crocus or daffodil bulb. The bulb fits snugly in the upper, bowl-shaped part, and the roots grow through the constricted neck down into the water in the lower part of the glass.

Begin forcing treated bulbs for water culture in early autumn, at room temperature and in semi-darkness. Fill the glass with water to just below the neck and add a few lumps of charcoal to keep it sweet. Set a bulb in the neck, above the water line, and cover the tiny growing tip with a paper cone.

When root growth is obvious, and top shoots well developed, remove the paper covering and move the glass closer to good light.

Crocus corms and small narcissi bulbs can also be grown in pebble and water trays. Wedge the bulbs on the pebbles and top up with water to just below the bulb bases. Discard after flowering.

Crocus pots, available in clay or plastic, have a number of holes round the sides, each for a single corm, and a few can also be planted in the top. Treat like any other container, but be even more careful with watering.

Garden bulbs indoors

Certain other spring flowering bulbs can also be used as house plants for the short period they are in bloom. Pot them in autumn in well-crocked clay pans containing John Innes No. 1, choosing small bulbs which will allow a fair number in each container.

Stand the pans in the open and bring them indoors in spring when the plants are just about to flower.

The best types are miniatures, such as *Convallaria majalis,* lily-of-the-valley, not a bulb but with sweetly scented white flowers; *Galanthus nivalis,* the familiar snowdrop; *Muscari armeniacum,* the grape hyacinth with short dense spikes of blue flowers; and *Scilla sibirica,* squill, with intense blue bell flowers. White and blue, dwarf irises are also suitable. After flowering, plant them out in the garden.

Hydroculture

Soil is not always necessary for growth, it can be replaced with plain water and specially formulated plant nutrients

Soil-less cultivation – or hydroculture – of house plants has only become accepted in Britain since the mid 1970's. Soil is not necessary for successful plant growth; it often serves merely as a reservoir for water and nutrients, while at the same time providing support for the plants.

In hydroculture, soil is replaced by an aggregate, usually porous clay granules, which supports the plant. The roots grow directly into a water and nutrient solution.

Most hydroculture systems consist of an outer container, of conventional shape and usually made of durable, non-transparent plastic. Inside this container is suspended a smaller, free-draining pot with clay granules.

Water and fertiliser are added to the outer container through a tube, with the water level reaching about a third of the way up the plant pot. A gauge indicates not only the need for more water, but also when the precise level is reached.

Hydroculture overcomes the problem of over and underwatering house plants; it is less messy than soil cultivation, and the risk of soil pests and diseases is minimised. It does not, however, obviate the need for other cultural requirements, such as correct heat, humidity and light. Growth is often more rapid and lush than in ordinary cultivation methods, and heavy and frequent pruning may be necessary to prevent top-heavy plants from falling over.

Plants grown by hydroculture are offered by high-class florists and are fairly expensive. It is also possible to purchase kits consisting of granules, a plant pot, nutrients, gauges and outer container.

Various brands are available, each with specific instructions on the strength of nutrients and the number of feeds to be given.

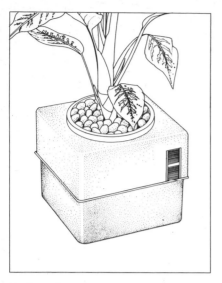

Hydroculture overcomes watering problems. The water level in the aggregate is indicated on a gauge.

Starting with hydroculture

Plants grown in a water and nutrient solution develop thick and fleshy roots rather than the thin feeding roots in soil cultivation. For this reason, plants which have been raised in soil are rarely able to adapt to hydroculture.

Not all plants are suitable for hydroculture, and as yet it has not been possible to explain satisfactorily why certain plants succeed and others fail. Among the successful plants are Aglaonema, *Cissus antarctica*, Coleus, *Dracaena sanderiana*, Hedera, Philodendron, Scindapsus and several palms.

Hydropots

These are simplified hydroculture systems and comparatively new on the market. The special pots, available in various sizes, have a water reservoir base, and the nutrient solution is watered on to the granules which support the plant.

Repotting

Hydroculture permits an exact and trouble-free watering programme, and fertiliser applications are restricted to one or two annually.

In time plants outgrow their special pots and will need repotting though less frequently than soil-grown specimens. Usually the need for repotting is determined less by root than by top growth when the aggregate becomes unable to support the plant.

Repotting follows the usual procedure: the pot containing plant and granules is removed from the container, and the aggregate tipped out with as little damage to the brittle roots as possible.

Use a new pot – and outer container – one or two sizes larger. Set the plant on a fresh layer of granules, deep enough to raise the crown to its former level in the pot. Thereafter continue as before, filling in with more granules round the stem and suspending the pot in a fresh water and fertiliser solution.

Always use water at room temperature and fertiliser specially formulated for hydroculture. Standard liquid fertilisers may be used at half strength but generally lack essential trace elements.

It is not, of course, possible to transfer a water-grown plant to conventional soil cultivation.

RAISING CUTTINGS FOR HYDROCULTURE

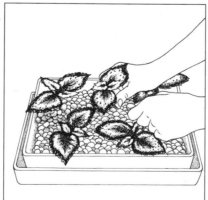

Choose an aggregate of fine-grade clay granules and spread in a 2 in layer over the base of a shallow, waterproof

container. Insert soft stem cuttings among the granules. Make up a nutrient solution, at a third the

strength recommended, and pour over the aggregate. When rooted transfer the young plants to hydropots.

Index

Figures in bold type indicate a main entry;
those in italics refer to an illustration